Assaulting with Words

Assaulting with Words *Popular Discourse and the Bridle of* Sharīʿah

ABDULLAHI ALI IBRAHIM

Northwestern University Press

EVANSTON, ILLINOIS

1994

Northwestern University Press
Evanston, Illinois 60208-4210

ISBN: 0-8101-1081-4

Library of Congress Cataloging-in-Publication Data

Ibrāhīm, ʿAbd Allāh ʿAlī.

Assaulting with words : popular discourse and the bridle of sharīʿah / Abdullahi Ali Ibrahim.

p. cm. — (Series in Islam and society in Africa)

Revision of author's thesis (Ph.D.)—Indiana University, 1987.

Includes bibliographical references.

ISBN 0-8101-1081-4 (alk. paper)

1. Evil eye—Sudan. 2. Jaʿaliyyīn (Arab tribe)—Folklore. 3. Jaʿaliyyīn (Arab tribe)—Social life and customs. 4. Discourse analysis, Narrative—Sudan. 5. Magic, Islamic. 6. Metaphor—Religious aspects. 7. Sudan—Religious life and customs. I. Title. II. Series.

GN652.S93I27 1994
133.4′3′09625—dc20 94-22065
CIP

The paper used in this publication meets the minimum requirements of the American National Standard for Information Sciences—Permanence of Paper for Printed Library Materials, ANSI Z39.48-1984.

To Khalda
with love

Contents

Acknowledgments

This book is a revision of my Ph.D. dissertation, which I completed at Indiana University in 1987. My studies at Indiana were made possible by a senior scholarship from the University of Khartoum, Sudan. Both the Graduate School and the Institute of Asian and African Studies of Khartoum University generously financed my fieldwork among the Rubāṭāb people in 1984. I would also like to acknowledge a timely grant-in-aid from the graduate college of Indiana University. I should also like to thank Professor Budour Abu ʿAfān of the Social Research Council for her support during the early stages of revising the dissertation for publication.

My special thanks are due to the members of my research committee: Professors Hasan El-Shamy (Chairman), Richard Bauman, Linda Degh, Michael Herzfeld, and Anthony Seeger. I am grateful to Professor El-Shamy and Dr. Susan El-Shamy for their care during my stay in Bloomington and ever since.

I would also like to thank Ambassador ʿAbdalla Ahmad ʿAbdalla, Yusuf Fadl Hasan, ʿAwan al-Shareef, Jim Faris, William Y. Adams, Ivan Karp, Ruth Stone, John Macdowell, John Johnson, Ahmad A. Nasr, William Murphy, Talal Asad, Dale Eickelman, Mette Shane, Mahammad Isa, John Godfery, Akbar Virmani, Hans Panofsky, David Easterbrook, *al-Asatidhah* al-Tayyib M. al-Tayyib, and ʿAbdullahi al-Shaykh al-Bashir, all of whom took time to answer my queries.

I owe a great deal to those fellow students at Indiana University who let me burden them with my "exotic" topic. Nancy Michael listened to hours of unprocessed thoughts and helped shape them. Moira Smith, especially, was a constant inspiration and an intelligent, friendly critic. Regina and John Bendix were always available to help with translations and editing.

ACKNOWLEDGMENTS

I wish to thank the late Osman Hasan Ahmed and Ustadh Mahjoub al-Badawi, the Sudan Cultural Counselors in the first half of the 1980s, for their understanding and support.

Drs. Idris Salim al-Hasan, Muhammad Ahmad Mahmud, Luise White, Laurence Michalak, Neil McHugh, Teriab Ash-Shareef, and Ibrahim Muhammad Zein read either the whole work or parts of it and offered helpful suggestions. I gained invaluable insights from discussions following the presentation of portions of this work to the meetings of the Sudan Studies Association, the American Folklore Society, and the American Anthropological Association, and at the University of California at Berkeley and Northwestern University.

John Hunwick and Robert Launay, the editors of the Islam and Society in Africa series of Northwestern University Press, gracefully saw the manuscript through the scrutiny of many eyes and minds. I owe much of my speed (they may have another assessment) to their "benevolent editorial harassment." Susan Harris, the managing editor of Northwestern University Press, put me to shame by strategically indulging in the make-believe world of my deadlines.

I am also grateful to Professors Lila Abu-Lughod and Margaret Drewal, the reviewers co-opted by the Press, for persuasively talking me into performing the unwelcome task of *naqdh al-ghazl,* that is, revising my dissertation to make it readable and appealing to a wider audience.

A timely grant from the Ford Foundation (The Middle East Research Committee, Cairo) and the African Studies Program, Northwestern University, landed me in the Institute for Advanced Study and Research in the African Humanities, Northwestern University, to conduct research on colonialism and Islam. In addition to bringing me in ambivalent proximity to my publisher and editors, my term with the Institute exposed me to a mind-boggling updating of and taste for the scholarship on representation and modes of writing. I am grateful to Professor David W. Cohen, Director of the Program of African Studies and Secretary of the Institute, and his wonderful staff, headed by Roseann

Mark, Linda Kerr, and Sheri Carsello, for their unfailing support, sensitivity, and solidarity. The fellows of the Institute were the epitome of congeniality, eloquence, and fun. Amal Fadlalla, my wife, was a tremendous source of inspiration, support, and joy.

The generosity and interest of the Rubāṭāb of the villages I studied and other Rubāṭāb made this research a growth experience. I hope this book reflects my respect and appreciation for their culture, as well as my enjoyment of it.

A Note on Transliteration

In transliterating Arabic words, I used the *International Journal of Middle East Studies* system. Rubāṭāb pronunciation of terms, proper names, and names of geographical locations is closely followed except in cases where convention has it otherwise. All the proper names of Rubāṭāb referred to in the text are actual names except for "Nasr," which is my invention. Conventional usages such as "Ghazzali" and "Ansar" survived the transliteration process.

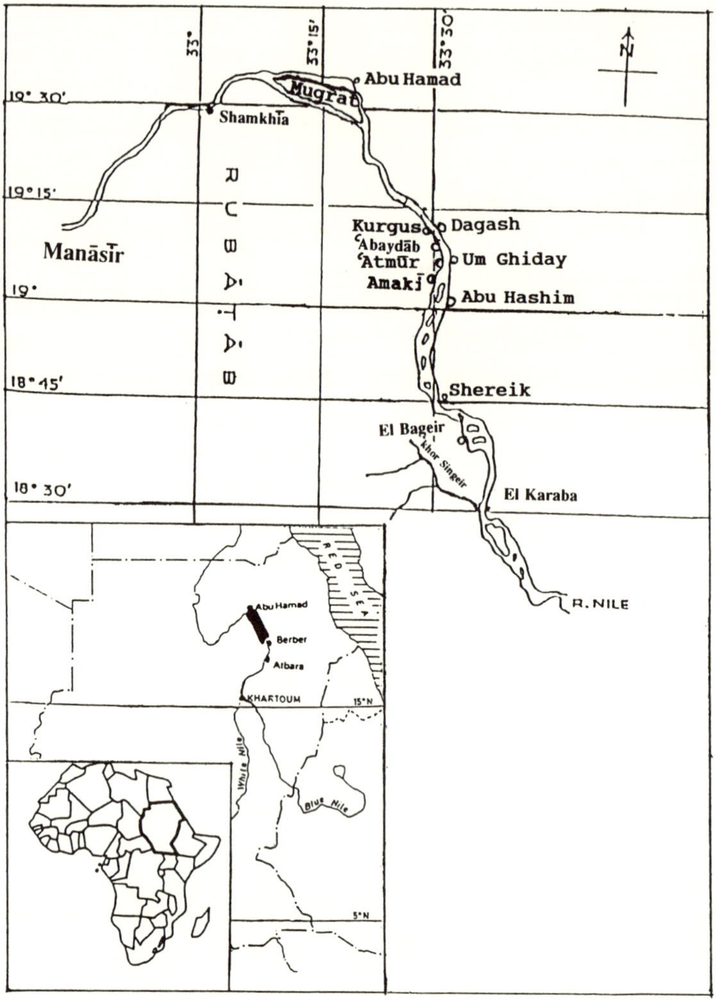

Rabāṭāb homeland: Details of the shaded area on the map of Sudan in Africa.

Introduction: The Politics of *Sharīʿah*-mindedness

This book studies the metaphors inherent in the practice of *saḥir* among the Muslim Arab Rubāṭāb[1] of the Sudan. *Saḥir* is intricately bound to belief in the evil eye, and the metaphors are believed by some to cast the evil eye. A common situation in which these dramatic metaphors are used is a speech event consisting of the speaker of the metaphor, known as the *saḥḥār;* a victim, the subject of the metaphor; and an audience. An account of *saḥir* is called *saḥrah.* In a *saḥir* situation a *saḥḥār* attempts to cast, or "shoot," the metaphor at persons or objects by comparing them to something else. A victim may then try to counteract the shot by uttering protective invocations. The victim's later account of the event in which the evil eye was cast upon him or her will include subsequent misfortune and perhaps justification for personal failure. For example, a *saḥḥār* saw two healthy children dressed in red shorts and shirts. He said to their father, "Your children look like Union Carbide batteries." The children were said to have caught a strange stomach disease and died two days later. Rubāṭāb debate the efficacy of *saḥir. Saḥḥār*s view their similes as products of an irresistible impulse to speak figuratively, likening this overwhelming impulse to a hiccup. Their victims argue that *saḥir* stems from *fakar* (lit., seeing and thinking in envious terms) to deny the *saḥḥārs*' claim to spontaneity. Lastly, the audience laughs at good similes, though not unaware of the evil consequences that may result, or which the victims claim to result, from *saḥir.*

The material for this inquiry results from fieldwork conducted among the Rubāṭāb in 1984. The Rubāṭāb, numbering about 38,000, are farmers inhabiting and cultivating the banks and islands of the middle Nile region, which lies between Sinqayr (lat. 18°30′, long. 33°41′) and Shamkhiyyah (lat. 19°30′, long. 33°) (see the map on page xiv). They are Muslims, and Arabic is their mother tongue. They belong to the broader Jaʿalīyyīn[2] group of northern Sudan who claim an Arab descent from Al-ʿAbbās, the paternal uncle of Prophet Muhammad. In the most common version of the broader Jaʿalīyyīn genealogy, their ancestor Ibrāhīm Jaʿal begot ʿArmān, the ancestor of the proper Jaʿalīyyīn, Shāīq of the Shāīqīyyah and Rubāṭ of the Rubāṭāb. The scholarly discourse that has dealt with the identity of the broader Jaʿalīyyīn since the turn of the century characterizes them as an Afro-Arab "bastard" (MacMichael 1922, 1:235; for a rebuttal see A. Ibrahim 1988, 1989), a product of the intermixing of the indigenous Africans and Arabs who came to the Sudan between the ninth and fourteenth centuries. Scholars describe this "hybrid" as having bastardized Arab blood (MacMichael 1922, 1:195, 199, 208, 233, 318, 336), paganized Islam (Trimingham 1949, x), and "creolized" Arabic (e.g., see MacMichael 1922, 1:196). Unlike previous studies of the Jaʿalīyyīn, this study accepts the Rubāṭābs' views of themselves as a valid ethnographic fact. This seemingly simple procedure of taking the Rubāṭābs' word for their identity legitimizes studying their culture in its Arabic and Islamic milieus, as will be shown later.

This book studies *saḥir* in its living social contexts. Accordingly, the narrative of *saḥir* is described with reference to the "expressions and the expressive intentions of dramatic players" (Asad 1986, 9). The sociopoetics of *saḥir* is thus analyzed in terms of the tensions resulting from the different evaluations of these intentions and expressions by those engaged in the *saḥir* encounter as a communicative event. Crucial to the understanding of these evaluations is Muslim speech economy, to which we will turn shortly.

We will see that each and every *saḥir* event reenacts Rubāṭāb culture. Debates evoked after such an event juxtapose Allah's wholesome world with the sorcerous renditions of it, humans with cannibals, language with gibberish, reality with fiction, work with leisure, cause with effect, intention with convention, playfulness with solemnity, incidence with coincidence, power with vulnerability, colonial spaces with colonized spaces, and excess with moderation. *Saḥir,* true to Evelyn Early, is a graphic illustration of the "emergence of culture in a communicative act" (1993, 24).

We will delineate the polemics of *saḥir* in which *saḥḥār*s, their victims, and audiences vigorously engage. In underlining their purity of intentions and being men of words, the *saḥḥār*s, as senders of the allegedly evil metaphor, emphasize the expressiveness and poetics of *saḥir.* The targets of *saḥir,* on the other hand, who suspect the intentions of *saḥḥār*s and view the content of their metaphors as evil, pose as victims and foreground the referential function in the *saḥir* communication. Again, *saḥḥār*s, who are upset at being accused of casting the evil eye, deploy meta-*saḥrah*s to defend the *saḥir* event as innocent and funny. In their ambivalence, the audiences, caught between the humor of *saḥir* and its anguish, experience the multiple functions of a *saḥir* event in intricate ways.

In its focus on the sociopoetics of discourse, this book anchors a plethora of emerging scholarly pursuits. As an ethnography of witchcraft it links up with the new writings on this seminal ethnographic interest that abstain from decoding what is said and strive to understand who is speaking and to whom (Favret-Saada 1977, 14). In these writings witchcraft is dealt with as spoken words pregnant with power rather than containing knowledge or information. In this perspective, the witchcraft event is a site of total war waged with words. The ethnographer has, therefore, to make up his mind to engage in another kind of ethnography (1977, 12).

This book also draws on new trends in the study of literature (Fabian 1990; Barber 1991). These new trends explore not how oral literature "mirrors" social relations, but rather the processes whereby knowledge of society is created and communicated between people (Furniss 1992, 271). Making sense of life for actors in oral literature is a process of speaking out in the explosions of the special language of ambiguous speech such as *saḥir.* By doing so, these actors capture for themselves and for others the interplay between the thought and experience (1992, 271).

In studying the sociopoetics of a discourse of an Arab, Muslim community, this book anchors specifically to an emerging paradigm in the ethnography of the Arab people, one that emphasizes both the study of Arab discourses and the indispensability of Islamic "high" texts to the understanding of the practices of average Muslims long held to be an aberration of, if not antithetical to, these texts.

Previous ethnographies of the Arab people have been criticized for presenting actors who "do not speak, they do not think, they *behave* [emphasis in the original]" (Asad 1986, 8; see Caton 1987, 82–86; Abu-Lughod 1986, 28). In these ethnographies, Arab eloquence—especially the spell of poetry on the Arab people—is pointed to, but little effort is made to study this eloquence in living social contexts (Caton 1987, 88; Abu-Lughod 1986, 28). Those ethnographers of Arab communities who are interested in language rarely ventured beyond lexicon (Caton 1986, 291). In view of the negligence of the "said" in Arab ethnographies, this emerging paradigm calls for the study of Arab discourses with the aid of a model of dialogue wed to a model of form, illuminated by poetics, wrestling with "the relationship among esthetics, language, and diverse functions of communication" (Caton 1987, 77).

In bringing Islamic texts to bear on *saḥir* practice, this book ties in with the emphasis on the complementarity of these texts and practices made in recent scholarship on Arab societies (Eickelman 1985; Messick 1986; Abu Zahra 1988; Caton 1986). Abu-Lughod takes exception with previous ethnographers, for, like the people they have commonly studied, they lapsed into illiteracy. Therefore they have neither access to nor interest in texts of Islam "high" culture or those in the communities they study. Abu-Lughod calls for more attention to be paid to "the interplay between . . . everyday practices and discourses and the texts to which they are referred, the histories of which they are part, and the political enterprise of which they partake" (1990, 113). The histories and political enterprises of both rain rituals (Abu Zahra

1988) and greetings (Caton 1986), viewed as "folklore" (Westermarck 1926) and a form of social etiquette (Irvine 1974; Youssouf, Grimshaw, and Bird 1976), respectively, are better illuminated when studied in the light of textual discourses of Islam.

The book analyzes *saḥir* with reference to a perceived conflict between it and what Hodgson has called "*sharīʿah*-minded" piety or discourse (1974, 1:350). This conflict rests on an indigenous perception of the tension between *saḥir* and such piety among the Rubāṭāb. I owe this research strategy to my many "uncooperative" informants who, citing this conflict, declined to be interviewed or used the occasion of the interview to disown the reputation of being *saḥḥārs*.

Hodgson defined *sharīʿah*-minded piety as the complex of attitudes characterizing Muslims and derived from *sharīʿah,* which has unrivaled primacy in religion and in life (1974, 1:351). Although it is not the only form of Islam, according to Hodgson, *sharīʿah*-minded piety enjoys a special prestige because it legitimizes or delegitimizes all other tendencies as being consistent or inconsistent with Islam (1963, 244).

Hodgson named this piety "*sharīʿah*-mindedness" to distinguish it from "orthodoxy," as misleadingly applied by Islamicists to it (1974, 1:350–51). "Orthodoxy," as is well known, did not sit well with scholars as a category describing the Islamic processes of legitimation (Smith 1957, 20; Eickelman 1981, 213). Extreme positions were taken by scholars to either do away with the category or replace it. To understand the diversity of Muslims' experiences, "orthodoxy," that is, "Islam" with a capital "I," is dissolved as a concept in order to understand the diversity of Muslim "islams" (El-Zein 1977, 227). Furthermore, Islam is viewed as a realm of orthopraxy (commonality of practices) rather than of orthodoxy (commonality of belief) (Eickelman 1981, 204, 1; Ahmed 1987, 220). However, Asad argues that there is a domain for orthodoxy in Islam "wherever Muslims have the power to regulate, uphold, require, or adjust, *correct* practices and to condemn, exclude, undermine, or replace *incorrect* ones [emphasis in the original]" (1986, 15). Orthodoxy, as he sees it, is a discursive tradition in which even unlettered Muslims participate by identifying and adhering to the correct model. As such, orthodoxy is a "discursive relationship—a relationship of power" and not merely a body of opinion (1986, 15). In this definition of orthodoxy, the *ʿalīm* (jurist), previously perceived as the custodian per se of the Islamic texts and their interpretation, becomes—in Gilsenan's words—"but one string to the bow" (1982, 46).

Like Asad, Hodgson reserves use of the term "orthodoxy" to Islamic practices in which this disciplining power of religion is in evidence. In his view, orthodoxy applies to discourses in which a "given position may be regarded as established, either officially or socially—and such usage will by no means always coincide with *sharīʿah*-mindedness" (1974, 1:351).

For the purposes of this study I adopted Hodgson's concept of *sharīʿah*-minded piety, one that caught like fire (Turner 1974, 105; Eickelman 1981, 221; Bousfield 1985, 207; Launay 1992, 85), to refer to the *sharīʿah* dogma of speaking bearing on Rubāṭāb *saḥir* discourse. In its repudiation of eloquence, this dogma is characteristic of this piety, which is intolerant of discourses not purposely enhancing one's religion or livelihood. Hence it emphasizes "what is useful, rather than what is ornamental; what helps oneself and others to get properly and decently through the tasks of family living rather than what embellishes that living or perhaps interrupts it" (Hodgson 1963, 233). In this emphasis, *sharīʿah*-mindedness detests "lush folkloric imagination" and is basically opposed to "frivolous indulgences" (1963, 235). Its matter-of-factness cultivates common sense, "with low tolerance for abstractions or imaginative symbols" (1963, 228). As such, *sharīʿah*-minded discourse can be viewed, in Bakhtin's terms, as a centralized discourse, which he defines as the "tendency toward the stability and completion of being, toward one single meaning, one single tone of seriousness" (1968, 101).

The polemics of other Islamic pieties against *sharīʿah*-minded devotion espousing this single tone of seriousness is both old and interesting. Ibn ʿAbd Rabbih, an Islamic writer who lived in the tenth century, described this centralizing piety as puritanically suspicious of everything pleasurable. The advocates of this piety refuse such food as white flour in general abstinence from this world (Nelson 1985, 44).

In the realm of the arts, Nelson (1985) and Kishtani (1985) have forcefully delineated the polemics of *sharīʿah*-minded discourse against the arts as *laghw* (idle talk).[3] Nelson dealt with the authority of this discourse in its repudiation of *samaʿ*, the art of reciting the Koran, as singing unworthy of the words of Allah. She perceptively analyzes the authority this piety enjoys in terms of the social identities, tone of piety, and rhetoric constitutive of its polemics against reciting the Koran. In the sphere of the art of humor, Kishtani briefly accounts for the rise and flourishing of the industry of eloquence and humor during the time of the Abbasids—from the eighth to the thirteenth century—with reference to the polemics of the *ẓurafā* (jesters) and *mutazamitīn* (dogmatists). The latter, who were one of the favorite targets of the former's humor, denounced humor itself as unworthy of Muslims.

However, *sharīʿah*-minded piety is too complex to be dismissed as a reactionary dogma. Neither can it be said that the arts in Islam evolved despite it. Akbar Muhammad has pointed out that this piety held fast to the racial equality of all believers before Allah and did not condone the negative attitude among some elite in Muslim society against Africans and other minorities (1985, 65). Furthermore, this piety remained an ideal ethical system, constituting at least a potential threat to the empirical reality of political power (Turner 1974, 116). On the other hand, by arguing that Islamic arts are Koranic arts, the Faruqis (1986) make a good case against those who long viewed Islam as an iconoclastic and conservative religion. However, in their defense of Islam as prescriptive of and not prohibitive of creativity, they dismiss the prohibitive streak in Islamic piety, represented by the *sharīʿah*-minded discourse, as a misunderstanding of the efforts of jurists and the Islamic nation "to guide aesthetic participation toward certain forms and types of art, and away from others" (162–63). Even if that were the intention of learned Muslims, the arts are nevertheless obviously delegitimized by *sharī'ah*-minded piety. In his call for the Muslim brotherhood in the Sudan to participate Islamically and fully in the modern arts of dance, art, singing, and so on, Hasan al-Turabi, the leader of the brotherhood, points out that the early recruits to the movement did not like to make any initiative in this regard, and for two reasons. First, they were too full of their own religious spirituality to need the arts. Second, they internalized the *ḥaraj* (embarrassment) that surrounds the production of these arts in their religion and did not want "to engage in activities frowned upon by the *figh* [jurisprudence] traditions" (1989, 165). I believe, therefore, that a differentiation of the pieties constitutive of Islam, a research strategy pursued in this book, is more akin to the Faruqis' project of rehabilitating the Islamic arts (long banished from or viewed as illegitimate products of their religion) in Islam. However, such research should not defeat its purpose by accommodating those discourses in Islam—and in other religions, for that matter—that have no place for the arts in their scheme of worshiping and living.

On the personal level this book crowns a cultural praxis I have engaged in since the 1960s, to fathom and rescue the *imaginaire social,* in Mohammed Arkoun's terms, against both *shari'ah*-minded and modernist discourses. Both of these centralizing discourses, identified with interpretive rigidity and political power, subordinate and manipulate the *imaginaire social,* identified with freedom, spontaneity, change, or *differance* (in Binder 1988, 164; Arkoun 1988). In this praxis I was provoked by the image of the Muslim, Arab Sudanese in modernist discourses as sullen, somber, and humorless. Evolutionary models are deployed to account for the solemnity of the Sudanese. A renowned psychiatrist, in a typical evolutionist argument positively correlating laughter and the degree of civilization a people attain, attributes this lack of humor characterizing the Muslim Sudanese to their nomadic and rural idiocy (*Al-Sahafa,* 22 Aug. 1983). Islam per se is held responsible for stifling the Muslim Sudanese sense of humor (Muḥammad al-Makkī Ibrāhīm, *Al-Rai al-'Am,* 15 Dec. 1963). Even as late as 1991, an anthropologist, whom we will see identifying *saḥir* exclusively as a belief in the evil eye, traces the rise and political successes of Islamic "fundamentalism" in the Sudan to the pathetic and somber Muslim, Arab Sudanese (H. Ibrahim 1991, 143–45). Fundamentalism is here equated with people suffering "from too little fun" (*New York Times,* 2 Sept. 1992).

I date my engagement in rebutting this flawed sociology of humor and Islam to an article I published in *Al-Haya* weekly in about 1970. Drawing on a genre of humorous *ṭiry* (satire) poetry, I argued that the Sudanese sense of humor is in place and functioning well. When an opportunity for sustained research presented itself in the form of a Ph.D. dissertation, I decided to study *saḥir* as an ambiguous exercise in social interactions in which humor and anguish are inextricably blended. In studying *saḥir* in the light of the centralizing *sharīʿah*-minded piety, I am interested less in how this piety stunted Muslims' sense of humor than in how the *imaginaire social* survived the onslaught of a piety that delegitimizes humor and shuns playfulness.

Sharīʿah-minded Islam has occupied center stage in international, transnational, and national politics and polities since the 1970s. Crucial to the investigation pursued in this book is the manner in which *sharīʿah*-minded discourse has been deploying intimidating *fatwahs* (legal opinion) to bring cultural and narrative discourses into line, exemplified by the execution of Mahmud M. Taha (An-Naʿim 1986; Taha 1987), the Sudanese modernist reformer, for his unsettling metaphors—for imagining a textually finished past and envisioning a concluded future. The *fatwah* and intimidation against Salman Rushdie and other minor practitioners of "narrative sorcery," such as Akhter H. Khan (*New York Times,* 20 Aug. 1992), Alla Hamid (*New York Times,* 18 Nov. 1992), Adil Imam (*New York Times,* 18 Nov. 1992), and Sembéne Ousmane (Cheréacháin 1992, 241–47), add to the urgency of studying this piety in the realm of culture.

This might be the time to test the usability of the distinction Hodgson makes between *shariaʿah*-mindedness and orthodoxy. The "orthodoxizations" taking place in international, transnational, and national Islam can be fruitfully analyzed with reference to this distinction. We need to determine how this dominant piety in Islam seeks, realizes, and maintains consensus for its beliefs, and what degree of success it obtains.

Research in the areas indicated will, in turn, require from ethnographers a diversification of their training to include familiarity with Islamic texts. Such training will undoubtedly put in jeopardy the division of scholarly labor envisioned by Robert Redfield. Redfield envisages the interaction of the "Great" and "Little" tradition as a rendezvous between Von Grunebaum, the Islamicist, who studied the authoritative, documented tradition, and Westermarck, the ethnographer, who studied the popular and the superstitious (1985, 48–49). Unlike the rendezvous of belief and superstition, Islam is confronting scholars as a totality, as a menace or an annunciation. The system and discourse of Islam can thus be entered and explored from any point in that system, "for there are no absolute discontinuities anywhere within it—there are no autonomous entities and each point within the system is ultimately accessible from every other point" (El-Zein 1977, 251–52).

1

On Men and Genres

Getting Lost

Rubāṭāb men born in the second and third decades of this century experienced at a high price the drama of the push and pull of the labor market that opened up in the wake of the establishment of the colonial administration in 1898. The lure of that market was seductive, but migrating to work in it—especially for the sons of the relatively well-landed families—involved symbolic and patriarchal disciplinary hurdles. It became formulaic in the initiation songs—*sōmār,* the showcase of the lineage prestige—to praise those young people who held firm to their ancestors' *ḥaq* (property and legacy) and did not degrade themselves by drifting to *kirāyah* (i.e., becoming a hired hand) along with the landless Rubāṭāb and ex-slaves. The fathers of these young men, who were already losing their slaves through colonial abolitionist acts, stood resolutely between their sons and migration. Consequently, the lives of most of these young men are characterized by an episode or more of *shurād* (escape) from the village, efforts that were often stifled by the watchful patriarchy.

Wad al-Tōm, the renowned *saḥḥār,* had two unsuccessful escapes before making it on the third try. In my interview with him, I asked why he had been so determined to leave the village. He said:

> I really did not know then. I believe I needed a kind of a change in my life. I just could not understand it then why I should spend all my life tied to those cows, herding and milking them. Those of my age who migrated started sending letters and stuff to their families in the village. I thought I could have migrated and sent a letter myself.

The lives of many of the men of the Rubāṭāb generation I studied are characterized by intermittent migrations to the labor market and back again to the village. These migrations are identified by these people as *ṭashīsh* (losing one's way), in recognition of both the diabolic enticement the labor market represented and the reality of the village as their ultimate anchorage.

I asked Jādallah, a blind, elderly man and a poet, if he ever "got lost." He replied:

> I have never left this village, but I "got lost" all the time. I drank water from all rivers. There wasn't a single well I passed without lowering my bucket into it to get water. We never left a stone unturned for eking out a living. We ran all over the place looking for work until we grayed on the road and the sap of life was siphoned off us. We cast our net wide for a catch of a livelihood. We knocked on all doors for work. By Allah, we sometimes despaired of ever returning to our folk, but Allah again and again extracted us from the whirl of *ṭashīsh* and took us back to our villages.

However, *ṭashīsh* migrations, which were taxing, were not as uncharted as the poet would have us believe. These Rubāṭāb migrated to niches in the labor market that had historically attracted ethnic Rubāṭāb. Besides involving largely unskilled, strenuous work, these niches were characterized by recruitment on an ethnic basis and sometimes by patronizing terms of service. The following is a list of these niches and a summary of their ethnic constitution:

1. Rubāṭāb could be railroad workers for the Sudan Railways. Yūsif Takonah, a Rubāṭābī occupying a high position in the railroad department, was responsible for hiring most of the Rubāṭāb there. Those appointed as railroad workers tended to stay at the job, but many Rubāṭāb worked for the railroad on a short-term basis on the line extension projects in western and southern Sudan.
2. They might also work as porters in Port Sudan, hired by al-Tijānī, a labor contractor from Berber, the administrative headquarters of the Rubāṭāb.
3. They worked for the Qash Project in eastern Sudan, digging irrigation canals.

4. They crossed the border to Eritrea, occupied by Italy in the years 1935–41, to work on road construction. They also worked as farmers with Wad Ḥāj Raḥama, a Rubāṭābī whom the Italians contracted with to cultivate onions and bananas in western Eritrea. Rubāṭāb were hired for the cultivation season and provided with room and board. The remainder of their income was withheld by Wad Ḥāj Raḥama to be sent directly to the farmer's family or given to the farmer when he returned to his village at the end of the cultivating season.
5. They would trade in firewood from the southern parts of the Blue Nile to Khartoum as rafters on the Blue Nile. They also worked as peddlers around the major line construction of the railroad department. Some of them would contract with this department to provide it with baskets. These contractors would cut *dom* leaves and hire their womenfolk to weave them into baskets.

The moral and physical scars these *ṭashīsh* migrations left on these men are legion. I asked Bajūrī of al-ʿAbaydab village to comment on his *ṭashīsh*. After praising Allah for returning him to the village and for the many successes he had had since then, he said: "I was in Atbara town working and leading a life of hooliganism. I was a hooligan through and through. No one could emulate or exceed my hooliganism. I also worked as a porter in Port Sudan. I carried sacks of sugar and cement on my back like a beast of burden."

The Peanut Miracle

From the late forties onward the Rubāṭāb villages I studied underwent far-reaching economic change. The process forcefully connected them to the money economy set in motion by the colonial administration since 1898. This connection brought the villages in daily contact with the "dizzier heights" (Geertz 1988, 94) of Europe, and this contact dramatically reconfigured their landscape, putting in sharp relief the relation between the past and the present and animating the social memory to mediate the emerging tensions of living dangerously in the nexus of the "traditional" and the "modern" worlds. *Saḥir,* along with other Rubāṭāb discourse genres, have been engaged in imaginative play (Comaroff and Comaroff 1987, 203) with categories of Rubāṭāb culture to help the Rubāṭāb create a sense of themselves in the throes of change.

The introduction of the water pumps in Rubāṭāb farming in 1947 was singularly responsible for this economic change. The possibilities of irrigation opened up by water pumps were immense compared to the limited lift of the waterwheel previously in use. ʾAḥmad Kiriz, a village merchant and farmer whose fortunes might have improved by distributing rationed provisions for the colonial government after World War II, is credited with installing the first water pump. He persuaded the owners of *sāqyah*s (waterwheels, metonymic for farms) to collectively irrigate their farms from his water pump and pay dues for the water. In 1951, Muḥammad ʿAlī Muṣṭafah, from the Mayāyyīs lineage of ʿAtmūr village—and industrious, as future reference will indicate—established his own pump at Um Ghiday, on the east bank of the Nile opposite ʿAtmūr. Irrigation by pumps proliferated, turning water, which was a common resource accessible by the family waterwheels, into a commodity.

The introduction of the pumps coincided with the heavy rains of 1950 that flooded *wādī* ʿAtmūr (1500 feddans), running at the back of the villages in view. People cultivated the *wādī* that year, and their harvest was considerable. Disappointed by the constraints that the limited land of the *sāqyah*s and the conflicts over its ownership imposed on his entrepreneurial drive and management, Kiriz turned his attention to the agricultural possibilities of the *wādī.* He applied to the government, which formally owns the *wādī,* to be given the right to develop it on a tenancy basis. The majority of the villagers, who had valid claims to the *wādī* by the right of *quṣād* (the right to have prior claims to lands that correspond to one's *sāqyah* land), supported Kiriz's application and were given tenancies on their *quṣād* to cultivate and pay water dues to Kiriz.

The changes resulting from the *wādī* project were phenomenal. Kiriz belonged originally to the Khatmiyyah religious *ṭarīqah* (brotherhood), which dominates among the Rubāṭāb and the riverain Sudan at large. However, the Khatmiyyah leader, who was approached by Kiriz to support his economic project financially, was not responsive. Kiriz then sought the help of the leader of the Ansar brotherhood, the archrival of the Khatmiyyah. The Ansar leader, vying with his rival for influence, was eager to assist Kiriz to make a beachhead in a region known to be sealed to the Khatmiyyah. Additionally, the leader's support of the Rubāṭāb project was recommended by Kiriz's Rubāṭāb, Ansar in-laws, who lived in Omdurman from the time they migrated in the 1880s to support the Mahdī, the grandfather of the Ansar leader.

Affronted by the Kiriz/Ansar linkage, the Khatmiyyah went on the offensive. Their local leaders petitioned the government to revoke Kiriz's right to the *wādī,* and accused Kiriz of fraud. They complained that their signatures, which he had solicited to get the government's approval of his *wādī* project, were given on the understanding that he needed them in order to demand an increase in the rationed provisions allocated to the villagers. Kiriz was infuriated by this, and when he met with the local Khatmiyyah leader he reprimanded him:

> I said, "Why didn't you show the same zeal in objecting to *khawājah* [European] Karkor?" [a Greek merchant who started an agricultural scheme in the vicinity of Atbara town immediately to the south of the Rubāṭāb region]. I cared for the Rubāṭāb whose lot was drudgery for the railroad as line section gangs and makers of baskets and ropes. I wanted to introduce some decency and respect into the way Rubāṭāb earned their living. The Khatmiyyah leader was not impressed and insisted that Karkor was more acceptable to them than the Ansar leader.

Kiriz proceeded with his project, using his ethnic and Ansar connections to ease his way through red tape. Through Mufaḍal, the extremely manipulative and humorous *omdah* (mayor) of Abū Hashīm district of the Rubāṭāb, Kiriz secured the support of Mr. Arber of the colonial administration in the northern province for his scheme. Mufaḍal had made the acquaintance of Arber in Kassala in eastern Sudan in the aftermath of World War II when Mufaḍal was engaged in *barashōt* (ostensibly from "parachute"; the illegal border trade between Ethiopia and Sudan). Arber was then in charge of Kassala and well disposed to accept the bottles of whiskey Mufaḍal gave him as presents. In addition, two Ansar officials in the northern province, a district commissioner and a land surveyor, readily and enthusiastically expedited Kiriz's project through the government bureaucracy.

The Ansar leader entered into partnership with Kiriz and provided him with the water pump. However, he later decided to end this partnership and sold the pump to Kiriz at a reduced rate and easy installments. Kiriz and his inner circle, to whom the project was a calling as well, switched allegiance to the Ansar brotherhood. This rethinking of political affiliation did not stop here. Bābikir, the sheikh of ʿAtmūr village in 1984, told me how he deserted Kiriz's camp when they denied him a tenancy despite the ardent and loyal services he had rendered to the project. Bābikir was also infuriated by the way an Ansar businessman cheated him in a colocynth deal. Subsequently, he switched to the National Unionists, a party that split from the Khatmiyyah in the mid-fifties. His resignation from the Ansar group had a deep resonance among the Unionists. Bābikir recalled specifically a telegram from the Taxi Drivers' Union, dominated by the Unionists, congratulating him on his most welcomed change of heart.

Rubāṭāb groped their way to the money economy unaided. Most of the other communities on the Nile were ushered into this economy by the government agricultural schemes dotting the Nile. These were equipped with water pumps and produced cotton, wheat, dates, beans, and peas. Rubāṭāb had only their dates, which are best when eaten fresh, to ship to urban markets.

With the irrigation of the *wādī,* the villagers grew a Virginia breed of peanuts and exported them to West Germany. Kiriz reminisced with me in 1984 about his relative who lived in Germany then. This relative wrote to him that they were not getting their money's worth for their peanuts because they sold them for the same price as the Sudanese local breads. Kiriz made a trip to Germany and negotiated an increase of price for the Rubāṭāb peanuts with the German importers. On the worth of their labor in German cuisine, however, Kiriz said, "I was amazed to see that our peanuts were only good as appetizers for beer-drinking Germans."

The extra money Kiriz got for his peanuts was the beginning of the end of his enterprise. In 1970, the government, led by President Nimmeri in his leftist phase, accused the exporters—the majority of whom were foreigners or Sudanese of recent foreign extraction—of subverting the national economy. The two-tiered price system for peanuts was cited as disguising shady transactions to illegally drain the country's foreign exchange. Subsequently, Kiriz's peanuts were sequestered in Port Sudan and a government corporation was instituted to handle the marketing of peanuts. Although Rubāṭāb blame Kiriz for shoddy administrative practices that led to the demise of his business, it was the government's aggressive intervention in the marketing of peanuts that killed his project.

The financial returns the Rubāṭāb had gained from sale of their peanuts were instrumental in major reconfigurations of the landscape of the villages. Villagers were encouraged by these returns to release or reclaim more land for cultivation. Aided by the water pumps, which could irrigate parts of the *sāqyah* previously unreachable by the waterwheel, the villagers employed two plans to increase their arable land. First, Rubāṭāb moved their houses from the farm to the ridge that separates the *wādī* from the arable strip of land along the Nile. On this land they intensified the planting of palms, the traditional cash crop. Second, they reclaimed more and more stretches of their land on the east bank of the Nile, land they had earlier abandoned to the creeping grip of the desert. To reclaim it the farmers literally chased the sand hills into the Nile using strong water jets from hoses. Muḥammad ʿAlī Muṣṭafah, a pioneer in such land restoration, said laughingly that the Egyptian military was only copying them when they pulled down the Barlev Line using water hoses in their 1973 war against

Israel. On these reclaimed lands the Rubāṭāb grew peanuts, fenugreek, and *ḥarjal* (African rye).

Patriarchy, which was undermined by the *shurād* (escape) of young people to urban or salaried careers in the newly introduced labor market, made a significant comeback in the aftermath of the changes the Rubāṭāb villages underwent. It has been successfully utilized to effect economically sound decisions in allocating land to the members of the patriarchy as well as the corporate running of the farms. The case of the ʿAlī Muṣṭafah family of the Mayāyyīs lineage is instructive in this respect.

Muḥammad ʿAlī Muṣṭafah's father died when Muḥammad was a boy, leaving him in charge of his many brothers and sisters. With the help of his brothers he reclaimed the family land on the east bank of the Nile. While increasing the family holdings of land, he obviated the fractionation that results from applying the Islamic laws of inheritance. Their ʿAtmūr farm was given in its entirety to Khiḍir, who turned it into an economic and social success. Muḥammad and his other brothers achieved comparable successes in their east bank possessions.

Patriarchy also proved to be efficient in the running of the agribusiness complexes these men developed. Sons either showed no interest in pursuing other than farm careers or resigned from government jobs to work on the farm and related businesses. Two of Khiḍir's sons, Bakrī and ʿUthmān, teachers[1] in government primary and intermediate schools, respectively, quit their jobs to look after the expanding family business. They are now jointly responsible to their father for managing the store (which distributes government rationed provisions such as sugar and flour to village merchants), the bakery, the truck, and the water and electricity ministations. On behalf of their father, they supervise the work on the girls' high school, built on Khiḍir's initiative by self-help, and oversee the reception of guests in the family *daywān* (guest house) together.

With the tightening grip of patriarchy, a male's marriage to a paternal uncle's daughter is being enforced, with the option of a second or more marriages always available. Later on we will see

Mayāyyīs and other young men complaining that the patriarchy took the fun out of marriage ceremonies.

The Club of Those Who Did Not Make It

The economic boom engendered by farm income not only made farmers less dependent on nonagricultural resources but also made some Rubāṭāb return to working the land. Nonetheless, the money that emigrants to Saudi Arabia and the Gulf countries sent is still crucial in the budgets of individual families, family investment plans, and in supporting the communal plans such as building schools and establishing electricity plants. However, villagers, disadvantaged by lack of skill in urban contexts, decided to return to the villages to partake of their boom. Al-Shaykh Hamza, who worked in menial jobs in Port Sudan, came back to his village in the early sixties to work on the tenancy allocated to him in the *wādī* and has never left the village since.

Villagers realize that they have been doing better than their kinsmen who migrated and joined the labor market. In Qundasī, villagers mockingly dramatize the misery of those who retired from government service and returned to the village by assigning them to an imaginary club called "*Nādī al-Nās al-Māshīn Lwaara*" ("The Club of the People Who Are Walking Backward," i.e., those who did not make it). The villagers especially pity the retirees of the railroad department because hard work sapped their energy.

The way these retirees and other urban kinsmen suddenly remember land they own in the village amuses the villagers. They tell of an urban kinsman who came to the village for the first time to claim land he inherited from his father. His land was allegedly swept away by the river long before he came to the village. On asking to be shown his land, a villager took the man to the riverbank. The villager bent down, picked up a rock, threw it far into the water and said, "There is your land." I also encountered a former railroad worker and trade union activist, dismissed by Nimmeri's regime after the general strike of 1981, who was indignant over a land property denied to him in Qundasī village. In deploring the injustices that are rampant among the Rubāṭāb, he said, "I have been to every corner in the Sudan, and I have never seen a place so lacking in fairness and forthrightness as the Rubāṭāb. They just don't recognize a right thing for what it is." The villagers teased him by frequent references to his dismissal by Nimmeri. His trade union experiences were cited by the villagers as good qualification for him to head the club of those who did not make it.

To alleviate the worsening urban living conditions, some Rubāṭāb are sending their families to live in the villages. About 20 percent of the families in ʿAtmūr village have their male earning spouse in an urban or salaried position. Villagers accuse these urban Rubāṭāb of hypocrisy because they never state honestly why they have to return their families to the village. When asked, these Rubāṭāb usually say that they did so in order that their children would receive a good education, since urban schools are not as good as they used to be. Villagers still remember how these same villagers took their families away from the village because schools were lacking there. Villagers suggest that the real reason is that these urban Rubāṭāb are finding it difficult to cope with the rising standard of living in the towns.

Look Back in Anger

The tangible change these villagers experienced in their lives inclined them to polemicize uninhibitedly with the past. Ancestors became the target of cynical bashing. Embracing the present, these Rubāṭāb never seem to shed a nostalgic glance at the past.

They hold some of their ancestors guilty of bad decisions that disadvantaged them as descendants. These ancestors are thus denounced and mocked in various ways. Rubāṭ, the ancestor of the Rubāṭāb, whose alleged grave lies in Kurgus village across from Kiriz's pumps, is blamed for settling in this ridgy, rocky country that can be cultivated only sparsely and with difficulty. The tillable land fell to the ethnically related riverain—Jaʿalīyyīn, Shāīqīyyah, and Mīrāfāb—whose ancestors knew better than to inhabit a desolate place. A *saḥrah* compares the rocky Rubāṭāb land to the plain land of the other riverain, distant kinsmen. In the *saḥrah* the former land is described as bony meat, whereas the latter is seen as the boneless meat of the thigh.

This ancestor bashing is further manifested in cases in which descendants judge the occupation of these ancestors as worthless. A story is told about a man who appointed himself the custodian of the tomb of a *walī* (saint) whom he claimed as an ancestor. As custodian, the man eked a living from the gifts presented to the *walī.* To bless sheep and goats, people milked them in a *daḥlūb* (a stone carved as a receptacle) at the *walī*'s grave. In the story, the custodian's brother came to the village and asked to visit the *walī,* his ancestor. His brother gladly led his visit. When the man reached the grave he asked where the *walī*'s head was positioned. No sooner had his brother indicated the place to him than the man lifted the rock *daḥlūb* and threw it where the head of the *walī* was supposed to be. He then addressed the *walī,* "Rise! What makes you lie waiting for goats to be milked at your head when other ancestors passed on multistoried buildings to their descendants?" In the same vein, the grave of Abū al-Zīynah, a dead Rubāṭābī *walī,* was struck by an angry, drunken great-grandson. The story goes that this man passed by Abū al-Zīynah's grave in the company of carousing young men. Intoxicated, the man beat the grave with his stick, saying, "Men are having all the fun on the earth and you stay put here."

*Walī*s are also bashed by young Rubāṭāb influenced by religious groups critical of belief in *walī*s (i.e., saint veneration). In the 1980s some Rubāṭāb high school students attended a youth camp organized in Khartoum by Ansar al-Sunnah, a Saudi-inspired or -supported group that has been active in denouncing saint veneration as antithetical to Islam. Inspired by the education they received in the camp, these students attacked the tomb of Abū Qayzān, the highest structure in the cemeteries in the villages I studied, and started bringing it down. A Rubāṭābī man who was nearby did not like what the boys were doing and chased them away from the tomb, saying, "You are just ungrateful. Your fathers should have told you that they could have starved to death had it not been for the bread visitors left on Abū Qayzān's grave."

A Sandwich Generation

The generation of the Rubāṭāb under consideration perceives the change they effected by weighing the ways of their fathers against their ways as fathers. In appraising their lives, these men see themselves as the victims of both their fathers and their sons. Without specifically mentioning the concept, they strongly suggest that they are a "sandwich generation." They argue that they worked hard as young men to support their fathers and families and as a result were deprived of an education. Now, illiterate as they are, they have to come to grips with the changing times. In order not to repeat their fathers' errors they have been sending their sons and daughters to schools, but by doing so they are not only deprived of the work their children could have performed on the farm but also have to provide for them for as long as it takes them to complete their education. Muṣṭafah al-Hadaʿ of ʿAtmūr village described their predicament:

> We *khadamnah* [served] our fathers and now we're serving our sons. Our fathers did not have to work hard on the farm when they were young. The slaves relieved them from expending themselves on the farm. The slaves were emancipated at the time we were growing up, so the work on the farm fell entirely on us. Our fathers had it the easy way: the slaves did the work for them when they were young, and we did it for them when they grew old. Our sons go to school now and we are still working hard, determined that they will never do for us what we did for our fathers.

No small wonder that these men are expansive, and even celebratory, about their changed lives and landscapes. They are embracing these changes soberly and with conviction. They believe that the change they brought into their lives is a *niʿmah* (blessing) for which people should thank Allah. They are not hesitant in this conviction, nor do they seem to throw nostalgic glances to the past. Khiḍir, an illiterate man who spearheaded the building of the girls' high school by self-help, said, "In the old days we used to have *khalwahs* [Koranic schools]. We have now an ever-increasing and expanding modern school system." As the owner of the most prestigious *daywān* (guest house) in the villages, he said, "These are good times. We have enough food to entertain guests." In our discussions, Khiḍir described the authoritativeness and aloofness of their fathers as *isti'mār* (colonialism). I asked him whether *saḥir* was common among their fathers' generation, and he said, "How would I know? We did not mix with them enough to even know what they talked about."

In describing the patriarchy they grew up under as "colonialism," these men are competent to substantiate their description. They indicate that in the old days slave women were required to take their headdress off when they passed men. On the other hand, women had to take their shoes off on meeting men, even during the night. Children riding on jackasses were supposed to get off the animals' backs until they were at a distance of respect from men. I was told the story of the boy who finally managed to ride a jackass after several bruising attempts. Immediately after riding he ran into a man. Recognizing both the imperative to descend to demonstrate respect and the difficulties he had encountered before riding the jackass, the boy implored the man, "Uncle! I will get off the back of the jackass, but you promise to help me ride it again." Finally, if a boy was allowed to eat with his seniors he was expected to hold the food tray with one hand and eat with the other. He was not allowed to rise until the last man had risen. He was then required to carry the pitcher and help the men wash their hands.

The Joy of Giving in Public

Khalīfah Muḥammad 'Aḥmad of 'Atmūr village was celebratory about how things had changed in their lives as a result of the developments that came in the aftermath of the introduction of the water pumps. He enumerated spooky spaces that were believed to be haunted by jinn and which have been put to good use by including them in the expanding farms. He said that when he was growing up the villages were sparsely populated and consisted of isolated groups of houses. Villagers used to have rooms without a *ḥōsh* (enclosure), but some rooms might have a *rākūbah* (verandalike shelter consisting of a grass roof without walls). He concluded, "The one who was better off in the village might have a *khalwah* [a guest room]. The *daywāns* [guest rooms or guest houses] were not known then."

Daywāns, a conspicuous enlargement of the men's domestic space, characterize the new family compounds built on the ridge. As sites displaying generosity, they supplant or supplement older forms of honoring guests in the villages. Such honoring was associated with religious families or with the relatively landed, "native" administration families. *Khalwah* refers to these older forms or sites of generosity. *Daywāns* came to exist in connection with the growth of the native administration in the thirties. The *omdah*'s (mayor) *daywān* was the place for government officials to stay during their rural treks.

The rising agribusiness class in the villages has appropriated the *daywān*—as the location for the politics of generosity—from the native administration families, which either joined the new class or were eclipsed by it. However, some religious families are still holding fast to their *khalwahs*, which are visited largely by wayfarers such as Fulani peddlers, Manāṣīr daub builders, Shāīqīyyah itinerant *muddāḥ* (Prophet's praise singers), individual gypsies, fugitives from southern Egypt, and other Rubāṭāb villagers soliciting help for projects they are undertaking. *Khalwah* is believed to be less restrictive than the *daywān.* In contrast to the former, a Rubāṭābī defined the latter as the institution where you need the permission of its masters before you are admitted into it. However, Khiḍir, an owner of a guest-house type of *daywān,* was clearly upset when someone repeatedly knocked on the already wide-open door of his *daywān.*

Some *daywāns*, like Kiriz's and Khiḍir's, in which I stayed in 1966 and 1984, respectively, are guest houses rather than guest rooms. Both senses are covered by *daywān,* though. This may explain why Khiḍir was not happy with the person who sought his permission to enter his guest house, supposedly open for all.

These *daywāns* are roomy, spacious bed-and-board facilities equipped with all the modern amenities, such as running water, water closets, and electricity. They are separate, but accessible from the women's quarters, where food for the guests is served. Guests, who come largely from the government or business communities, stay for the night or longer until their mission is done. In 1966, Kiriz's *daywān* was for all intents and purposes the administrative center of his agricultural project. In 1984, Khiḍir's *daywān* housed the teachers of the new girls' high school until their residences were built. Parents who brought their daughters to the school would stay in the guest house until they arranged to go back home. Villagers—especially the schoolteachers—also come to the *daywān* for business and socialization and would have there whatever meal was served during their visit. There was always enough food for the people present, and the cuisine was overtly urban.

Anthropological literature conceives generosity, this intentional transfer into the other (Bourdieu 1977, 82), in terms of alms (Mauss 1967) or symbolic capital (Bourdieu 1977). In all cases it is an economy, albeit archaic (Marx 1964; Engels 1972; Mauss 1967; Bourdieu 1977), for concealing the reality of its economic acts and refusing to acknowledge and confess itself as such (Bourdieu 1977, 172). Alms, according to Mauss, are the results on the one hand of a moral idea about gifts and wealth, and, on the other hand, an idea of sacrifice. In this perspective, generosity is necessary because otherwise nemesis will take vengeance upon the excessive wealth and happiness of the rich by giving to the poor and the gods (1967, 15). However, Bourdieu takes generosity as a social investment of people in people and calls it "symbolic capital," that is, a capital spared economic calculation. This calculation, according to Bourdieu, appropriated the "naked self-interest economies," whereas it dreaded extending its "icy waters of egoistical calculation to the sacred islands of symbolic capital" (1977, 177–78).

Although the *daywān* evokes the "simple grandeur of the ancient gentile society" (Engels 1972, 101), it does not belong to an archaic economy. Rather, it crowns and decorates the steadfast enterprise of an agribusiness rural class whose rise we highlighted earlier. In trying to understand the politics of the *daywān* in the light of the sociology of generosity, the theology and economy of this politics are perceived as inextricably bound. Rubāṭāb, who do not dread extending economic calculation to the corporate *daywān,* are nevertheless overwhelmed by its grandeur. Bourdieu was not impressed by this splendor because he did not take the theology of the community he studied, the Kabyle, seriously. He discounted Islam from their habitus understood as a system of dispositions which, integrating past experiences, functions at every moment as a matrix of perceptions, appreciations, and actions, and makes possible the achievement of infinitely diversified tasks (1977, 83). Simply put, habitus is history turned into nature (1977, 78). In ignoring the role of Islam in structuring Kabyle dispositions, Bourdieu made Islam the part of their history that remains untranslatable in their nature. His treatment of the Islam of the Kabyle (1977, 41, 55, 106, 122, 173) leaves one with the impression that it is either irrelevant or artificially superimposed. In their relation to Islam, Kabyles were made to look at best as the spectators of a state cult, at worst its victims (Sahlins 1981, 53).

Rubāṭāb are not oblivious of the economy of the *daywān.* It is not without significance that they call Khiḍir's *daywān* the *baladīyyah* (town hall) in recognition of the business that takes place in it. Appeasing and manipulating the state, which rations provisions and gasoline, issues permits to carry firearms, and even controls access to *hajj* (pilgrimage to Mecca) through quotas, have always been crucial in the rise and successes of this class. We have seen how Kiriz's project collapsed when it was fatally struck by the state in one of its periodic fits of misguided concern over public money. The state officials who have the power to make and break businesses need to be impressed and "domesticated." The *daywān* apparently accomplishes this. To maintain a quality service, the *daywān* is unconditionally open to government officials. Even the bus driver of the new school was accommodated there.

However, a far less glamorous room, built of local materials and attached to the *daywān,* is reserved for the kind of people usually hosted in a *khalwah.* This *daywān* hierarchy should not be viewed as insulating people like Khiḍir from their guests in the minor *daywān.* I encountered in Khiḍir's *daywān* an old man from the Beja people who comes annually before the date harvest to guard the palms of a villager. When he came for the 1984 harvest he got sick on the way, and his patron refused to take him. The Beja man then moved to Khiḍir's minor *daywān,* where he was lodged and treated for his ailment. I was walking with Khiḍir one day when we saw the Beja man coming out of the minor *daywān.* Khiḍir said to me: "Look there, the Beja man is already on his feet. What a pity! His patron let him down." Khiḍir cannot be accused of not being courteous to minor guests as well.

Villagers are outspoken in their criticism of Khiḍir's *daywān.* A highly politicized relative of his said Khiḍir's zeal in building the girls' high school was not simply altruistic because he wanted the food contracts of the school for himself. A woman poet blamed the lack of sugar in the villages on Khiḍir and those like him who take the village rations and send them to other places to sell on the black market.

There are times when villagers succumb to the marvel of the *daywān.* It strikes them as indivisible, wholesome, and magnanimous. At times—depending on the occasion, the frame of mind of the speaker, and the genre at his or her disposal—people do not apply Bourdieu's "icy" calculation to the *daywān* because it just does not feel right to do so. Generosity, as a "sacred island," has its worshipers in and of itself. In the poetics of manhood among the Rubāṭāb, generosity, the epitome of being a man, is couched in idioms of bellicosity and vigilance. Women's *sōmār* songs, sung on the juncture of men's initiations in circumcision and marriage, emphasize, by the power of their senders and message, generosity as a beautiful risk or duty. A generous man is described as *ʿwaj al-darib* (the one who twisted the road), for no traveler can pass by his village without paying a visit to his place to lodge, eat, and drink. It has become formulaic in *sōmār* to describe the opulence and watchfulness of a would-be Rubāṭāb man as "the one who hosts the late-night guests." For generosity to be forceful and aggressive, guests, in the parlance of *sōmār,* are made to appear as an attacking party choosing the small hours of the day for charging. Rubāṭāb acknowledge those among them who live up to the standards of the poetics of manhood. Those who missed the joy of having close combat with generosity, as people such as Khiḍir do, are vulnerable to their grandeur.

Two experiences of Khiḍir's *daywān* stand out in my field notes. In Abu Hamad town I was sitting in a coffee shop with Al-Bashīr ʿUmar, a poet, retired school teacher, and member of a defunct mayoral family, when he suddenly asked me:

"With whom were you staying in ʿAtmūr village?"

"With Khiḍir."

"Al-Khiḍir [Elijah]! I have never before composed a poem praising a man. It just does not feel right to me. However, I am considering writing praising Elijah. The generosity of this man is beyond cognition. How would you feel about that?"

The other experience took place in Khiḍir's *daywān* one evening. An elderly woman, a guest of Khiḍir's womenfolk, entered the *daywān.* Apparently she was under an irresistible impulse that made her ignore the gender boundaries. She stood, gave her back to the men, and looked around. Finally she said to no one in particular: "This, then, is Khiḍir's realm." I could hear her heaving a sigh of relief on retracing her steps to the women's sphere. I assumed that she was perhaps pleased to have scanned with her own eyes Khiḍir's *daywān,* the verbal miracle generations of women of *sōmār* singers have been putting together.

The poet and the woman were struck by the light of dreams coming true. Turner has admirably argued that religious myth constitutes a dramatic process model, acquiring, in influencing social behavior, a strange inevitability inherent in the model itself, "overriding questions of interest, expediency, or even morality once it truly gains popular support" (1974, 122–23). This is perhaps why economic calculation of a phenomenon such as the *daywān* is not always applicable.

Modernity: Looting as Accommodating

Daywāns, à la Kiriz or Khiḍir, dramatize aspects of the variegated, unsettling Rubāṭāb encounter with modernity. With their architecture and amenities, they represent a successful appropriation of modernity. Needless to say, the promises of modernity made to villagers by colonialism and postcolonial authorities went unfulfilled. The villages in view, with their desire to catch up with the world, had no running water. The government project to supply them with water was stalling, and a *saḥrah* (which will be mentioned later on) was shot to criticize the government's failure to deliver. Villagers chipped in to buy a generator, but electricity was only supplied for the early hours of the night and use of electrical appliances was prohibited. Against this background the *daywān* stands as a triumphant incorporation of modernity. The following *saḥrah* captured this single victory over modernity against the utter failures in the village at large:

> Al-Shaykh al-Ṣāyim, a *saḥḥār,* spent the night at a *daywān* at Um Ghiday village. He woke up in the morning to go to the water closet and to the bathroom to take a shower. Struck by the amenities he enjoyed in a village context, he commented, "Waking up in this *daywān* is like waking up from a wet dream."

As a site for male, communal consumption of food, the *daywān* mediates complex social desires of the generation of Rubāṭāb that built it. Influenced by ways of modernity, these young Rubāṭāb men went on picnics, copying the practice of the few schools in the region staffed by urban teachers. These men would go either to the desert lying at the back of the village to hunt rabbits and gazelles or to an island in the Nile to feast on a sheep. They would also take along alcohol for the many among them who drank.

This mode of food consumption was in conflict with the Islamic interdiction against alcohol and against Rubāṭāb norms informed by Islam. Regarding Islamic prohibitions, these young men were discriminative by giving themselves the right to decide what to uphold and what to violate. This ambiguity of accommodating a religiously unsanctioned supping in the picnic context was the subject of the following piece of Rubāṭāb dry humor.

A man widely known for his biting tongue came late to a picnic to find the men drinking but the butchered sheep unskinned. When asked why, the men said:

"We *ḥarjamnah*" (i.e., it was not killed in the strict Islamic way).

"And what is wrong with that?"

"*Ḥarām*" (it is forbidden by Islam to eat it).

Pointing to the bottles of alcohol, the man said, "Did you ask yourselves who sanctioned these?"

Rubāṭāb domesticity abhors eating at any but one's own home. They call this *kadāyah,* which is narrowly and aptly defined by one woman as "food not prepared by one's womenfolk and which children are woken up from their sleep to partake of." The emphasis on home as the culturally sanctioned space for the consumption of food is deftly made clear here. The hardworking Mayāyyīs lineage of ʿAtmūr village were known for their love of *kadāyah.* A *sōmār* song expressed the hope that a circumcised child, who belonged to the Mayāyyīs through his mother, would avoid taking to them:

> If you took to the Mayāyyīs
> they are a folk that indulge in *kadāyah*

Censuring *kadāyah* goes hand in hand with censuring drinking. A *sōmār* praised a man for not brewing beer or eating *kadāyah:*

> Listen O girls to the descriptions of his valor
> He does not indulge in *kadāyah* festivities and gain weight
> And does not waste his money drinking alcohol.

Those men knew that their picnics were culturally polluted, but they needed them to satisfy their claim to a modern youth. A man admitted that what they were doing was *kadāyah,* but to soften its image for the participants they rechristened it "alcommodation" (accommodation) in reference to reserving a compartment in a sleeping car on railway trains in which both bed and board are provided.

Concrete for the Ancestors

Rubāṭāb are apparently upset by a government that cares for their past more than their present, a present they have been forging on their own. Al-Ṭayyib Abū Sin, my classmate Rubāṭābī in the sixties, a folklorist who wrote his master's dissertation on the verbal art of his ethnic group, and a minister in the government of the northern region, to which the Rubāṭāb belong, proposed to Kiriz to commemorate Rubāṭ, the Rubāṭāb ancestor. Rubāṭ is buried in Kurgus village, and his grave lies just across the street from Kiriz's water pumps. The minister asked Kiriz to build a tomb for Rubāṭ on which the minister could hang a placard containing the genealogy of the Rubāṭāb. Kiriz's sons, who blamed Rubāṭ for coming to live in this rocky place, were not impressed by the minister's proposal. Instead, they suggested to their father that concrete be poured on his grave so that he would stay where he is, even on the day of resurrection. The implications of this attitude toward the government for my own mission, which could only be conceived as governmental, will be treated shortly.

Rubāṭāb are turning their dry humor on the government not only for failing to deliver but also for blaming them for these failures. The governor of the northern region, a Rubāṭābī and a former university professor, told me how in 1983, a time of extreme gasoline shortages, he blamed a group of Rubāṭāb farmers for not applying themselves conscientiously to their work and threatened to invite *fellahin* (Egyptian farmers) to come and farm their lands for them. A Rubāṭābī farmer asked the governor to allow him to comment, and when he was given the opportunity he said, "We won't object to your bringing Egyptians to farm our land for us, but I have a question for you: Would you provide them with gasoline, or should they bring their own from Egypt?"

People were determined to manage without the government, so they began building schools and introducing electricity on their own. The running water and the hospital projects undertaken by the government were going nowhere, and no one seemed to view the government as relevant to the kind of trouble they were going through. I attended a social occasion on which villagers were discussing the irrigation problems of their farms. They were appreciative of the good that came in the sixties with the big water pumps, but they were not nostalgic about these days, since they admitted that the experience had met a natural death. The owners of the pumps had been poor administrators, and the people were too unruly to observe the discipline required by a cooperative. Furthermore, the increasing farm income encouraged farmers to disengage from cooperatives and buy and install small Lester water pumps on their farms. In ʿAtmūr village alone they counted thirty-two Lester pumps, which were unjustified considering how little land farmers had at their disposal and the government's failure to deliver gasoline. An old man was trying to persuade the group that they should negotiate with Kiriz, whose big pumps were still in place, but Kiriz's business was in disarray and Kiriz himself was feebly surviving a stroke. However, the group was not at all impressed by his proposal and soon killed it by moving to another topic.

The government, which was espousing traditional values—augmented with a return to the rulership of God by Nimmeri's 1983 Islamic laws—was accused by the farmers of disregarding traditional land tenure practices. The *quṣād* right, the right of *sāqyah* owners to the government land bordering their family holdings, was being undermined by legislation before the regional assembly. This piece of legislation was pushed by those investing in water pumps, who, as developers, wanted to be given these government lands. The emergence of a capitalist class of developers pushing their way through an Islamic rhetoric is still underresearched in Sudan and perhaps other Muslim countries witnessing an Islamic revival. Analysts only scratch the surface of the latter phenomenon when they perceive it as a backlash against modernity. The economy of fundamentalism needs closer scrutiny.

The Rubāṭāb of the villages under study were familiar with the kind of interest I have had in their culture from my first visit in 1966. Some of them had even read or thumbed through *Min ʾAdab al-Rubāṭāb al-Shaʿbī* (Aspects from Rubāṭāb Folklore), which I coauthored in 1968. But I could understand their mixed feelings toward my mission. My dedication notwithstanding, they were justified in looking at my mission as frivolous, since it was reasonably financed and equipped by a government wrapped in making virtue of its bankruptcy: the president of the country was undergoing a fit of authenticity, dismissing complaints about power shortages as sassy and asking people to go back to the old ways of riding on jackasses, in boats, and so on. I felt embarrassed when my mission was occasionally perceived as having a direct utilitarian relevance to the villages. A Rubāṭābī, who took me for an administrator with the Cooperative Department, approached me once to complain about the high price they paid for sugar, which was rationed and, as such, had a fixed price.

To overcome their ambivalence toward my mission, the Rubāṭāb deployed their wit and charm to polemicize with it. My interest in *saḥir* was acknowledged by subjecting me to caustic *saḥrah*s, making me the victim of my own passion. Moreover, my claim on their time for interviews was seen as interfering with the serious farming work at hand. Thus they marked my work as trivial and constantly played on this comparison to subvert as well as sustain my mission. Some told me to my face that my mission was misguided, and they argued their case admirably.

In the *saḥir* launched at me, the *saḥḥār*s analogized the mechanics of my work among them to the work of medical doctors and nurses and to Sufi practices. Here are some of these *saḥrah*s: In the *daywān* where I stayed in ʿAtmūr, people hang out for a variety of reasons, and I made use of this situation to conduct minor interviews. One day I called someone for a short recording session. Later I called someone else to explain a Rubāṭābī idiom for me. Immediately after the second call one of those present shouted to me, "Doctor! They killed you!" "How?" I said, hating to be the victim of the metaphors I set out to collect. He replied, "Someone here just said the physician began calling numbers." The reference is being made here to the practice in private clinics by which nurses admit patients to see doctors in the order of the numbers they were given on arrival to the clinic.

A *saḥḥār* who saw me carrying my recorder all the time compared me to nurses who carry the water kettle in which they boil water to sterilize syringes every time they use them.

I interviewed a *saḥḥār,* and he recommended that I should also meet with another *saḥḥār.* I heard later that the first *saḥḥār* sent a message to the second one saying that the doctor would operate on him the day after his own operation was performed. A fourth *saḥrah,* in which my work was compared to Sufi ritual, will be described in chapter three.

The Rubāṭāb farmers I encountered also weigh their past against their present in terms of work and time. With the expanding economy, they have no time for leisure. In contrast, their fathers' generation lived a life of relative leisure. Whereas they make trips strictly for business reasons, their fathers took long trips to visit their relatives.

To index my work among them as *fāqah* (having no work to do, leisurely), Rubāṭāb played on their *shaghalah* (absorption in work) over and over again. A successful farmer from the Mayāyyīs lineage was surprised that I should care to collect riddles and *maqālāt* (old, repeated stuff; folklore). When asked to record *saḥirs*, *saḥḥārs* would excuse themselves for forgetting them due to absorption in work. A Rubāṭābī would introduce me to another saying, "Don't you have a *saḥrah* to deliver to him?" In answering this question, a Rubāṭābī once said, "I never thought the day would come when *saḥir* would be in demand." Muḥammad ʿAlī Muṣṭafah, the patriarch of the Mayāyyīs lineage, defined the *wannās* (performer) as the one who pulls out jokes and anecdotes that arouse laughter. "But," he said, "that requires leisure." Madīnah al-Ḥāj, whose charm as a performer we will see in chapter three, said that folktales disappeared with the death of their old folks. Those who survived them, she continued to say, turned into people of "*ḥash* and *qash*" (weeds and weeding) and hardly had time even to attend to the work at hand. Finally, in concluding an interview I had with her, Zaynab al-Fakī complained, saying, "Had it not been for your interview I could have made headway attending to my *shaghalah.*"

The real or imagined demands upon the villagers' time resulting from this new economic activity is generally felt and expressed by farmers. I asked Khiḍir once if he had been to Egypt. He said that he had not but would have liked to.

"What prevents you?" I said.

"Not before it [i.e., *shaghalah*] lets go of my hand."

A *maqālah* (folklore or proverb) says that a father ordered his son to beat his sister, who was fighting with him. The father was unaware that his daughter had overpowered her brother and was tying up his hands. The son said helplessly to his father, "Not before she lets go of my hand."

I asked Muṣṭafah al-Hadaʿ, a *saḥḥār* from a family known for *saḥir,* if I might accompany him to the island where his family lives to record *saḥrah*s from them. "*Ṭarīqatnah* [our Sufi religious brotherhood] in the island is *marayq* [a variety of grain sorghum]," he said. With this answer, in which he, a diligent farmer, denied any knowledge of *saḥir,* he was alluding to a story about an older relative of his. In the heat of the religious and political controversies that followed the independence of the Sudan in 1956, this relative was asked about the *ṭarīqah* (brotherhood) he belonged to. Known to be "good at ploughing, good at farming," he curtly replied, "My *ṭarīqah* is *marayq*" (i.e., "all I know is farming").

The interviews I requested from Rubāṭāb were usually dismissed as a waste of time. On one occasion I asked a woman to define *wanasah* for me. She defined it as whiling away time by casual talking. Significantly, she considered my interview with her to be a kind of *wanasah* and started pointing to those attending the interview as people who had abandoned their *shaghalah* to while away time. She even pointed to me as one of the loafers. I objected laughingly, "I did not abandon my work. This *is* my work."

"Aha! You are attending to your business then. But what about the rest of us? Cousin, you made me abandon my *shaghalah.*" I remember that she was visibly worried at the time because some of her lambs needed to be tethered.

My mission was openly censured by an elderly Rubāṭābī into whom I ran unplanned and decided to interview on Rubāṭāb discourse genres. He was extremely negative in his views on folktales and *wannās*es (performers). He described the latter as "talkative" and the former as nonsensical and pure inventions, like "someone waking from a dream." I asked him how he would define a *buda'ī* (*wannās*, performer). At this point he could not take any of my questions anymore and apparently wanted to get my mission straight. He said to me:

"What good do these discourses of past people [old wives' tales] contain to deserve your interest?"

(Laughingly) "I want *al-buda'* [the fun of them]."

"These discourses are worthless in this time of ours. What really matters are today's discourses. Past people's discourses are futile. They are like folktales, like someone narrating a folktale. I just cannot stomach such narration because they are like waking from a dream. These discourses have no *zibdah* [butter, point]."

"Pardon."

"Milk produces butter when curdled. Nay, the stuff of old days." He turned to those around who were having the fun of their life from this encounter and said, "Discourses of people past are nonsense. Or isn't that so?"

I asked, "But where do you think *zibdah* lies now?"

"In discourses of today that are sound, pointed, and pragmatic. Past discourses lack *sīyāsah* [politics, acumen], shrewdness and discernment. You will find even the average person of today adept, pragmatic, and discriminative."

What If I Stole with My Left Hand?

Rubāṭāb are conscious that religious practices, especially prayers, are observed more now than they were before. More people perform the Friday communal prayer in mosques than in the past, when the quorum (twelve adult men) for holding this prayer was not reached. Laxity in performing this prayer in the past was a subject for Rubāṭāb humor. I was told of a group who wanted to pray but found that they were one man short of the quorum.

They spotted a man on his way to his farm and asked him to join them to make their prayer ritually valid. Pressed to pray for the quorum's sake, the man said, "I will do it for you today, but what are you going to do next Friday?"

This village religiosity of the men I studied stems from a cultural sobriety that comes with age, growing in the responsibilities of heading households in times of opportunity, strain, and change. The business/domestic successes some of these Rubāṭāb achieved translated into a religious idea of God's design and man's mission and the indebtedness of the latter to the former. Bājūrī, whom we have seen leading a life of "hooliganism" in Atbara town in the forties and fifties, succinctly made the convergence of age, family, success, and religion as follows:

> Praise to Allah, I returned to the village and planted dates, built a stone mill, praise the Lord. I married four wives and begot children. [He enumerated four or five of his many children, two of them university graduates.] I moved my house from the farm to the ridge across from the road. I believe I did well. I built a spacious family compound on government land. I praise God by following his orders and abstaining from his prohibitions.

The age factor in this religiosity characterizes it with sobriety and a stark sense of realism. This realism is in evidence in a comment by a Rubāṭābī on the drying of the country that came in the wake of the Islamization undertaken by Nimmeri in 1983. The man, who stopped drinking just before the laws prohibiting drinking, said, "Drinking becomes unbearable when one advances in age until the time comes and you kick the habit. Nimmeri [famous for carousing and excessive drinking long after he assumed power in 1969] reached the age of kicking the habit and I see no reason why he should dramatize this personal decision and make it a state law."

I conducted my fieldwork in 1984 when the process of Islamization, which had begun the year before, needed the emergency laws of 1984 to be effected. Rubāṭāb were not enchanted by this state Islam and played with their notions of Islam and politics to question its sincerity and applicability. It is true that some villagers were closely and hopefully following the severe measures taken by the newly created Islamic state against sections of the merchant class involved in smuggling goods across the eastern borders of Sudan or taking rationed provisions from one region of the country to another to sell them on the black market. A Rubāṭābī was appalled that a school was asking him to pay fees for his children when the government coffers were filled with the huge fines those merchants were asked to pay. The fear that struck the wealthy from the severe emergency laws made a Rubāṭābī say, "These are one of the rare times a poor man is envied."

However, Rubāṭāb were apparently convinced that the state's application of *sharīʿah* law was too good to be true. A Rubāṭābī said that embezzlement, nepotism, and dishonesty were so rampant and entrenched that weaning those who practiced them was impossible. They were not enchanted by *sharīʿah* degenerating into a "witch-hunt" for drunkards and fornicators, whose public floggings were broadcast on the nine o'clock radio news. *Saḥir* comes in handy to Rubāṭāb to mediate their ambivalence over a *sharīʿah* that went awry. A *saḥrah* criticizes the obvious political uses to which Nimmeri was putting *sharīʿah.* It describes his recourse to *sharīʿah* as a swimmer drifting in a place of strong current and not having a rope to hook to a tree or rock for support. The aggressiveness of *sharīʿah* emergency courts against minor actors such as burglars, fornicators, and drunkards was noted in a *saḥrah* by al-Shaykh al-Ṣāyim of Mugrat Island. In the *saḥrah* he analogized the undue emphasis of Nimmeri's *sharīʿah* on alcohol and drinking to a *sāqyah* that has one *farīdah* or *inqāyah* (plot, row, or side). For a *sāqyah* to deserve the name or justify the investment it has to have more than one plot of cultivation.

The Rubāṭāb were affronted or puzzled by aspects of the application of *sharʿiah* in 1984. To counteract or play with these aspects, they recalled episodes from a repertoire of irreverence that the generation I studied had developed in its youth. Performers like ʾAḥmad ʾAbd al-Qādir and ʾAḥmad Ḥunbuliyyah dominate this literature as tricksters to whom nothing is sacred. A Rubāṭābī was aggravated by the government, in its Islamic drive, imposing *zakah* (alms tax) on the people. He was arguing that the government had no right to tax them twice: to ask them to pay the usual taxes and *zakah*. He said, "If the government would not cancel the taxes we would just refuse to pay *zakah*." Another man commented, "If you are plagued by the miserly make up for the loss by resorting to the generous." People understood immediately that the man was suggesting that as long as the government (the miserly) insisted on taking its taxes, people had no alternative other than not paying *zakah*, God's (the generous) alms.

The statement recalls a similar situation that took place in the late forties or early fifties. At that time Kiriz and ʾAḥmad ʾAbd al-Qādir, the trickster, were fledgling village merchants entrusted with distributing sugar, a rationed item after World War II, to their customers. ʾAbd al-Qādir complained to Kiriz that some villagers insisted on having their right share of sugar regardless of the loss of sugar that resulted from the wear and tear of the sacks. Kiriz threw at him this common aphorism of the miserly and the generous. However, Kiriz discovered that ʾAbd al-Qādir started to decrease the villagers' shares of sugar across the board. ʾAbd al-Qādir understood from the aphorism that he should resort to God's right, that is, to cheat in the weight, an action strictly prohibited in the Koran. Kiriz explained to him what he meant by the expression: to take from those who understood his problem to avoid getting in trouble with the stingy customers.

Some conventions of *sharīʿah* sentences intrigued people. Wad al-Tōm, a *saḥḥār*, was puzzled by the fact that it was the right hand of a thief that was cut off. He wanted to know why the left hand was spared from blame. A villager argued that people use their right hands to steal things. Wad al-Tōm replied, "What if I said that I stole with my left hand?" In this context, people recalled a story about Khālid, the humorous shaykh of Abu Hamad town. As a witness before a court, Khālid was asked one day to take the oath on the Koran. Khālid extended his left hand and took the oath. A common belief warns that false oaths lead to hands ultimately suffering from paralysis. Khālid, not especially known for being truthful, explained his decision to use his left hand instead of the right one, often used for this purpose, by saying that he would prefer his left hand to suffer if his oath proved false. This in turn recalled a story about a Rubāṭābī greeting a man he hated by extending his left hand. The man did not like that and asked why the other man did not use his right hand. The Rubāṭābī said, "What gives you the right to discriminate against one of my hands?"

Genres of Rubāṭāb Discourse

Rubāṭāb identify an array of their discourse genres as *maqālāt* (sing. *maqālah*). *Maqālat* is the passive participle of *qāl* (said). The mechanics as well as the ethical status of these discourse genres are implied by the way they are categorized. These genres are described as "*kalām ba'id aw tārīkhī aw qadīm*" (past or historical or ancient discourses). An informant even broke down *maqālah* to its root, *qāl*, and repeated "*qāl, qāl, qāl*" to emphasize the mechanics of transmission in *maqālāt*. To bring the point of transmission home, a literate informant referred to the Prophet's *hadīth* tradition in which *'an'anah* (handing down of tradition) is used to explain the relaying of *maqālāt*. Telling about your first-hand experience, according to an informant, is not a *maqālah* but a *wanasah* (casual talk).

Maqālat are characterized by the anonymity of the author, reproduction by application to current situations, and uncertainty regarding occurrence. Regarding authorship, an informant said a *maqālah* is handed down and "*maqtū'ah min al-rās*" (lit., cut from the head, not created by a known individual). Anonymity is defined by another informant as the futility of trying to *tasnidah* (attribute it) to a particular individual. Three processes are mentioned in the reproduction of *maqālāt* in the present: *ta'qīb* (repetition), *jar* (pull out, apply), and *ḍarb mathal* (to analogize). One would say "*y 'mlāt al-maqālah*" (as the *maqālah*) as a key to applying a *maqālah* to an emerging situation. The veracity of the *maqālah* is held in doubt by the Rubāṭāb. An informant said the *maqālah* can be "*ḥāṣlah wa mā ḥaṣlah, māfī zūl yaqdar yaqūl*" (it could have happened and it could have not. No one can be certain). An informant said a *maqālah* can be truthful, but he did not feel contradicted when someone else said it could also be false. In mode of transmission as well as anonymity of authorship, *maqālāt* can be seen as a "a folk gloss on the learned idea of folklore itself" (Herzfeld 1983, 1–2).

The ambiguity of *maqālah* is enacted in a Rubāṭāb folktale and in a conversation I had with a Rubāṭābī man and woman: A young man did not find a match in any of the village girls paraded to him by a matchmaker, an old woman. In desperation, the old woman rebuked him saying:

"You will only be married to al-Luʿayb, I think."

"And who is this Luʿayb?"

"Don't be ridiculous. This is mere *maqālah*."

"You wouldn't have mentioned her to me had it been only so."

The young man cajoled the old woman to reveal the place of al-Luʿayb. Understandably, he got her after being subjected to severe trials and tribulations.

I asked a woman, unusually literate for her age due to the religious education she had received from her father, about an "unorthodox" formula allegedly recited by women before starting their prayers. The woman started reciting it, and her cousin Khalīfah, who was attending our conversation, objected to the formula:

"Who starts his prayers with this formula?"

(Taken aback, confused) "What?"

"This formula you are reciting is sheer *maqālah*."

"But this is exactly why this man is here."

"At any rate this recitation is a *maqālah*."

(Condescendingly) "I can't agree with you more. It is not religion. It is a *maqālah* performed by illiterate women who don't know better."

"This is a *maqālah* you find among the *ʿArab*" (nomads).

However, *maqālāt* become pure fiction in two distinct cases. *Ḥujah* (folktales), a form of *maqālah* performed largely by women narrators, is seen by men as a collection of fantasies. Men variously described *ḥujah* as "lies," "fiction," "myths," and "*maqālah* of old wives, based solely on lies." Women are said to "cut it from their head." The Koranic "*habāun manthūr*" was used by an informant to judge the worthlessness of *ḥujah.* The women I talked to were less interested in the ethicality of lies and truths than men were. Instead, women foregrounded the mechanics of the genre as *maqālāt* not attributable to anyone in particular and handed down from one generation to the next. A woman narrator said that as a mother she found *ḥujah* handy in *ghashghish* (lit., deceiving, taking one's mind off something) her children of supper until it was ready.

Fiction creeps into *maqālāt* also through the embellishment of the wordy entertainers. These entertainers, who pepper *wanasah* (casual talk) with their arts, are described as *maqālāt* tellers, humorists, mimics, and *buda'ī,* that is, tellers of *buda'*. *Buda'* is defined by a Rubāṭābī as discourses an entertainer creates. It is again defined as saying things, understood largely to be humorous, that have never been said before. However, the *buda'ī* builds a creation on kernels of realities or occurrences or *maqālāt.* The process by which the creation is spun off is called *ta'līq* (comment) or *talḥīn* (embellishment). A *buda'ī* is defined by a Rubāṭābī as one who makes a short story long by embellishment and ornamentation.

I asked al-Shaykh al-Ṣāyim, a *buda'ī,* about how stories come to him. Below is how he embellished a story to apply to an emerging situation he found himself in:

> He lived once for a month or so in a Rubāṭāb hostel in Atbara town. For dessert after lunch the cook served bananas every day. Al-Ṣāyim refused to take his bananas one day. Asked about the reason, al-Ṣāyim told the story of the homosexual, the bananas, and the monkey. In the story the homosexual would invite boys to his place, give them bananas, and have sex with them in front of his monkey. One day his date did not show up and, in desperation, he ate some of the bananas and threw some to the monkey. The monkey revoltingly swung his head, body, and hands and refused to take the bananas.

I asked al-Ṣāyim about how he came to learn the story. He said he heard it from Salmān, the head of the Rubāṭāb "native" administration. However, in reproducing it in the hostel context, he took only the frame of Salmān's story and improvised the rest of it. The story he heard was about a blacksmith, a kid goat, and a monkey. The blacksmith wanted his monkey to learn how to fan the fire with bellows. To teach it by example, the blacksmith would bring a kid, order it to fan the fire, and beat it when it failed to do so. The blacksmith did this with the kid repeatedly and ultimately killed it with a knife when it failed to learn. The "moral" of the story did not escape the monkey. Asked to work the bellows, the monkey, having learned the lesson, complied and did well.

Although *saḥḥār*s, like *buda'ī*s, are largely *maqālāt* tellers, *saḥir* is not viewed as a *maqālah.* Wad al-Tōm, a *saḥḥār* and a *buda'ī,* denied any retention of *maqālāt* or *ḥujah* to circumvent any suggestion that *saḥir* is a *maqālah.* At any rate, *saḥḥār*s argue that *saḥir* is emergent and describe it as a "repartee," a "direct comment," "quick-wittedness," a "joke," and an "analogy." Muḥammad 'Ayyūb, a young *saḥḥār,* said that his "*saḥir* is not premeditated or planned. It is something that I have neither studied at school nor discussed in a *wanasah.* It is innate, you are born with it. You see something and there is this urge to analogize it to something else."

2

Saḥir and the Fantasy of Difference

So far we have only mentioned that the Rubāṭāb identify those among them who cast the evil eye as *saḥḥārs*. Chapters four and five will be devoted to elaborating and analyzing the dynamics of these accusations. In this chapter, in order to discuss aspects of their identity in terms of the way they "other" people near to and far from them, we will deal with other people the Rubāṭāb identify as *saḥḥārs*.

We have already indicated that the Rubāṭāb are Muslims and that Arabic is their mother tongue. We have also mentioned that they belong to the Jaʿalīyyīn group of northern Sudan, who claim Arab descent from Al-ʿAbbās, the paternal uncle of Prophet Muḥammad. In the most common version of the Jaʿalīyyīn genealogy, their ancestor Ibrāhīm Jaʿal begot ʿArmān, the ancestor of the proper Jaʿalīyyīn, Shāīq of the Shāīqīyyah, and Rubāṭ of the Rubāṭāb. Islam, Arabism, and a farming economy, in conjunction with the Sudanese state structures that mushroomed in their region of riverain central Sudan, gave the Jaʿalīyyīn the privilege of defining the Sudan as we now know it. The Jaʿalī elite, for example, are believed to have monopolized political and economic power since the independence of the country in 1956. Mansour Khalid bashes this ruling elite for failing the country "because of myopia, dogmatism, ethnocentricity, factionalism and, in the case of some, religious bigotry" (1990, 11). From this position of power we will see how the Rubāṭāb brutally deploy *saḥḥār* to "other" (Ashcroft, Griffiths, and Tiffin 1989, 103) neighboring communities and fix identity as the fantasy of difference (Bhabha 1985, 94).

In being called a *saḥḥār*, the one who possesses the evil eye is automatically categorized with an order of actors and actions that define his person and power. These orders and actions, to which *saḥḥār* are also applied, are as follows:

1. The nomad Manāṣīr "Arabs" are accused of practicing a form of *saḥir* called "knotting" in which a Manṣūrī's property (a camel, for example) is rendered irremovable by thieves.
2. *Saḥḥār* is applied to persons who transform themselves into crocodiles and attack and eat people.[1] Those especially accused of this *saḥir* are the Danāqlah, a non-Arabic-speaking Muslim community inhabiting the Nile region immediately north of the Jaʿalīyyīn homeland.
3. The cannibals and ogresses and ogres of the folktales are also identified as *saḥḥārs*. These cannibals, who are seen involved in plots to entice, elope with, or eat women, possess the ability to transform into animate and inanimate forms.
4. *Saḥḥār* is also applied to some "Sudanic," non-Arabic-speaking communities to the south and west of the Jaʿalīyyīn country. These Sudanic groups are believed to transform themselves into cannibals, vampires, and ogres, and to disembowel human beings.

In the three latter senses the *saḥḥār* is conceived of as a regular cannibal. This association between *saḥir* and cannibalism evidences itself in the ballistic and homicidal idioms in which the audience to the *saḥir* performances express their delight of its exactitude, as will be discussed in chapter five. An audience appraising his power of comparison would say the *saḥḥār* shot the target of his metaphor dead. Audiences normally punctuate their laughter with expressions such as "he killed him," "*qaraḍōk*" (bit, tore with his teeth), and "*yaqrush*" (crunch). The evil bite of a *saḥḥār* is compared to the sting of a scorpion.

This association between *saḥir* and cannibalism was strikingly brought home to me in an interview in which an informant described a Rubāṭābī as an evil *saḥḥār* who missed no opportunity to bewitch and cause needless misfortunes. This *saḥḥār* was reported to have said, "At times I taste blood in my mouth when I conjure up a *saḥir*." And the informant commented, "When this *saḥḥār* bewitches someone his mouth tastes of blood exactly like a regular *saḥḥār* [i.e., a cannibal]." Another *saḥḥār* (evil eyer) was described as having black spots on his tongue and as smacking his lips when he uttered a *saḥir*.

Ethnographers of cannibalism are not embarrassed to question the existence of the object of their study, that is, the practice of cannibalism. They occasionally find it necessary to ask if their scholarship is not about, in Luise White's words, the "things that never happened" (1993, a1). Arens (1979) argues that ethnographers must be skeptical about the actual existence of cannibalism because no one has ever observed this purported cultural universal. His assertion that the attribution of cannibalism is sometimes a projection of moral superiority has been accepted by ethnographers (Sanday 1986, 9; Brown and Tuzin 1983, 3). Nonetheless, these ethnographers believe that the existence of cannibalism is borne out by the evidence of the extant literature. Importantly, they dismiss the actual occurrence of cannibalism as of little import (Poole 1983, 6; Sanday 1986, 3). What analysis should address, in their view, is an interpretation of the symbolic, metaphoric, or ideological dimension of the reported act of cannibalism or beliefs (Poole 1983, 6). Sanday argues, "Cannibalism is never just about eating but is primarily a medium for nongustatory messages—messages having to do with the maintenance, regeneration, and in some cases, the foundation of the cultural order" (1986, 3). Accusations of cannibalism, Sanday continues, can constitute a cultural order in various ways. If projected outward they become a feature of the ethnic landscape and can provide an idiom for deranged and antisocial behavior. They become an idiom of dreams, possession states, and other fantasy formations in case these accusations are projected inward (1986, 6, 8). Cannibalism, in Lindenbaum's view, "emerges less as a single form of behavior located in a number of out-of-the-way places, than as an activity to be comprehended by reference to its place in particular cultural orbits" (1983, 95). Poole maintains that different constellations of the cultural construction of cannibalism are woven from different ideas about reproduction, ethnicity, or other elements. He also says that images of enemies, sorcerers, witches, and wild animals are implicated in the construction (1983, 30). White identifies the vampire accusations in southern Africa as an "epistemological category" with which Africans described their world (1993).

White (1992, 1993), Coplan (1992), Strathern (1982), and Lewis (1989) have been studying situations in Africa and other places where Europeans were accused of being vampires, that is, situations in which the cannibals are "writing back." Chief among the emerging issues from these studies is the manner in which magic is inextricably juxtaposed with cannibalism. Lewis convincingly argues for exploring this connection for a meaningful understanding of cannibalism. He starts off by pointing out the "anthropological paradox" (1989, 234) in dealing with the dynamics of witchcraft and cannibalism. Anthropology, according to Lewis, assumes a disinterested (if not disbelieving) external perspective regarding witchcraft, concentrating on the accusation and the accuser. However, anthropology is credulous when it comes to cannibalism, concentrating rather on the accused (1989, 332). Anthropology is thus prevented from studying witchcraft as it dovetails into cannibalism. For, if we want to fully understand the dynamics of cannibalism we have to set it in context "as a part of a wider constellation of ideas concerning mystical powers and witchcraft in particular" (1989, 233). Lewis also says that African and many other peoples believe that "witches eat people" (1989, 233).

The juxtaposition of witchcraft and cannibalism calls into question the independent status each enjoyed as a separate field of ethnographic inquiry. And a realization that they belong to a unified domain of activity may set right misconceptions that arise from dealing with them independently. The two ethnographies, for example, have been faulted for exhibiting diametrically opposed tendencies. Evil eye studies, as a subcategory of witchcraft scholarship, were criticized for eschewing theory and presenting too many examples (Spooner 1976, 280). The ethnography of cannibalism, on the other hand, has been criticized for premature theorizing on inadequate reporting (Brown and Tuzin 1983, 6).

Manāṣīr Nomads as Saḥḥārs

Sōmār songs, in which the noble ancestry of a Rubāṭāb family and wealth are praised, painstakingly delineate the property bases of the Rubāṭāb identity as *nās al-balad* (village people). *Sīd* (owner of) is formulaic with this kind of songs. A man is described as the owner of the *sāqyah.* In a problem-ridden land (because of claims and counterclaims), these songs describe a man's ownership as certain and unchallenged. The boundaries of such farms are said to be "faultlessly drawn." The Rubāṭāb, who claim to be "sons of Arabs," hire "Arabs"—denoting nomads per se and including the non-Arabic-speaking Beja of the Red Sea Hills as well as the Manāṣīr Arabs—to work on their land on a seasonal basis, pollinating their palm trees and cutting their dates. Pejoratively, "Arab" connotes landlessness in Rubāṭāb idioms.

Rubāṭāb invest in livestock, too. This mixed economic enterprise of the Rubāṭāb is metonymically represented in the *sōmār* songs by praising a man for owning the "palm date tree" as well as the "young she-camel." The palm date tree stands for the agricultural component of that economy, whereas the young she-camel stands for the pastoral component. In the latter component the Rubāṭāb hire "Arabs" for herding their livestock. A Rubāṭābī describes the Manāṣīr Arabs' dependency on the Rubāṭāb as follows:

> The Arabs bore wells in the watercourse at the back of the village. That was unacceptable to us because the land of the watercourse is ours. It is even more expansive than our river land. And it is fertile too. It has silt and, as a sign of its fecundity, *ʿushar* shrubs grow on it. In olden times the river used to fill that watercourse. Our grandfathers witnessed the flooding of the watercourse in their times. This is the reason why we asked the Arabs to destroy their wells if they wanted to live in peace with us. And they did.

Manāṣīr are accused by the Rubāṭāb of practicing a form of *saḥir* for which they are called the *fanqāsah,* from the verb *fanqas,* meaning to kneel and stick one's butt out. The variety of Manāṣīr *saḥir* is of the "knotting" type, in which a property of a Manṣūrī is protected against theft by tying it to a location through witchcraft and rendering it irremovable. To effect his *saḥir*, a Manṣūrī would ritually kneel and stick out his butt to the redness of the sunrise and sunset.

At the mica factory in Al-Shrayk West I asked the non-Rubāṭābī technician in charge if the Rubāṭāb *saḥir* interfered with the technical operations. He said, "It sure does. *Saḥir* incapacitated the water tanker. A Rubāṭābī asked me to do him a favor and I refused. He did not like that and told me that I would soon regret it. Soon the tanker broke down, and it hasn't worked since." The Rubāṭāb who were present asked the technician to name the Rubāṭābī who bewitched the tanker. The Rubāṭāb identified the man the technician named as a Manṣūrī rather than a Rubāṭābī.

Stories abound among the Rubāṭāb of how knotting works. One story tells about an animal thief who wanted to steal a Manṣūrī's camel. The thief looked for a saddle to put on the camel, but he could not find one. In lieu of a saddle he took off his pants and filled them with sand. He then put this sand saddle on the camel and prodded it to move, but to no avail. The thief sweated all night trying to stir the camel to move, but he failed miserably. At daybreak the Manṣūrī—the owner of the camel—came to check on his camel and found the thief naked, exhausted, and fixed to his impossible task. The Manṣūrī pitied the thief, saying, "Poor you! You tried hard all night, but you stayed put." The thief implored the Manṣūrī to break the spell and lend him pants to put on because his were ripped apart from riding the knotted camel all night.

The spell a Manṣūrī can cast on someone is best illustrated by what an ex-mayor of the Rubāṭāb told about his relationship with a Manṣūrī politician. The ex-mayor met casually with the Manṣūrī, who was running for election in a constituency that included the Rubāṭāb region. The ex-mayor found himself drawn to the Manṣūrī and joined his political campaign. The mayor said, "The candidate just bewitched me. I worked for him for forty-five days, abandoning my family and business."

Manāṣīr are apparently careful to act as good clients to the Rubāṭāb patrons. They deploy their witchcraft to rectify relationships with the Rubāṭāb when they turn sour. A Rubāṭābī said the Manāṣīr would knot their livestock lest they graze the Rubāṭāb farms. Mughdād, a village skeptic, told me about a Manṣūrī camel that terrorized the village people and would not cool down. Incensed by this incivility on the part of the Manāṣīr, the Rubāṭāb sent them an ultimatum, that they must either control their camel or leave the village. A Manṣūrī, annoyed by the ultimatum, came running in the direction of an elderly Manṣūrī with whom my informant was talking. The elderly Manṣūrī was asked by the other Manṣūrī to restrain the camel. The elderly Manṣūrī said:

"But you well know that I no longer do such things" (knotting, i.e., witchcraft).

"You would not expect me to buy this from you, eh! Do you know that the village people are determined we either control the camel or they will evict us from the village?"

The elderly Manṣūrī gave in and asked the other Manṣūrī to bring a handful of dirt taken from the hoofprints of the camel. When that dirt was brought the elderly man held it in his hand, and instantly the camel cooled down.

However, Manāṣīr might use their *saḥir* to avenge themselves against insulting Rubāṭāb. A common curse formula among the Rubāṭāb originated from such an encounter between a Manṣūrī and a Rubāṭābī. When a Rubāṭābī is extremely mad at someone and wants him to disappear forever he would say, "God causes you to take the non-return trip of Wad ʿAjīb." Tradition has it that Wad ʿAjīb, a Rubāṭābī, was on bad terms with the nomads. A nomad came to Wad ʿAjīb's waterwheel and found the man driving his oxen around watering his farm. The nomad sprinkled the dirt he had in his hand all over the farm. When Wad ʿAjīb finished watering the farm, he stopped the waterwheel and headed home, and that was the last anyone saw of Wad ʿAjīb. He mysteriously left the village, never to return to his farm, and his waterwheel was ultimately devoured by termites.

Danāqlah as Saḥḥārs

Danāqlah, that is, the people of Dongola, a seat of the historical Nubian Christian kingdoms of medieval Sudan, also figure in Rubāṭāb discourses as *saḥḥār*s. *Saḥḥār* Nāwī (Nāwī being the first Danāqlah village across from the Jaʿalī/Shāīqi homeland) is proverbial among the Jaʿalī community representing the monsters next door. The mutual contempt in which the Shāīqīyyah and the Danāqlah hold each other is succinctly described in al-Shahi (1986, 68–90). In what follows we will give two narratives delivered by Rubāṭāb on the "amphibian" Danāqlah *saḥḥār*s who live in water and on land, and who meticulously perform their obligations as kin and families. A third narrative will explore the connection between Danāqlah and Rubāṭāb *saḥir.*

Khalīfah, a Rubāṭābī, tells about a helmsman (a profession filled exclusively by Danāqlah) who approached and negotiated with his *saḥḥār* relative while Rubāṭāb were watching:

> Boats used to come from *aṣ-Ṣaʿīd* [south] to our region carrying sorghum and cooking oil to be traded for dates. Railroads had not yet taken at that time the transportation of dates. Crocodiles were known to live not far away from the boat port. One of these boat people was seen wading into the water in the direction of the lair of the crocodiles. A crocodile came to meet the man. The man was overheard talking to the crocodile/*saḥḥār,* whom he was reprimanding for abandoning his children and family. After two hours of conversation with the crocodile, the man returned to his boat.

Jaqalaybah, a Rubāṭābī from ʿAtmūr village, tells of the *saḥir* experiences of a Rubāṭābī who went to a Danāqlah village to visit the children of a relative who had married into the Danāqlah:

> A Rubāṭābī married into the Danāqlah of Al-Qolid village and had a son and a daughter before his death. A cousin of the Rubāṭābī traveled to Al-Qolid to visit the family of his relative. In Al-Qolid he met a non-Dunqulawī who had lived with the Danāqlah for a long time and who told the Rubāṭābī of his encounters with them. He told him

about the Danāqlah who ate the meat of a dead cow and would not listen to him when he suggested that they dig a ditch for the corpse and bury it. The man also told the Rubāṭābī about the time he saw trays of food being carried from a wake to the river and how they were returned empty and spotlessly clean. Clearly, the ritual food was taken to their crocodile/*saḥḥār* relatives, who took time to wash the dishes. Weary of his fears of *saḥḥār*s living in the river, the people of Al-Qolid identified a spot on the riverbank from which the man could safely take water for his household purposes. He went to take water from the spot they identified, but the place scared him to death. Subsequently, he asked a Dunqulawī to come down with him to that spot in the river to experience for himself the dread of the place. No sooner they arrived at the place than a crocodile jumped out of the water, snatched the Dunqulawī, and reentered the river with its catch. The terrorized man ran to the village and broke the story to the people, who went about their usual business unperturbed. To the man's great astonishment, the Dunqulawī resurfaced and was walking around the village in one piece. [The narrator is apparently suggesting that the Danāqlah planned to get rid of the inquisitive, unnerving man, but the crocodile took instead his relative, the Dunqulawī, and returned him when he discovered his mistake.]

Undeterred by what he heard from the man who lived among the Danāqlah long enough to experience their *saḥir,* the Rubāṭābī went to a relatively isolated place on the riverbank. In the water he saw a man whom he described as "red" (white) in color, surrounded by young crocodiles. The red man was patting the young crocodiles on their backs in the water, thus producing a "*ṭubuj, ṭubuj*" sound. The Rubāṭābī took to his heels.

The subversive power that the *saḥḥār*s set loose is so engaging that the search for a theory of *saḥir* is a continuing process among the Rubāṭāb. The theories I came across encompass notions on causation, disposition, intentions, envy, agency, coincidence, and predestination. Ḥasan Jaqalaybah, of ʿAtmūr village, an uninhibited theoretician, argues that *saḥir* originates in the Rubāṭāb preference for crocodile meat. However, some crocodiles are believed to be men *saḥḥār*s who, failing to pay the excessive taxes imposed by governments, transformed themselves into crocodiles and preyed on women to take their gold ornaments. Such a crocodile, known also as a *saḥḥār,* would mate with a proper female crocodile and impart his witchcraft to his offspring. In eating one of these offspring, a Rubāṭābī would imbibe its *saḥir* and become a *saḥḥār,* that is, one who casts the evil eye. In the following statement Jaqalaybah expounds his theory, its sources, and how he verified it and found it adequate to explain the phenomenon of *saḥir.*

I was once talking to a Dunqulawī man on the train about the ways we hunt and eat crocodiles in the Rubāṭāb region. The Dunqulawī man said, "Hey, brother, you should not eat crocodile meat."

"You just say that. If you tasted it once you would never eat anything else."

"You'd better heed my words, don't eat it."

"Just give me one good reason. I tell you it tastes great and the hides sell good. Eating crocodile meat is like dessert for us. We hunt crocodiles after having our dinner. If you are lucky to catch one you would barbecue it. I once caught six crocodiles with six fishing rods. The length of the crocodiles I caught ranged from two to three feet. I swear by Allah we ate the six crocodiles in just two days. I tell you, man, no one can have his fill eating crocodile meat. You eat it and you want more of it."

"Nonetheless, I warn you. It is no good."

"You are not giving me a single good reason, though."

"You asked for it. Of course, you heard about men who transform themselves into *saḥḥārs* and everything. Perhaps you don't believe in this. But take it from me. It is true that some people can transform themselves into *saḥḥārs*. In olden times some people chose to live in the river because of their failure to pay their taxes. To live in the water away from the grip of the government, these people transformed themselves into crocodiles. A crocodile from this category would hide close to the river bank to attack women wearing gold. A crocodile would not attack a woman to eat her, nay, it is the gold that the crocodile wanted. This is true, man. A *saḥḥār* would prefer residing in the river to living in this problem-ridden land. In water the *saḥḥār* would mate with a female crocodile, thus imparting witchcraft to his offspring from his *saḥir* root. However, his offspring would not be *saḥḥārs* the way their father was. They would have the *saḥir* root in their constitution, though. If you ate one of those offspring you had in your catch it would pass its *saḥir* root to you for you to become a *saḥḥār* in your own right. If, for example, you would look at a plump, young goat with a puffed-up, fat tail and started saying to yourself [Jaqalaybah actually started talking to me the way one would talk to one's self], 'What a feast this goat will make!' You would say that desiring the goat for yourself. You rest assured this goat is done for. There would either come guests the same day and the goat would be butchered for their banquet, or it would fall somehow and break its neck. The coming of the guests or the falling of the goat were incidental to the demise of the goat. The real cause for the misfortune of the goat was in fact the *saḥir* you imbibed from eating the *saḥir*-infested crocodile. Take another example. You might be visiting a family who has a chubby, well-dressed child. If you gazed at him even without having any envious feelings, the child or his family would eventually suffer a misfortune. The child would throw up or come down with diarrhea."

Jaqalaybah was impressed by the man's theory and found that he could substantiate it from his own observations in his Rubāṭāb community. Jaqalaybah then said,

> By divorce [i.e., I swear on the bane of being separated from my wife that what you said is true], you hit it right on the head. Like you said we at times sit to drink coffee prepared by one of our womenfolk. For no obvious reason, the coffee pot would be spilled and burn the child of that woman. We might also be sitting and we would see goats fighting each other with their horns and one of them would end up being killed by the others. We come by the event and wonder and fall short of a convincing explanation of what we encountered. What you said explained it for me.

Ogres and Ogresses as Saḥḥārs

Amnah Dafaʿ al-Sīd is the ethnographer of cannibalism par excellence in the Rubāṭāb villages I studied. She not only contributed a varied body of narratives on cannibals but also claimed, on the basis of her actual encounters with *saḥḥārs*, an ethnographic authority of the "I was there" variety. Here I will discuss one of her folktales and two stories.

Amnah recorded a folktale about *saḥḥārs* marrying the daughters of a king and two narratives on her personal encounters with *saḥḥārs*.

Amnah Dafaʿ al-Sīd's folktale was entitled "Ant Skin and Louse Skin." In this tale a king raised an ant and a louse in a water jar until they grew big enough to break the jar open. The ant and the louse were then skinned, and their "hides" were stretched on the top of the king's copper drums. Subsequently, the king announced that he would marry his two daughters and give half his kingdom to those who would recognize the animals from which the drum skins were taken. People repeatedly tried to identify these animals, but to no avail.

Worn out by the arduous chores required by this identification process taking place at the king's palace, the king's slave women, who were bringing water from the river, wished that a man would soon come and recognize the skins as belonging to an ant and a louse and bring the festivities to an end. Two *saḥḥār*s were in the river when the slave women made this revelation, and they appeared before the king and identified correctly the skins of the drums as belonging to an ant and a louse. The *saḥḥār*s were hence married to the king's daughters, declining to have their shares in the kingdom because they wanted to take their wives back to their country. On the journey home the *saḥḥār*s ate up the camels and the cows their father-in-law had given them. Next they ate one of the wives, who was pregnant at the time. When she was assaulted by the *saḥḥār*s her unborn baby asked them to reserve his mother's kidney for him because he would share it with nobody. Finally, the second wife managed to escape back to her family. However, the *saḥḥār*s followed her to return her to her marital home. They were well received by their father-in-law, who now knew about the nature of his in-laws. Late that night the guest house in which the *saḥḥār*s were lodged was set on fire and the *saḥḥār*s and their offspring were burnt.

Sudanic Communities as Saḥḥār*s*

Amnah Dafaʿ al-Sīd's first story regards her encounter with a *saḥḥār* in the "Sudanic" belt of Sudan, which lies to the south of the Jaʿalīyyīn territory. In the 1940s she took the train to Khartoum, the capital of Sudan, on her way south to Sennar to join her husband, who lived in a village in the vicinity of Sennar. Sennar, the capital of the Funj Kingdom (1504–1821), is known among the Jaʿalīyyīn as the "Black Kingdom," and is a railway juncture that lies at the southernmost part of the Jaʿalīyyīn frontiers with the Sudanic (indigenous, black Africans) communities. In Khartoum she paid a *ziyārah* (visit) to Lady Fāṭnah of the Khatmiyyah holy family. In acknowledging the awe and sacredness of this visit, Amnah said, "You don't address Lady Fāṭnah by word of mouth. You just make your heart talk to her and she instantly grasps your *sir* [concealed wish]. I let my heart speak to her. [Her heart said] 'O Lady Fāṭnah, let my neighbors be sweet to me, honor me in my [marital] home, shorten my sojourn away from my [original] home, and protect me from the *saḥḥār,* because I'm leaving for Sennar.' You hear me now uttering these wishes in words. But to Lady Fāṭnah it is only my heart which pronounces my wishes."

Lady Fāṭnah was prompt in responding to Amnah's wishes. When the train arrived at Sennar she discovered that a Rubāṭābī was on board. The Rubāṭābī read her what was allegedly written on the placard of Sennar station: "Passengers, this is Sennar station. Beware of the *saḥḥār.*" The timely appearance of this Rubāṭābī was interpreted by Amnah as a sign that Lady Fāṭnah had responded to her request and provided her with this kinsman to protect her. From the window of the carriage she called for Bisharah wad Nōh, from the Jaʿalīyyīn community, whom Amnah's husband had asked to take care of her until he got to Sennar from where he lived. Bisharah was there and he welcomed her. His fellow Jaʿalī railway workers impressed upon Bisharah his duty to take good care of Amnah because she, in kinship terms, was his cousin. Jaʿal, the ancestor of the proper Ja'līyyīn, they reminded him, was the full brother of Rubāṭ, the ancestor of the Rubāṭāb, and Shāīq, from whom the Shāīqīyyah descended. Bisharah promised to act as an honorable kin, and kept his promise.

Bisharah took Amnah to live close to a Jaʿalī family and hired people to bring her water, do her laundry, and cook for her. One day when she was visiting the womenfolk of her Jaʿalī neighbor, a peddler was heard announcing his merchandise, "*Hatab* [firewood], *hatab, hatab* . . ." From the way the peddler spoke the word he was marked as a non-Arabic speaker. One of the Jaʿalī women laughed at the man's horrible accent, and she immediately fell down to the ground. The peddler was a *saḥḥār,* and he disemboweled her. The terror-stricken women sent for the men in the marketplace to hurry up and help them. The men took no time to get to the scene and called the *fakī* (Muslim educator, leader of prayers and healer) to cure the afflicted woman. Three men held the woman, and the *fakī* burnt a *bakharah* (a piece of paper on which Koranic verses and other healing formulas are inscribed) and fumigated the woman with its smoke. Soon after the fumigation the *saḥḥār*'s voice was heard in his horrible accent imploring the men to put out the fire that was burning him. The *fakī* ordered the *saḥḥār* to get out of the woman's body, and the *saḥḥār* complied. The men then turned to look for the peddler and soon found him and beat him up.

Amnah Dafaʿ al-Sīd's second story is extremely important for its dialogic character. In this narrative Amnah gives her version of the incident of the *saḥḥār* who came to the village in 1950. Bābikir, the mayor of the village at the time of my fieldwork in 1984 and an eyewitness of this incident, recorded his version also. In her version, Amnah took Bābikir to task for failing to identify the *saḥḥār* for what he was. We begin with Bābikir's variant, in which he is extremely cautious in reading the incident as cannibalistic—a misreading for which he earned Amnah's wrath.

Rains were exceptionally heavy in 1950 in the Rubāṭāb region. Torrential streams destroyed the railroad, and the area was isolated from the rest of the country. People ran out of foods such as sorghum, sugar, and tea. On one evening of those miserable days, Bābikir and his cousin were sitting in front of the *khalwah* waiting to be served a modest dinner. Bābikir says:

> A group of ten or twelve men came to where we were sitting. They were seminaked, each wore pants and threw a piece of cloth over his shoulders. [He answered a question I posed about the identity of those people.] I really don't know. I would guess they were Masālīt

from western Sudan, Namnam [cannibals], I believe. I would not say they were Fur [of western Sudan]. They speak a *ruṭānah* [a gibberish] anyway. They were peddlers carrying their merchandize of beads and cowries on forked sticks. We invited them to stay in the *khalwah,* spread a mat for them to lie on, and brought them water to drink. No sooner had our womenfolk started preparing their dinner than I heard a child crying nonstop. I thought he was sick or something. I noticed simultaneously that one of the visitors was lying on his abdomen [suggesting that the man was a *saḥḥār* and was working on the crying child]. I took the dinner to the guests. The dinner consisted of *balīlah* [boiled beans or grains]. [We both laughed because serving *balīlah* is a clear indication of lack of proper resources of hospitality.] But, mind you, that was a lot of *balīlah.* On my invitation the men rose and partook of the food, except for the one lying on his abdomen.

They were speaking their gibberish among themselves. I asked them why the *faqīr* [their fellow traveler; lit., a man of religion and piety] was not partaking of the food, and they told me that he was not feeling well. I waited on them until they were done with their dinner, served them water, and bade them good night. At one o'clock the next day I was awoken by a kind of a scream, a very scary screech that woke up the village. The sound, which was coming from the *khalwah,* resembled the crowing of a cock. No, it was louder than that. The sound was closer to the one of a whining dog, but more penetrating. I would say it resembled a duck quacking in the water, but more assertive. I tell you it was really, really scary. I went in the direction of the *khalwah* and found my guests running toward the river and collectively hitting one of them, *lab lab lab.* I was alarmed, and I carried my stick to safeguard against an attack on me. My father took his spear. When we approached the men they were still conversing in their gibberish. My father asked me to keep my distance from them. At this time the child stopped crying, since his mothers [his mother and aunts] took him to one of the rooms in their house and tightly closed the door. We returned home, seeing no reason to pursue the men, who were leaving the village anyway. When we woke up late the same morning the men were gone and the people of ʾAmakī village told us that they saw them crossing their village just before daybreak.

Amnah Dafaʿ al-Sīd's version runs as follows:

CHAPTER TWO

Five men, including a *saḥḥār,* came one night to the *faqīr*'s [Bābikir's father] *khalwah.* They were served dinner. Four men partook of the food, but the fifth declined because he had planned to attack and eat the people of the village. The *saḥḥār* planned to eat the daughters [she used the diminutive, "daughterlets"] of Abū al-ʿAbbās, whose house was across from the *khalwah.* The *faqīr,* who wanted to be recompensed by God for humility and hospitality, waited on them in person, carrying dinner to them and filling their cups with water from the water jar. The *faqīr* himself told me later saying, "Daughter of Dafaʿ al-Sīd! I swear by Allah that four of the men had dinner and the fifth alone refused to dine. Whereas the four men were lying on one of the big mats of the mosque the *saḥḥār* lay on a separate mat." You might as well know that I [Amnah] had been to Sennar and recognize a *saḥḥār* when I see one.

I told the *faqīr* when he described to me later the encounter with the *saḥḥār* that, judging from the way the fifth man acted, that he was a *saḥḥār.* Obviously he was planning to attack the village and eat one of the daughters of Abū al-ʿAbbās. These daughters were his targets, wearing as they were their yellow dresses and their red headdresses and with their door just across from the *khalwah.* Late in the cool of the night, on the day of the encounter with the *saḥḥār,* a sound was heard: o ooOo OOOO OoOOO, from low to high pitch. The man started to *yisaʿlaw* [a verb derived from *siʿlwah,* ogress, to transform into a *saḥḥār*] to snatch one of the girls. His fellows did not like it and started beating him, *daz daz daz.* He had to run in the direction of the river to evade his pursuers. At that very same moment I called the *faqīr* to express my concern of what was going on, but he assured me that the *saḥḥār* would not be able to eat anyone in the entire village. The *faqīr* then began snapping his rosary this way, that way, and all around, reciting from the Koran to protect the villagers. The men eventually disappeared from the village scene. The one who ran toward the river did not return, and those who stayed behind left the *khalwah* that very night.

What do you think our Bābikir did and thought of this? He came to us with his stick in his hand. We asked him what was up, and he said that the men in the *khalwah* had quarreled with each other and left one of them beaten up and crying. I told him to give us a break. I lived in Sennar and I know a *saḥḥār* when I see one. The man was not beaten and left crying. He wanted rather to *yisaʿlaw* and eat one of the daughters of Abū al-ʿAbbās.

These accusations of casting the evil eye and cannibalism construct the Rubāṭāb cultural order woven from different ideas of ethnic diacritics, reciprocity and lack of it, religion and magic, clients and patrons, nomads and farmers, peddlers and customers, language and gibberish, taxes and evasion of paying taxes, slaves and their treacherous access to domestic space, travel and ethnographic authority of knowledge, gaze and utterance, children and vulnerability, misfortune and causation, pagan times and Islamic times. Images of evil eyers, men of words, cannibals, ogres and ogresses, and crocodiles are implicated in the construction.

Saḥir *as an Epistemological Category*

Attribution of cannibalism in our case study is clearly about "othering." However, the process of "othering" described by the attributions is more encompassing than Arens has suggested. Arens argues that such attributions are a rhetorical device used ideologically by one group to assert its moral superiority (1979, 46). These attributions among the Rubāṭāb connote this superiority in intergroup as well as intragroup situations. They are, as I have argued, an epistemological category that can be projected inward and outward to describe the cultural order of the Rubāṭāb. If projected inward, the attributions provide an idiom for describing deranged and antisocial behavior such as the casting of the evil eye. If projected outward, however, they describe an ethnic landscape of Muslims and non-Muslims, Arabs and non-Arabs, gibberish and language, and the landed and the landless.

Finally, cannibals and witches are intertwined constellations. Any attempt to single out one constellation as impinging on or determining others is counterproductive. Obeyesekere, for example, traces the British belief in cannibalism to the ways European children grew up scared of witches, and to a sailors' subculture in which survivors of a shipwreck eat the flesh of their dead colleagues (1992, 635–36, 641). In historically accounting for the British belief in cannibalism, that is, in writing a history of the idea of cannibalism, Obeyesekere precludes a discourse approach to beliefs in witches and cannibals as recommended by the Rubāṭāb material. Although Rubāṭāb adult males dismiss the magic world of the folktale—including the childhood fantasy of witches and cannibalism—as lies woven by idle women, they participate variously in other cannibalistic and witchcraft discourses. Hence the production of cannibalistic discourses is not ipso facto locked into what Obeyesekere called "the primordial fantasy" (1992, 641). We have seen how the theory linking cannibalism to *saḥir* emerged in a discourse in which strict rules of reasoning and, later, verification were required and observed. Furthermore, thirty years after an incident in which a man allegedly transformed himself into a cannibal and was on the verge of attacking some children in the village, Amnah Dafaʿ al-Sīd and Bābikir, the village mayor, were still at loggerheads regarding the veracity of the allegation. In the narrative I recorded from Bābikir he only vaguely suggests that cannibalism might have been involved. Amnah did not like Bābikir's story the first time he related to her what had taken place in the *khalwah* in 1950, and her narrative apparently has always contained a rebuttal of Bābikir's misreading of what transpired at the *khalwah*.

3

Discourse and the Bridle of *Sharīʿah*

This chapter examines the Rubāṭāb discourses from the perspective of the community's Islamic beliefs. The Rubāṭāb poetic and narrative genres and their speech events will be dealt with individually and broadly to bring into focus the tension between the hegemonic *sharīʿah*-minded discourse and these forms of verbal art. The discussion is intended to demonstrate that the Rubāṭāb's attitudes toward fiction (e.g., metaphors), verbal art (including poetic inspiration), and reproduction (such as the process of transmission) are not only informed by a strict religious code of truth but also articulated in a socioeconomic situation that places unprecedented claims on the community's time.

"The Saḥḥār *Is Coming!"*

Siḥr, the standard Arabic for the Rubāṭāb *saḥir,* is a category that covers magic, witchcraft, sorcery, and talisman. It is unbelief, and Muslim jurists differ only on the sanctions to be inflicted on its practitioner, the *sāḥir* or *saḥḥār.* Execution is an extreme but well authorized form of sanction (al-Rāzī 1872, 1:753). The Rubāṭāb identification of *al-ʿayn* (the eye, evil eye) with *saḥir* is in line with those jurists who consider *al-ʿayn* a category of *siḥr.* They call it the *siḥr* of "the owners of [compelling] *ʾawhām* (fancies), imagination and strong psychic power" (1872, 1:640). People of such imagination are said to plant phantasms, images, and pictures in the world of elements and consequently exercise an influence upon these elements. (Ibn Khaldūn 1956, 1:926) Furthermore, *ḥasad* (envy), which the Rubāṭāb believe to be the root of evil eye *saḥir,* is found to be comparable to *siḥr* in that they are both inspired by *shayṭān* (devil) (Ibn al-Qayyīm, 2:234). Importantly, Koran often refers to *ḥasad* and *siḥr* together (2:233).

In view of this strong religious and social disapproval, one would imagine that speaking *saḥir* must be a stigmatizing experience. In this connection I was repeatedly told in utter revulsion that Wad al-Tōm, the dean of *saḥḥārs*, had *saḥr* (cast the *ʿayn* on) two of his sons and that one "died" as a result. One of his sons, the story continues, succeeded in continuing his school education, while the other failed and ended up farming with his father. The situation of his two sons was likened by Wad al-Tōm to clothes; the successful son, with an urban career ahead of him, was likened to clothes you wear to religious and social occasions, whereas the other was likened to work clothes. An informant added that Wad al-Tōm had never been the same since the death of his son. Not only had he grayed quickly but he had also lost a great deal of his jovial spirit.

I wanted to ask Wad al-Tōm about the veracity of the story without seeming insensitively inquisitive. Finally I asked, "Have you described (spoken *saḥir*) anything and had results that caused you to repent?"

"Not exactly, but I was on my way to Kurgus village one day when I ran into some kids. They started pointing to me and asking among themselves, 'Who is that?' A kid finally said to them, 'That is the *saḥḥār* man.' And the kids took to their heels. That was all I heard from them."

"What was your feeling then?"

"I felt like I was someone, or something, that scares children [to death]. It dawned on me that it [speaking *saḥir*] is not right and that indulging in it draws [negative] attention to you."

That incident took place in 1980, and in 1984 the indomitable Wad al-Tōm had not given up *saḥir* yet. Nevertheless, this incident and the indelible mark it left on Wad al-Tōm's psyche are important.

With this socioreligious complexity surrounding *saḥir* speaking, I was not in the least surprised to find two of my potential informants uncooperative. One of them granted me an interview in which he courteously and firmly refused to record *saḥrahs*. The other *saḥḥār* flatly refused to be interviewed. Whenever I tried to make an appointment for an interview, he would talk about either the technical problems of his water pump or his future plan to accommodate his sons and daughters after their marriages in the family compound he was building on the ridge. The reasons for this uncompromising, businesslike attitude of his became clear later. At one point, as I was insistently asking him for an interview, he excused himself by saying, "I spoke *saḥir* when I was young. I have realized since that it is prohibited by the religion. People don't like it either. Thus, I *tubtah minuh* [renounced speaking it]." The people around him, however, said they did not believe that he had renounced speaking *saḥir*. Nonetheless, I decided to stop harassing him for an interview. I thought it would be more productive to read his silence than coerce him into talking.

The concept of folklore as artistic communication (Ben-Amos 1975, 10) tends to make folklorists focus on the aesthetic, on the ritually and calendrically scheduled (Bauman 1977, 28), and on the areas where speaking and speaking folklore are positively regarded (Bauman 1983b, 10). In other words, the focus is on the collectible. This focus has precluded the exploration of the constraints put on folklore by the authoritative moral discourses within which it usually operates. Richard Bauman has perceptively called for the investigation of what he calls the relationship between ethics and aesthetics to understand both the repute and the disrepute of performance (1977, 29). Regrettably, little has been done in this direction. Performance has been commonly presented as taking risk at a display of competence. The audience is described as the "jury, the guardian of folklore aesthetics" (Yankah 1985, 135). A successful performance is said to be rewarded by a measure of power, prestige, and control over the audience (1985, 135). Entrusting the audience with folk aesthetics is very risky, however. Audiences do not necessarily prize competence in each and every performance. Sometimes, as in the case of the *saḥḥār*s at hand, ethical considerations override aesthetic ones and competence is viewed as offensive.

By abandoning the aesthetic considerations in favor of the ethical ones, the Rubāṭāb *saḥḥār*s emphasize how crucial the Islamic model of speaking is to the understanding of Muslim folklore.

With respect to narration, El-Shamy has suggested that the stigma surrounding narration of tales in Egypt, and why certain genres of tales are told rather than others, can be adequately interpreted with reference to that model (1967, 78–81).

This chapter will broadly examine the Rubāṭāb discourses from the standpoint of the community's beliefs, values, and attitudes, which are grounded ultimately in Islam. This examination is carried out to provide "a vantage point which might bring out most saliently the respect in which ways of speaking constitute symbolic forms" (Hymes 1981, 46). This symbolic milieu of discourse will be utilized to better understand the construction of *saḥir* as a voice in Rubāṭāb discourse.

The Bridle of Sharīʿah

I was jealously guarding the tapes that were recorded from women informants by cooperative young school-educated relatives of theirs. I did not want the people of Khiḍir's *daywān,* with whom I stayed during my fieldwork in ʿAtmūr—and who had access to other tapes—to listen to them.

I was apprehensive about unveiling the vulnerable voice of a woman in this male-dominated situation. The tapes contained songs or statements that were purposely or inadvertently critical of people and practices, and which could have caused trouble for those who delivered them had I played them in public. Any such incident would have scared off my helpers and blocked the only access I had to women informants at that time.

Khiḍir, however, overheard the *ḥujah* (sing. *ḥajwah,* folktale) on one of the tapes and asked me very gently to play it again. I could not turn him down. However, the session in which I played the tape turned out not to be so bad after all. In fact, it turned into an interesting feedback interview. The tale was about the newborn baby who helped his mother lift a bundle of firewood onto her head. "*Bidaʿ*[1] [unheard of], by Allah!" said Khiḍir in disbelief. The raconteur continued to tell about the girl who was planning to escape for her life from the ogre's dwelling. To gain time, the girl asked the ogre to bring her a drink of water from the river using only a fishing net or a whole gourd. "None of these will hold water," Khiḍir said again very matter-of-factly. When he rose toward the end of the session to attend to some business, he described my mission as the collection of "*saḥir* and lies." Khiḍir was definitely not bored by the *ḥujah.* He was probably refreshed by that reminder of his childhood. His literal and negative responses, however, were intended to demonstrate his prized manhood, which starts early and abruptly for a Rubāṭābī.

Khiḍir was also present once when I interviewed Wad al-Tōm. I asked Wad al-Tōm if *saḥir* was of any practical use to him or to those around him. "Not in the least. It comes close to being useful when you run into somebody who is upset and you speak *saḥir* by way of a *mathal* [example or proverb] to him. It will make him laugh and forget about his worries," he said. Khiḍir said laughingly, "It has no harvest whatsoever." Wad al-Tōm modified Khiḍir's statement significantly by saying, "It does not have much of a yield."

Khiḍir's uneasiness with what Hodgson had labeled the "lush folkloric imagination" (1963, 235) of the raconteur and his utilitarian idiom regarding *saḥir* are typical manifestations of that prevalent piety in Islam, which Hodgson named "*sharīʿah*-mindedness." According to Hodgson, this variant of Islam is basically opposed to frivolous indulgences (1963, 233). In reading the fantasy of the *ḥujah* literally, Khiḍir exhibited the factualism of that piety which cultivates common sense and matter-of-factness and which has "low tolerance for abstractions or imaginative symbols" (1963, 228). The concerns Khiḍir showed in describing *ḥujah* and *saḥir* as lies and useless occupation are cut from the cloth of this piety, which focuses on what is useful, rather than what is ornamental, and what helps oneself and others to get properly and decently through the tasks of family living, rather than what embellishes that living or perhaps interrupts it (1963, 233).

Finally, the negative sense in which Khiḍir used *bidaʿ* is akin to the way *sharīʿah*-minded piety hurls the same term against innovations in faith, which are invariably condemned.

Al-Ghazzali's (1058–1111) chapter on *Afāt al-Lisān* (Harms of the

Tongue) (1965, 3:107–163) is the most systematic exposition of the attitude of *sharīʿah*-minded Islam toward speaking. In it silence is strongly recommended unless a Muslim has something good (in the religious sense) to say. One should speak just enough for the conduct of one's worldly livelihood (1965, 3:110, 115). These two occasions for breaking the virtue of silence are the edges of the "bridle of *sharīʿah*" needed to protect the tongue from the seduction of the *shayṭān* which tempts it to lie or talk frivolously.

From the perspective of *sharīʿah*-minded piety, eloquence in talk is held in distrust because it is attended by the eloquence of the *shayṭān* (al-Ghazzali 1965, 3:120). It is feared that lies creep into narration even though it might deal with religious themes (1965, 1:35). When all is said and done, narration is a waste of time even if it is faithful to reality (1965, 3:113). Jokes, if they are to be admitted at all, should not be excessive or rely on falsehood (1965, 3:128). Laughter is viewed as a sign of inattention to the Day of Judgment; only smiling "where the tooth is revealed and no sound is heard" is laudable (1965, 3:128). It is considered a violation of dignity to subject a fellow Muslim to ridicule and mimicry (1965, 3:131). Poetry is described as a mixed blessing, and prophetic traditions are quoted that describe it as pus and wisdom in the same breath. While its composition and recitation are not forbidden, making an occupation of it is objectionable. God's invocation is always a far better enhancement of one's life and afterlife than poetry is (1965, 3:126). *Sharīʿah*-minded discourse is clearly either opposed to or suspicious of verbal art performances. In its struggle for power and hegemony, this discourse undermines the legitimacy of verbal art. It apparently takes its injunction of silence literally and seriously. To acquire the habit of silence, a Muslim is asked by an extreme formulation of this discourse to constantly remember death or put a pebble in his mouth (1965, 3:114).

Don't Die in the Peanut Season

Recall that since the late 1940s the village of ʿAtmūr has undergone major economic and social changes that are finally integrating it into the national market economy. The Mayāyyīs lineage, to which Khiḍir belongs, are known for their industriousness and have contributed significantly to those changes.

I delineated in chapter one the real or imagined demands upon the villagers' time resulting from this new economic activity. A combination of *shaghalah* and religiosity (or *shaghalah* as religiosity) has made the Mayāyyīs lineage cut down considerably on rituals. Some of their young men complained to me that they were not looking forward to their weddings, in which they were supposed to marry a paternal uncle's daughter, because their elders had reduced them to merely formal religious contract ceremonies. The overtly sexual bridedance and the festive nights of the weddings were ruled out as irreligious and as a frivolous expenditure.

Similarly, residents of Um Ghiday, where the most ambitious and successful land reclaiming from the sand hills took place, live a real frontier life under the patronage of Muḥammad, a typical Mayāyyīs patriarch. A line from a poem composed to celebrate a successful yield at Um Ghiday eulogizes the frontiersmen of the village for not abandoning their work to attend the festive wedding processions. I heard a man from ʿAtmūr village saying to a man from Um Ghiday, "God forbid I die in your peanut-growing season. Muḥammad is sure to prevent you from attending my funeral. He would say as usual, 'What is the use of going to funerals? The dead won't rise from their graves anyway.'"

Furthermore, most the men in the villages I studied abandoned the ritual of cutting the first hair of their children on the tomb of their family or lineage *walī* (saint). The ritual, according to them, was sometimes not worth the trip involved. Wad al-Tōm said he could have sent the offerings of dates and money required by the ritual without taking the trouble to go himself. He said that although it was thought a child's hair would not grow if the ritual was neglected, the hair of his children grew so abundantly that he had to pay a lot of money to have it cut.

With this absorption in *shaghalah,* defined as work with a tangible yield, goes a strong contempt for practices that do not have this kind of yield. Professional performers and entertainers are hit hard by this contempt. It is said that a *maddāḥ* (an itinerant singer of the praise of the Prophet) was denied permission to perform at a Rubāṭābī's house because the Rubāṭābī wanted to know "In what respect is the Prophet deficient to make his praise known?"

Performers are fully aware of the low opinion in which their craft is held. For example, the poets in Abū Hashīm, a village on the east bank of the Nile, calls the place where they meet in the marketplace[2] "*Taṭwīr al-Fārghah*" (The Development of the Empty Words) to preempt the objections of people who would say—in the words of the renowned poet Ibrahīm al-Duqāq—"Oh man! These poets have nothing else to do besides singing poetry." The poet al-Kilaybāwī meant to ask *al-ghinah* (prosperity) from *lailat al-qadr* (the night between the twenty-sixth and twenty-seventh of Ramadan, the month of fasting, when the wishes of those to whom it is revealed come true), but he slipped and said *al-ghunah* (singing, composing poetry) (Ibrahim and Nasr 1968, 162). Thus poetry became his lot and the lot of his descendants. The pun indicates an interesting taxonomy of careers and their rewards among the Rubāṭāb.

Evil in a Hiccup

A comparison of the views of *saḥḥārs* and non-*saḥḥārs* regarding *saḥir* represents graphically the tension between verbal art and *sharīʿah*-minded notions of speaking. The speakers of the genre would prefer to be called *waṣṣāfīn* (sing. *waṣṣāf,* clever at drawing analogies). The function of the genre, as some *saḥḥārs* helped me understand, is humor; they would like the *saḥrahs* to be taken as jokes. *Saḥḥārs* view their similes as products of an irresistible impulse to speak figuratively. They liken this overwhelming impulse to a hiccup. Al-Duqāq, the poet, said, "I speak *saḥir,* but I am more cautious nowadays to avoid being accused of *saḥir. Saḥir* nonetheless comes out sometimes, despite my caution." He added, "The poet is basically a *saḥḥār* because if you do not imagine things poetry will not come to you."

Victims of *saḥir* and other Rubāṭāb hold a different view. *Saḥir,* according to them, stems from a *fakar,* which is the dialect form of *fakarah,* the standard Arabic term for "to think." In this context it connotes seeing and thinking in envious terms. *Fakar* is therefore used synonymously with *al-ʿayn* or *ʿayn ḥarah* (lit., a hot eye, i.e., an evil eye), and the speaker of the genre is known as *saḥḥār* or possessor of the *ʿayn.* The conflict between the *saḥḥārs* and their accusers of evil is best illustrated by the threat Wad al-Tōm felt when I asked him about the meaning of *fakar.* He denied knowing its meaning, though he heard people using it. He tried to persuade me that *fakar* is perhaps a form of *iftikār* (to recall).

The non-*saḥḥārs* and victims of *saḥir* clearly deny the *saḥḥārs*' claim to spontaneity. *Saḥir,* in their view, involves more than merely, in the words of John Ciardi, "the joy of guessing out analogies" (1972, 162). Their argument against the genre has a distinctly religious character. In fact, the earliest report of the genre is contained in one of the traditions of the Prophet, according to which the Prophet said to a Muslim who likened the soft skin of a fellow Muslim to that of a virgin, "Why should any of you want to kill his brother? Shouldn't one in these situations ask the blessing of Allah for his brother? The *ʿayn* is a reality" (al-Ṣuyūṭī 1969, 2:227–28).

A victim of *saḥir* said to me when I asked him about *saḥir,* "All *waṣif* [description, analogy] is evil. All kinds of talk are evil except talk about what Allah said and what his Messenger said. If you speak about anything other than your livelihood or 'Allah said, his Messenger said,' like describing a thing, it is evil."

A Ridiculous Test in Iblīs *Discourse*

Poetry is viewed by the Rubāṭāb as untruths inspired by *Iblīs* (Satan). The assumption that poets were liars was of long standing in Muslim writings; this attitude also had Koranic sanction (Cantarino 1975, 34). Verse 226 of the *Sura* of the Poets (Koran: XXVI) reads, "And they [the poets] say that which they do not do," and this is taken by the exegetes to mean simply that poets are liars (Shahid 1983, 6–7). The belief that the jinn inspire poets is pre-

Islamic and was reinforced by the hierarchization of jinn by Islam in which *Iblīs,* the angel that fell from heaven, is named the leader of the unbelievers among the jinn and the author of all sins.

When I entered the field a poem duel between al-Duqāq and al-Shāʿir (from the neighboring Manāṣīr community) was just concluded, and the poems exchanged and their occasions were on every lip in the Rubāṭāb district. The two poets are among the best in the popular genre of *aṭ-ṭirī* or *aṭ-ṭaryān*[3] (lit., mentioning in a negative sense). In this form a poet lampoons those who fail to show competence in vital skills or who break social taboos. A transgression or an inadequacy is reported to the poet. This report is called *balāgh* (notification), just like police usage of the term. The poet then warns the transgressor or "mentions" him in vague terms in a poem called sometimes the "c-c" (cubic centimeter, borrowed from pharmaceutical jargon). The transgressor is then expected to ransom himself through a special arrangement with the poet. The negotiation and its result are carried out under the watchful eyes of the audience. The poem-duel of *aṭ-ṭirī* takes place also when two poets are involved, either when a transgressor who would not admit his mistake appeals to another poet to come to his defense, or when a transgression committed by a poet is reported by the audience to another poet.

In the duel under consideration, al-Duqāq was reported to al-Shāʿir for carelessly allowing his jackass to fall from the ferry into the Nile and thus soaking the flour it was carrying. Al-Shāʿir sent his "c-c" to al-Duqāq, who denied responsibility in his reply and blamed the ferryman for the failure. Al-Shāʿir dismissed al-Duqāq's excuse as empty talk and insisted, "What I am saying is not mere talk. I know the tongue is crafty; it can turn wrong into right." These lines are obviously informed by the *sharīʿah*-minded model of speaking, which, as we have seen, suspects speaking as a fleshly faculty.

Al-Duqāq's next poem was physically aggressive. In it he imagined himself as a bull on the rampage, butting with his horns. In his reply, al-Shāʿir objected to al-Duqāq's aggressiveness and reasoned with him. In his next poem, al-Duqāq apologized for being carried away and said,

> Poets, indeed, are followed by *al-ghāwūn.*
> Let us not lampoon each other since the
> poet's mouth is haunted.

The first line is a paraphrase of verse 224 from the *Sura* of the Poets (Koran: XXVI), where *al-ghāwūn* is translated as an erring group of human beings following the poets (Shahid 1983, 2). Incidentally, Shahid suggests *al-shayāṭīn* (sing., *shayṭān*) to be the correct translation for *al-ghāwūn* (1983, 4).

Reference to *Iblīs* as the source of inspiration of poetry abounds in the duel form of *aṭ-ṭirī.* Thus the reference to the haunted mouth of the poet is best explained by a line from al-Bashīr, the poet who intervened to reconcile the embattled poets:

> It is indisputable that the cursed *Iblīs* has
> penetrated your ranks, causing you to fall
> foul of one another.

On another occasion, a fellow poet harassed al-Duqāq to write a poem in his praise. Al-Duqāq apologized to him, saying that poetry is essentially inspired by *shayṭān,* but that his *shayṭān* had deserted him. However, the other poet persisted. When al-Duqāq warned him to stop harassing him or he would satirize him, the second poet challenged him: "Didn't you say that your *shayṭān* had deserted you?" Next day al-Duqāq was reading the fellow poet a poem that began, "The *shayṭān* of my poetry, who was absent, did come back."

In an *aṭ-ṭirī* duel between al-Ḥassānī of Kurgus village and Ḥisayn al-Ḥāj of ʿAtmūr, the theme of *Iblīs* also dominates. At a certain point in the duel al-Ḥassānī decided to quit. Ḥisayn al-Ḥāj, however, pressed on and challenged al-Ḥassānī to solve some riddles he had inlaid in a poem composed for the duel. The riddles themselves were drawn from religious literature, and the persons Ḥisayn al-Ḥāj invited to arbitrate the duel were religious figures in the two villages. Al-Ḥassānī asked a nephew of Ḥisayn al-Ḥāj to reason with his uncle to bring the duel to a close. He said to him, "Singing of poetry is beyond one's control. If it is unwisely set on the loose it may cause the people of ʿAtmūr and Kurgus to fall foul of each other." The nephew replied that his uncle only wanted to give him a test. Al-Ḥassānī was furious and said, "Are we university graduates, or what? Isn't it ridiculous that he wants to test me in *Iblīs*'s talk?" In Islamic perspective, the two duelers are like two howling, agitated *shayṭāns* (al-Ghazzali 1965, 3:122). Al-Ḥassānī was apparently ready to admit this characterization in the face of an indefatigable opponent.

The dimension of *Iblīs*-inspired lies was brought up again in my interview with the jovial, vigorous old woman poet Madīnah al-Ḥāj. She is a singer of *sōmār,* and after reciting to me a *sōmār* that had been well received by the dancing men, she said, "I made them happy regardless of truth or falsehood [laughs]. Observing truth is not my business, as long as they were happy. All of it [the *sōmār*], of course, could not be true and all of it could not be false." I asked Madīnah how the *sōmār* came to her. She said,

> By Allah, this discourse . . . in actual fact *Iblīs* inspires this singing [laughs]. From the moment I stood up to sing *Iblīs* followed me, whispering to me, "Say [this] and say that" [those attending my interview with Madīnah laughed]. When I finally sat to sing he sat beside me. He would indicate to me to say this and to say that. It is none of my business which words succeed or fail. The one that succeeds is so desired by Allah to be effective and the one that fails . . .

Allah's intervention is to be seen here as helping the poet to succeed in her singing rather than as inspiration. Madīnah complained that her relatives usually ask her to sing *sōmārs* for their sons at the very last minute. Consequently, she would invoke Allah and his Messenger to make her succeed in her mission "and not disappoint her relatives, and the God of the people patches me a word from here and there in order not to disappoint them."

Iblīs not only inspires poetry but also seduces a reluctant poet into speaking it. Al-Ḥassānī said that after advancing in age he decided not to court women or eulogize them in verse. *Iblīs,* however, showed him a woman, "whose beauty he had never seen before," to make him go back to poetry. Introducing the poem he composed for that woman, al-Ḥassānī said, "My hair was graying and I had abandoned singing but when I saw her I said to myself, 'By Allah, buddy, *Iblīs* was right.'" And the audience laughed.

Between the Lie and the Laughter

The belief that the poet is a liar finds its foremost expression in the asides introduced by some performers during their delivery. In these asides, the performer sometimes refutes assertions made in the text or at least denies responsibility for the veracity of these assertions. For example, the singer Madīnah began one of her *sōmār*s, "The young deer of the meadow sings your praise," and said immediately and sarcastically, "No doubt that young deer of the meadows is me." The old poet herself could not believe the words the poetic discourse was putting in her mouth. On another occasion, she delivered an *aṭ-ṭirī* poem in which her brother, al-Ḥisayn al-Ḥāj, lampooned her other brother, ʿAradayb, for getting so drunk that he was swept away by the canal water. She commented, "The poet is, of course, a liar. Would anyone believe what he said about the man being swept away?"

The reflexivity of Amnah Dafaʿ al-Sīd in delivering her repertoire of *ghunah* (lyrical songs) and *sōmār* is unique. She was interviewed for me by a "text-hungry" (Dundes 1966, 512) assistant who would stop recording whenever the informant "derailed" from the text into asides. However, the few asides that persisted in the record are very indicative of the war between truth and lies waged by the poetic statement and its aside. She delivered the following two lines:

> My love to her began before her weaning
> And till *ʾIsrāfīl* [angel] blows the horn for the Day of Resurrection.

She commented laughingly, "He is a liar, boy. Would it enter your mind that he would love her till the day *ʾIsrāfīl* calls, 'Hey you!'" Repeating these lines later on, she said, "What a liar! Are you going to even hear what *ʾIsrāfīl* would say?"

She again considered a lie a line from a *sōmār* in which a man was praised for restoring order to things ruined by others. In another line from the same *sōmār,* the poet said that she had seen the galloping horses of a lineage she was praising. Amnah said, "She is the one who saw them. I did not," clearly refusing to be held accountable for the veracity of the line because she merely repeated it after the poet.

Lies and Farts

If oral discourses are defined by oral transmission, then by definition it is suspected by *sharīʿah*-minded Islam of ultimately producing lies. The Rubāṭāb consider "*qūlnah wa qālū*" (we said and they said) hearsay that discredits evidence. A related concept, *al-qiwālah* (telling somebody what someone else said about them), originates according to *sharīʿah*-minded Islam in *al-tafaruj bil hadīth* (talking for the sake of talking) and is condemned as the source of lies and disputes (al-Ghazzali 1965, 3:154).

In *ḥujah* (folktales), "*qālū*" (they said) is a formulaic beginning and is always followed by the disclaimer "*wa yakfinah Allah shar qūlnah wa qālū*" (May Allah prevent the evil that comes along with we said and they said). The negative attitude towards "*qūlnah*" is best illustrated by the metanarrative *ḥajwah* in which a sultan asks the people to compete in original lying and threatens to kill anyone who prefaces his lies by saying "*qālū*" (they said). Those who introduced their lies by saying "the *maqālah* said" met their deaths. The ethical implications of *qālū* are further demonstrated by a woman informant who mistakenly used *qālū* to refer to persons and events in a narrative of her personal experience. When she finally realized that she was talking about people and events she had experienced herself, she retracted and said, "They said, they said, [pause] they said, or was that all real?"

Moreover, the association made by the Rubāṭāb between lies and *fasū* (farts) is indicative of Islamic ethics of speaking. The genre of tall tales (*al-kiḍib* or *al-kalām al-ghulād,* fat lies or talk) is known also as farts, which also denotes lies. The binary opposition between truth, symbolized by the mouth (i.e., culture), and lies, symbolized by the anus (i.e., nature), is also found in Rubāṭāb discourses. It is said that a dog was asked why it howled and farted at the same time. It replied that it howled to scare people and farted because it was scared to death by them. Courage and cowardice tie in neatly with this opposition.

Fictionless Men

Michael Meeker described the Bedouins of North Arabia as men without fiction because to them facts play the role of fiction. The Bedouins, he says, did not tell the romances of Abu Zayd or ʿAntrah (1979, 52).[4] Instead, they told stories of their own participation in raids and wars, or stories of actual raids and wars that had occurred more or less within the memory of the living men (1979, 52). By their choice of the realistic *maqālah* as their one and only genre, the men of the Rubāṭāb are like Meeker's fictionless Bedouins. Furthermore, the *maqālāt* I heard in these men's sessions approximate the Bedouin's stories in time frame and concern for real occurrences. The early resocialization of these men away from women and *ḥujah* (El-Shamy 1980, lii), together with their enterprising, rational spirit, has banished the realm of the "numinous"[5] from their adult lives. The term "numinous" is used here to denote broadly and loosely the source of awe and reverence that introduces fictive elements in narratives. The past, ancestors, the *karāmāt* (miraculous manifestations of *walīs*), and the graves and haunted places are especially dismissed by this "busy, busy" generation of Rubāṭāb men.

As mentioned earlier, the Rubāṭāb men I studied showed very little nostalgia for the past. They considered their present to be far superior to the past. They did not hide their pride in transforming a rocky, narrow strip of a hardly cultivable land into an economically and socially viable place. Mention was also previously made of how these men bashed their ancestors for their bad decisions or hopeless careers, and their many regrets for being a "sandwich generation." We also noted how these men did not allow inherited spiritual loyalties to get in the way of their progress. Nothing remained sacred when they tasted the fruits of trading religious allegiance for economic and political gain.

The desire of the men of ʿAtmūr to extend their arable land brought cultivation right into the graveyards. The village has no central cemetery. At any time a farm compound may stop burying its dead at a nearby cemetery and start a cemetery in its own backyard. Burial apparently became a matter of convenience rather than ritual. Moreover, the extension of the cultivatable land demolished all haunted, enigmatic, and spooky places. Like Meeker's Bedouins, these men of ʿAtmūr have left almost nothing for the ethnographer to describe (Meeker 1979, 23).

Most of the dead saints of the Rubāṭāb have no relatives or disciples to continue interest in the dissemination of their *karāmāt*, a genre usually kept alive by just such people (ʿAbdalsalaam 1983, 108). My fullest record of legends and rituals came from the ʿĀbdāb saints of ʿAtmūr, who have a woman descendant actively officiating at their shrines. Zaynab al-Fākī still leads a following of mainly female believers through the ritual visit to the saints. In her formulaic invocations she recapitulates the saints' legends. I still remember clearly how she utilized our visit to the shrine to admonish her male relatives for doing nothing to rebuild their forefathers' shrines and *khalwah*s. The men, who had other priorities, nervously and noncommittally agreed to the appropriateness of what Zaynab had said.

When saints' legends are narrated by men, they often take the form of the antilegend, which is "destructive to the legend" (Degh and Vazsonyi 1973, 14).[6] The men who showed me a few saints' tombs or relics narrated what they knew about the legends with tongue in cheek. They expected us outsiders, "representing the judgment of society" (1973, 17), to confirm their disbelief in this mediating agency that stands illegitimately between them and Allah.

Generally speaking, belief in any fictive script is instantly demolished by ʿAtmūr men. ʿAlī al-Ṣāfī (thirty-seven years old) narrated an etiological legend about how the islands ʾArtōlī and ʾArtul came to their present positions to the south and in the center of the Rubāṭāb territory, respectively. The two islands, he said, were "twins" who got separated and drifted with the current toward the north, where they are now. ʿAlī was contradicted by ʿUthmān Khiḍir (twenty-three years old), who would not believe the legend. The conversation continued for a while until another young man narrated the legend about Dulumbabay island of the Rubāṭāb, which came to the Rubāṭāb land from the north in the footsteps of a certain saint. ʿAlī al-Ṣāfī was offended that ʿUthmān Khiḍir did not contradict this legend, too. He said to ʿUthmān, "Why didn't you say anything about what was told about Dulumbabay? It is unfair. You would believe that an island could go against the current but deny that an island can go with the current!"

Popular beliefs[7] were also dispelled quickly by their skepticism. A man came to a funerary wake and, as custom requires, took off his shoes, but he placed one shoe on top of the other. Another man pointed to the shoes and mentioned the belief that such a positioning of the shoes indicates that the owner has a trip ahead of him. The belief was instantly contradicted. The positioning of the shoes was explained by a number of those present by the fact that when one takes off his shoes he always uses one foot to take the shoe from the other foot and thus ends up having one shoe on the other. On another occasion, the belief that tomatoes do not succeed in summer because they are scared of clouds was also dismissed. Instead, a few of those present said that high temperatures caused tomato failures in the summer.

This brief survey of the place of fiction in Rubāṭāb culture demonstrates how Rubāṭāb men are, at best, wary of fictive texts. This lukewarmness to seduction through fiction will assume a special analytical significance in chapter five, when the metaphor of *saḥir* is interpreted as a fictive script.

Telling Lies about National Politics

Rubāṭāb speech events largely reproduce the *sharīʿah*-minded model of speaking. The commended "*qāl Allah, qāl al-Rasūl*" (Allah said, [his] messenger said) and the prohibited *qaṭīʿah* (backbiting) speech events put in relief the *sharīʿah*-minded injunction on silence, which may only be broken if something good for religion or one's livelihood is going to be said. On the other hand, *wanasah* (casual talk), where *maqālāt* transmission takes place, is the prevalent speech event. It is widely enjoyed, although it is suspected of bordering on and shading into *qaṭīʿah.* Moreover, when *wanasah* turns sour people fall back upon the "*qāl Allah* . . ." model to call that *wanasah* off.

The Koran likens the acts that the Rubāṭāb term *qaṭīʿah* to eating the flesh of one's dead brother (Koran 49:12). The abhorrence some people feel toward *qaṭīʿah* was brought home to me by an elderly woman who stopped us for a ride one midday on the road between ʿAtmūr and al-ʿAbaydab. When we stopped for her, the woman sighed in obvious relief, wiped the beads of sweat from her forehead and said, "I am having this unforeseen ride because I never backbite." Listening to *qaṭīʿah,* according to Islam, makes one an accomplice in the guilt (al-Ghazzali 1965, 3:145–46). This is why one young man, according to his father, would either fight with those who backbite in his presence or just leave. Ideally, one may make amends for backbiting by seeking forgiveness from the one who was slandered (1965, 3:153). In practice, however, people ask forgiveness from Allah. A Rubāṭābī would begin his *qaṭīʿah* by saying "*Istaghfir Allah*" (I ask forgiveness of Allah).

Wanasah is the least structured speech event with respect to place, genres, and themes. It covers a number of speech genres, the most important of which is a form of teasing known as *mulākadah* (lit., elbowing). Both women and men participate in *wanasah.* Although it can take place anywhere two or more people get together, funerary wakes and marriage ceremonies are its ideal situations. On such occasions the people—who sit on mats at wakes and on wooden beds and chairs in marriage ceremonies—may enjoy a single dominant *wanasah* or several simultaneous *wanasahs*, or they may alternate between the two depending on the popularity of the *wannās* (the adept *wanasah* speaker) involved or the genre taking place at one point in time. Some of the *saḥḥārs* I encountered in the villages I studied are singled out as adept *wannās* or *budaʿī. Wanasah* admittedly may border on *qaṭīʿah. Wanasah* is said to be a cup of coffee, and *qaṭīʿah* is the ginger that gives it the cherished taste and aroma. Madīnah al-Ḥāj, the *sōmār* singer, said, "Indeed, we can't claim that we don't engage in *qaṭīʿah.* We backbite people and they backbite us. Indeed! . . . Do you think we chew grass?" I asked her to repeat what she just said. She said, "Do you want us to eat grass?" Madīnah was alluding here to the proverb "The cud which people chew is other people," which indicates that speaking inevitably leads to *qaṭīʿah.* In other words, what people talk about is other people.

Mimicry, according to *sharīʿah,* is the worst form of backbiting because of its graphic portrayal of others (al-Ghazzali 1965, 3:145). Ṣiddīq al-Ḥibayl, a first-class *saḥḥār* and a *budaʿī,* is a very good mimic and performs at the risk of incurring the indignation of those he imitates.

The most distinct form of the "*qāl Allah*" speech event is the recitation of Koran on the third and last day of the funerary wake by *fuqarah* (sing., *faqīr,* Koran schoolteacher, maker of charms and medical cures, a holy or religious man, or all three of these in one). The recitation takes place parallel to and separate from the *wanasah* event. Although people believe it is the ideal speech event, they know that they cannot engage in it without the aid of a specialist in religion. This professional nature of the event is best illustrated by the story of the ex-*omdah* (mayor) who was reprimanded by an elderly relative for participating in one such recitation. The elderly relative said, "I thought to find you as an *omda* prevailing in the *wanasah* telling lies about national politics, and you are here sitting with the *fuqarah.* Don't you ever do that again."

The *ʿalīm* (preacher) circle is another form of the "*qāl Allah*" speech event, but such circles are sporadic and held mostly in the holy month of Ramadan. *Ṭarīqah* ritual *zikir* nights used to be included in the event, but they ceased to be regular occurrences in these villages.

The Audience as Censor

The Rubāṭāb internalize the speech preferences dictated by the *sharīʿah*-minded discourse and reproduce them in judging speech appropriateness. I observed on three occasions how the audience put the bridle of *sharīʿah* on a performer thought to be abusive or flippant about religious mores. On the first occasion Wad Ḥāj ʿAlī wanted to start a teasing of the *mulākadah* type with ʿAradayb al-Ḥāj in a *wanasah* at a funerary in ʿAtmūr. But ʿAradayb intentionally "misunderstood" the key for the *mulākadah* and rekeyed it into a *mukhātah,* a kind of verbal insult. The reason for this turn of events was the disparity of social status between ʿAradayb, the literate farmer, and Wad Ḥāj ʿAlī, the illiterate tenant. Teasing ordinarily takes place between people of approximately the same social status. The audience intervened consciously and consistently to prevent the dominant *wanasah* from turning into *mukhātah* by rekeying the defunct teasing or by creating byplays,[8] but to no avail. ʿAradayb pursued the *mukhātah* unflinchingly by attacking Wad Ḥāj ʿAlī's illiteracy and inferiority as a landless tenant and ended up calling him a jackass. Wad Ḥāj ʿAlī remained silent but was obviously perturbed, combing his beard with his fingers and drawing vague lines on the ground. His expression remained blank and his gaze was directed toward nothing in particular. Members of the audience started expressing their disinterest in the continuation of the *wanasah:*

MŪSAH: As a rule, this kind of talk has an unpleasant end.
HĀSHIM: People have abandoned talking about *qāl Allah qāl al-Rasūl.*

The metaspeech of Mūsah and Hāshim was followed by a relatively long period of silence. Someone used the chill precipitated by the authoritative statement of Hāshim to accuse ʿAradayb of being unfair to Wad Ḥāj ʿAlī. ʿAradayb denied any ill intentions on his part. The door was thus opened for a reconciliation between the two, which subsequently took place.

On the second occasion, Bajūrī of al-ʿAbaydab village was attending a wake in the village when news came that an elderly man was dying. Immediately Bajūrī said, "Couldn't he wait and die a week from now or so? We just can't afford to attend two wakes in a single week." This statement struck a man as blasphemous, and he rebuked Bajūrī for his false sense of safety in this ephemeral life, and added, quoting a proverb: "Al-ylqah hawāhū . . . [If the wind goes one's way what else should one do except . . .]" Bajūrī interjected: "Yaḍarit [to fart]." The man, then, said "Yaḍarī [to winnow], ya mughafal [you idiot]." "Believe me, I have always thought it 'to fart,'" said Bajūrī.

My interview with Madīnah al-Ḥāj of the ʿAbaydab lineage was the third occasion on which the tension between Rubāṭāb discourses and the *sharīʿah*-minded model of speaking was made clear by the audience. The interview took place during the afternoon, the celebrated time in a semidesert climate when the fiery, perpendicular grip of the sun is dislocated from mid-sky and shadows add meaningfully to the social space. Madīnah was beaming with happiness. Cognizant of being the focus of attention and surrounded by her kinsmen, she apparently intended to use the interview to showcase her talents in performance. She inlaid her delivery with asides and comments that were highly reflexive, as I have shown earlier. She even praised the *saḥḥār*s as being clever in drawing analogies, unlike the mute majority. She realistically admitted that *qaṭīʿah* is inseparable from *wanasah* and that it is segmentary in nature, that is, it is the bond of solidarity between those present which sets them against those absent. She also endorsed laughter and merriment with an adage from folk theology that is clearly patterned after the Prophet's traditions: "The soul with the wrinkled forehead and anguished heart is taken to hell." At one point Madīnah was indistinctly greeted by another woman, at which point she launched into a soliloquy:

> Allah wills it that I be blessed with health. Allah wills it that I live long and be blessed with health, O God. Allah wills it that I don't die when the goodies are abundant. Allah wills it I don't die [she laughs]. The okra is blossoming in the farm and the dates are ripe for reaping. Allah wills it I don't die at this time. Indeed, praise to Allah. I praise him again. Those around me [the audience] are all my sons and daughters. Whenever I feel like entering any of their houses I do and I eat and drink and I don't care. Praise be to Allah and I am grateful to him.

This soliloquy is blasphemous from a *sharīʿah*-minded perspective because her sense of safety on earth is a ruinous delusion (Hamori 1974, 54). *Sharīʿah* recommends silence to restrain exactly such satanic eloquence. However, Madīnah got away with it on this occasion. At one point, I asked her if she knew any *ḥujah* (folktales). She said, "*Ḥujah* was passed on from my grandmother to my mother. And my damned mother died and left us without *ḥujah* [laughs]." The male audience said in unison, "Say Allah, bless her rather." She condescendingly said, "Allah bless and forgive her [laughs]. She passed on very little *ḥujah* to us and went to her grave with the rest. Isn't that mean of her, anyway?" A silence ensued. Madīnah apparently did not quite make it this time. The audience's religious sense of the sanctity of the dead was offended, and they pressured her to use the invocation "Allah bless her" from the theologically disciplined language (Piamenta 1979, 20). But the indomitable Madīnah swallowed the pebble tactfully and restated her argument. The sanctity of the dead, to Madīnah, is just one way of looking at the victims of death. She is infatuated with life. She does not want to die "when the okra is blossoming," and she did not hesitate to ask Allah, who wisely instituted death, to leave her to enjoy life.

4

Saḥir Performance and Theory

The Predatory Eye and the Evil Mouth

Rubāṭāb *saḥir,* in which the casting of *'ayn* (evil eye) is attributed to the utterances of the *saḥḥārs*, is a category of the evil eye concept known as the "evil mouth" (or "hot mouth," "black tongue," "malalingua," "black mouth," "ill tongue," or "bad breath" [mouth]) (Elworthy 1895, 14, 16; Maclagan 1902, 8, 12, 62, 51; Seligmann 1910, 1:4–5; Flores-Meiser 1976, 149, 151; Maloney 1976, 131–32; Spooner 1976, 78; Dionisopoulos-Mass 1976, 44; Stein 1976, 198, 201; Donaldson 1981, 68; Harfouche 1981, 90, 93; Schoeck 1981, 196; Herzfeld 1981, 567; Galt 1982, 671). The evil mouth has been regarded as "subordinate to [the evil eye] and a marginal relative to it" (Flores-Meiser 1976, 160). Seligmann argues that bewitching with words is a form of an emanation of an evil gaze (1910, 1:5). The emphasis in evil eye scholarship has been on the gaze rather than on the evil mouth, perhaps because looking and staring are said to have a more constant and generally defined value than the utterance (Spooner 1976, 283). Thus Flores-Meiser warns the reader that her article on the hot mouth has little to say about the evil eye and apologizes for including it in a collection of articles devoted to the evil eye (Maloney 1976, 149).

The phenomenon of the evil mouth in Arab and Muslim contexts has been noted by Edward Westermarck (1926, vol. 2). He begins by pointing to the belief in the evil mouth among the Moroccans, who greatly feared the utterance when combined with a look (1926, 2:416). Interestingly enough, he relates four evil mouth events that sound like the best *saḥrahs* that can be collected from the Rubāṭāb today (1926, 2:416–17). With the progress of his exposition, however, he quickly loses track of the speech aspect of the belief and describes it exclusively in terms of the gaze, that is, the setting of the eyes, their relation to the brows, their malignant glance, and the way people represent them on prophylactic objects and charms (1926, 2:419–22, 427, 439).

The extent of the discrimination against the mouth (and, for that matter, against other value-laden symbols such as the tongue, the smell, the breath, and the bodily presence) is best illustrated by the question "Why the eye?" raised by scholars to account for the concept being specifically the evil *eye*. Various answers to this question have been proposed. Brian Spooner argues that the question is to be solved by a psychological rather than a sociological approach (1976, 283). The eye as the mirror of the soul (Maclagan 1902, 1; Maloney 1976, 134; McCartney 1981, 11) may be said to be at the root of the psychological universal espoused by Spooner (1976, 283). The eye is also foregrounded in Alan Dundes's theory in which the evil eye concept is seen to mediate the wet-dry opposition (1981, 266–67). In this perspective the eye is repeatedly cited as the symbolic equivalent to wet organs such as the phallus, breasts, vulva, or testicles (1981, 278–84). Similarly, Vivian Garrison and Conrad Arensberg describe the eye as the "ethogram of our species." They offer a sociological interpretation, theorizing that the evil eye concept is a symbol of interpersonal threat in societies that have completed their social stratification. Consequently, since the mouth and its cognates involve organs of communication that befit homogeneous or egalitarian society, they need no symbol as distinct as the eye (1976, 306–307).

The neglect of the verbal component of evil eye events has often led to a misunderstanding of the phenomenon. One such error is the common assumption that the evil eye is tied to praise. Students of the evil eye often gloss the utterance in the evil eye event as generalized, inadvertent praise, without analyzing and sometimes even without stating the particular instances (Barclay 1964, 194–95; Flores-Meiser 1976, 155, 159; Dionisopoulos-Mass 1976, 44; Stein 1976, 201; Schoeck 1981, 196; Dundes 1981, 258;

Harfouche 1981, 88; Herzfeld 1981, 567; Galt 1982, 671). However, in the rare cases when evil eye utterances were recorded in detail, they were often not expressions of praise at all. Frederick Elworthy, whose habit of narrating evil eye events at length needs to be emulated, relates how a man possessed of the evil eye said "It is difficult" to someone starting a journey and how misfortunes befell the man throughout the journey (Elworthy 1895, 20). Michael Herzfeld presents the case of a woman who was accused of casting the evil eye because she asked people she met where they were going (1981, 586). Anthony Galt describes an event in which a man said jokingly to an acquaintance, who was walking to his field in a new pair of work shoes, "You must sleep in those shoes for fear someone will steal them" (1982, 671). In all these cases praise is either lacking or inconsequential in understanding the actual evil eye events. These nonpraise versions of the evil eye have escaped our attention because we have taken the evil eye belief—a metaphor for a complex ritual of social avoidance—to mean literally the *eye,* disregarding its wider implications.

Verbal behavior occasionally proves to be crucial to the understanding of an evil eye event, even in the insufficient, fragmentary, and cure-oriented data we have at our disposal (Garrison and Arensberg 1976, 305, 319). In Italy an American anthropologist's wife who praised a cow for looking healthy was accused of giving it the evil eye, even though, the anthropologist said, she had been "thinking herself polite in a North American way" (Galt 1982, 672). It is clear that the threat of praise here does not arise from envy—which is held to be at the root of praise and evil eye (for example, Dundes 1981, 261)—but rather from certain rules of language use. This distinction is graphically demonstrated by the advice given to people traveling from cultures where praise is invited into cultures where praise is taboo—namely, to either refrain from praise or to offer it according to cultural prescription (Maclagan 1902, 76; Griffiths and Taha 1936, 75; Dundes 1981, 295). These examples show that the evil eye derives from rules of language use as much as from envy or evil gaze alone.

Aside from the few humane moments in which students of the evil eye have shown sympathy with those accused of possessing the evil eye (Schoeck 1981, 197; Oyler 1981, 85), evil eye scholarship has been faulted for failing to include the views of such people (Herzfeld 1981, 569; Siebers 1983, xi). It is worth noting that when students of the evil eye have found access to the perspective of the accused and, hence, the evidence to absolve him of the accusation, it has been only through the evil eye utterance itself. For instance, Maclagan maintains that accusations of afflicting beasts with the evil eye "have arisen in connection with men who talked freely giving opinions based upon hurried observation. Where silence would have left no ground for animadversion the wordy man had his sayings remembered against him" (1902, 74–75). Those accused of the evil mouth, according to Westermarck, were jokers having no feeling of ill will or envy (1926, 1:416). Further, we have already mentioned how Galt described a person accused of the evil mouth as a joker (1982, 671). It is the utterance that gave these scholars some evidence with which to analyze and explain the interaction. It is difficult, however, to imagine how the eye, the mute, predatory "window of the soul," could have offered similar access to the perspective of the accused.

Among the Rubāṭāb the theory of the subordination of the evil mouth to the *ʿayn,* or of the disassociation of the two, is untenable. Most instances of the evil eye occur during symbolic interactions in which speakers shoot metaphors at victims. In order to explain more fully the dynamics and poetics of this "hitting with sound" (Tambiah 1968, 176), this chapter will examine the speech component in the *saḥir* event in light of the indigenous semiotics described in the previous chapter.

Saḥrah *as Performance: A Display of a Deadly Competence*

Ideally, a *saḥrah* is a performance in which a competence, albeit deadly, is displayed. It involves an actor, an audience, a subject, and a judgment. As a performance, it is keyed and can be disclaimed (Bauman 1977, 15–16, 21–22). Besides the social risks that the *saḥḥārs* take, *saḥrah* involves the common risks of performance as an assumption of responsibility for a display of competence before an audience (1977, 11).[1]

A *saḥḥār* initiates the *saḥir* event by shooting a simile that likens the physical attributes and actions of a subject (person or object) to something else. When the subject is a person or the property of a person, that person will normally utter or perform traditional invocations to protect himself or his property from the adverse consequences of *saḥir*. The audience, on the other hand, laughs at good similes, though they are not unaware of the evil consequences that may result, or which the subject may claim result, from *saḥir*.

The *saḥḥār* may utter the *saḥrah* voluntarily or be pressured into uttering it. Understandably, *saḥḥār*s concur that they are at their best in the former situation. My informants agree that a *saḥḥār* wears on his face an expression that oscillates between a smile and a suppressed laugh when he has finished mentally conjuring up his simile. Recognizing this expression, the audience then urges him to utter his *saḥrah*. On one occasion I was recording narrated *saḥrah*s when I moved the microphone from one informant to another, who said he had remembered one. The people around me suddenly broke into laughter. Someone said "*Saḥarak*! [He bewitched you!]." More voices repeated the same words, and there was no mistake that they were addressing me. Some people asked ʿUthmān al-Māḥī, a non-Rubāṭābī who is adept in *saḥir*, to speak the *saḥrah* he had shot at me. One person asked him, "ʿUthmān, have you bewitched him?" And ʿUthmān said, laughingly yet very detachedly, "[Carrying the microphone from one informant to another looks like the situation in which] the Prophet's birth story is read." Laughter broke out again. The audience apparently knew from ʿUthmān's facial expression that my movement between the informants had reminded him of a comparable situation. The metaphor here is to the practice at the *zikir* circle of the Khatmiyyah brotherhood, in which the leader of the group takes the book containing the story of Muḥammad's birth from one reciter to another according to each one's favorite chapter of the story.

The *saḥḥār* may be invited to speak a *saḥrah*. Occasionally people ask him to *yasḥar* (bewitch) persons or objects that look a little odd or different. Ṣiddīq al-Ḥibayl was once asked to bewitch a sleeping fat man. He likened the man's belly, which seemed to be all over the bed, to an overstuffed mattress whose tacks had come off. On another occasion Wad al-Tōm was asked to bewitch the water filter that had been bought as part of the proposed village water plant but was left lying on the ground for a long time. Wad al-Tōm compared the cylindrical filter, with its three extended arms, to a pulled-out molar or wisdom tooth.

A *saḥḥār* may be provoked into saying a *saḥrah*. One man with curly, grey hair got on the nerves of Wad al-Tōm, who then said, "Get off my back with your hair that looks like the vapor arising from hot porridge." Those who are exceptionally scared of *saḥir* are the ones most exposed to this kind of *saḥrah*. In an attempt to avoid Wad al-Tōm's *saḥir,* a man sitting on a bird-scaring platform did not return his greeting. Wad al-Tōm teased him, asking, "What train is entering the station now?" in reference to the similitude between the platform and the railroad switch tower.

"A Saḥrah *Would Be Wasted on You!"*

There are two typical situations in which the *saḥḥār* may disclaim the performance. The first is when the audience has asked him to bewitch somebody or something. The *saḥḥār* may disclaim the performance by saying "*Asḥar layk*" or "*layh shinū*" (lit., What am I to bewitch you [or him] for; a *saḥrah* would be wasted on you [or him]) and then uttering the *saḥrah* all the same. The second situation in which disclaimers are used to preface *saḥrah*s is when somebody, either in anticipation of a *saḥrah* or because he is exceptionally afraid of *saḥir,* asks the *saḥḥār* in advance, "*Ma tasḥarnī!*" (Don't bewitch me!).

I asked Wad al-Tōm why he disclaims the *saḥrah* when people ask him to bewitch a subject. He answered: "In fact, people say in the *maqālah* [proverb] that the one who is incited to fight will not put up a good fight. When you feel that someone is asking you to bewitch something, you tend to disclaim [*tanaṣul*] what you are about to say; that is, you won't be as enthusiastic as when it [the *saḥrah*] comes naturally from you. You feel like somebody hired to say it." For example, I was told the story of a boy who was riding on the *tukum* of a waterwheel (the *tukum* is a forked log of wood, the forked part of which is woven with ropes to provide a seat for those who drive the oxen). When a *saḥḥār* approached, the boy implored, "By Allah, uncle. Don't bewitch me!" The *saḥḥār* said, "A *saḥrah* would be wasted on you, looking like a piece of meat on a spoon." The disclaimer " *'asḥar* . . ." echoes the "*ma tasḥarnī*," which is uttered by the potential subject of a *saḥir*. Although this disclaimer is widely used, other disclaimers echoing the subject's root statement are not uncommon.

*Saḥrah*s may also arise from a competition between *saḥḥār*s called for by leading practitioners of their art. Al-Ṭahir wad Ayyūb called for one such competition in which he asked some of the *saḥḥār*s to find analogues to a number of things, including the clock at Atbara's railway station. The jerky movement of the minute hand was likened by al-Ṭahir to a jackass jumping with its forelegs tied together. On other occasions *saḥrah*s arise during joking exchanges between two or more *saḥḥār*s. Wad al-Tōm and Muḥammad al-Khayr 'Umar, for example, frequently joke at wakes and wedding ceremonies, which is a kind of theatrical enactment of *saḥrah*s. Muḥammad 'Umar relates how once, on seeing Wad al-Tōm, he feigned annoyance at being bewitched by him and how they exchanged a series of *saḥrah*s after that. We will elaborate on these two *saḥir* performances in chapter six.

It is not uncommon for someone who is angry at a *saḥḥār* for causing him one misfortune or another to hire another *saḥḥār* to avenge himself. Wad al-Tōm likened this technique to throwing a male camel on another sexually excited male camel to cool him down—a procedure followed by the nomads to keep their herds under control. Thus a *saḥḥār* was hired to bewitch Wad al-Tōm. When he was finally asked by the one who hired him to say his *saḥrah*, the *saḥḥār* said, "Whichever way I turned him [Wad al-

Tōm], I found him inaccessible [to *saḥir*]. Your only alternative is to burn him and get charcoal from him." The reference here is to logs of wood that have so many bumps that they are useless except as charcoal. In other words, he could do nothing with him. Wad al-Tōm was *saḥir*-proof because of the lifetime he had spent practicing this art.

People of one village may also ask a visiting *saḥḥār* to compete in *saḥir* with their local *saḥḥār*. Thus the Rubāṭāb in Atbara arranged for a duel between Silaymān ʿAbd al-ʾAẓīm, their local *saḥḥār*, and al-Shaykh al-Ṣāyīm of Mugrat Island. The two *saḥḥār*s met in a store in Atbara market and were introduced to each other. Both fell silent. After a while Silaymān said, "I presume that the man [al-Shaykh] is a *qāṣir*" (someone who shortens his prayers), in reference to the Muslim practice of shortening prayers when one is on a journey.[2] In other words, Silaymān suggested that al-Shaykh would not speak *saḥir* as long as he was not in his original place. Thereupon both contestants left the store.

Saḥir *as a Way of Speaking*

Some *saḥrah*s are spoken in an intimate atmosphere or are so general that it is impossible, or at best difficult, to claim that they have a bad effect. In this way *saḥrah*s become a way of speaking. ʾAwlād (sons of) ʾAyyūb of the ʿAbaydab village and lineage are famous for this manner of speaking. Their family reunions, it is said, extend late into the night with members competing in making analogies.

A *saḥrah* that illustrates graphically this last category of *saḥir* is about two dying men, Shaykh al-Dīn and Bābikir of the ʿAbaydab village, who fell seriously ill on the same day. Shaykh al-Dīn's home was at the southernmost end of the village, whereas Bābikir's home was at the northernmost end (see fig. 1). A woman from the village likened them in their bedridden situation to two express trains that have been held back at different stations because of a heavy rain that is feared to wash out the railroad. A few days later Shaykh al-Dīn died. Drawing again on her train meta-

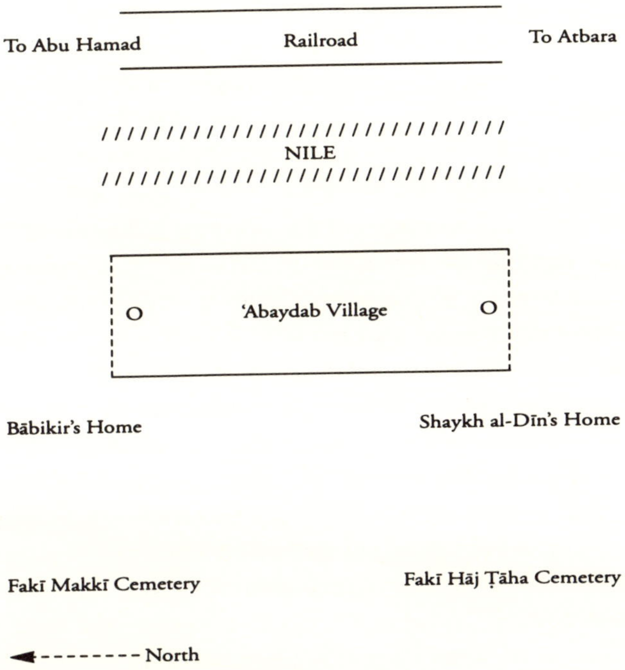

Figure 1 The Geography of a *Saḥrah*

phor, the same woman said that the northbound express was given the signal to move but not the southbound one. In another analogy, a young man from her family said that Shaykh al-Dīn, who died first, had been returned to his constituency. The two dying men here were pictured as candidates running for election in the constituency of death. When Shaykh al-Dīn died, another young man from the same family said that *fakī* Ṭāha, in whose cemetery Shaykh al-Dīn was buried, had "admitted" his man, but that *fakī* Makkī, in whose cemetery Bābikir, the other dying man, was supposed to be buried, had not. The reference here is to the system of entrance examinations in which elementary schools are grouped according to their geographical proximity and the pupils of each group sit for an entrance examination at a specified junior high school. This uninhibited, extended, and multivoiced *saḥrah* demonstrates how *saḥir* is virtually a way of speaking to certain Rubāṭāb.

Green Onions and Microphones: Perform and Run

The responses of the targets of the *saḥrah* range from laughter to actually fighting with the *saḥḥār.* Ṣiddīq al-Ḥibayl interpreted the laughing response of one of his victims by saying that the man had become accustomed to his *saḥir.* This is what the Rubāṭāb occasionally refer to as being *maṭaʿam* (immunized).

A laughing response, however, does not mean that the subject may not have second thoughts later about the effect of the *saḥrah.* Muḥammad Bābikir, a baker, told about how, one day, he rode his jackass early in the morning to sell his bread because that day he was not able to hire any of the boys he usually hired to sell for him. On his way he met Wad al-Tōm, who said, "Boys can't be depended on, eh!" This *saḥrah* was an allusion to the belief that *Iblīs* does not delegate his sons to persuade people not to perform the morning prayer. Such a seduction is *Iblīs*'s specialty; he attends to it in person. Muḥammad said they both laughed. A few months later Muḥammad went out of business. In retrospect, he thought that the *saḥrah* might have had something to do with his misfortune.

Occasionally, the subject of a *saḥir* reacts violently. Wad al-Tōm relates how Muḥammad ʿAlī Muṣṭafah, the patriarch of Um Ghiday, prayed against him and followed him in hot pursuit after a *saḥrah* was directed against his combine. Another *saḥḥār* once likened someone eating a green onion to somebody speaking into a microphone. The man threw away the onion, cursed the *saḥḥār,* and complained thereafter that his hand had never been the same. Another subject is said to have threatened to beat his uncle because he bewitched him. People intervened and asked the man to apologize to his uncle, which he did in the presence of other men.

A *saḥḥār* may actually find it necessary to flee the scene immediately after performing a *saḥrah* to avoid the target's retaliation. Wad al-Tōm said he had to leave a wedding party hurriedly because his *saḥrah* of a man with a certain disability had begun to spread among the guests. Wad al-Tōm had whispered the *saḥrah* to the person sitting next to him, who in turn had passed it on, and so forth. Wad al-Tōm was apprehensive about how the target, who was known for his bad temper, would react when the *saḥrah* finally reached him.

A subject may choose to reprove the *saḥḥār* for making him a target of the metaphor. He may firmly tell the *saḥḥār* that he is genuinely scared of *saḥir* and indicate the kinds of misery it caused him, such as headaches, fever, and the like. In this case, the *saḥḥār* might assuage the subject's fears and assure him that his *saḥir* is of the ineffectual kind, saying it is like the harmless sting of *ʿaqrab al-baḥar* (river scorpion, crab), not the venomous sting of the regular land scorpion. Another possible tactic for victims of *saḥir* is to complain to the *saḥḥār*'s elders. Ṣiddīq al-Ḥibayl, against whom such a complaint was made, said that he was asked by some people to bewitch for a second time the man who had complained of a previous *saḥrah.* He added: "I did that a week ago, and I know that I am in big trouble. People will, of course, tell him about it."

*The Vindictive Meta*saḥrah

In order to nip the *saḥrah* in the bud or to forestall adverse consequences after its utterance, the target or victim may perform various prophylactic formulae and rituals. The *saḥḥār*s, who are especially insulted by these prophylactic measures, make these countermeasures, in turn, the object of their ridiculing "meta-*saḥrah.*"

Māshallah is an element of the bridle of *sharīʿah* that people apply to the *saḥḥār* to deflect the evil metaphor. The *saḥḥār*s sometimes put this bridle on their own mouths to pacify their victims. Before or after a *saḥrah,* the audience or the victim may ask the *saḥḥār* to say "*māshallah*" (what Allah willed). The following is an example of how *saḥḥār*s may respond to such audience pressure by producing meta*saḥrah*s. Pressed hard by an audience who kept reminding him to say "*māshallah*" at every other utterance, one *saḥḥār* said, "You sound like people pricing a male sheep" (a context where this formula is often heard).

Wad al-Tōm, like some other *saḥḥār*s, does not share the subject's view that he should say "*māshallah,*" since according to him what he performs is not *ʿayn* practice. He argues that the real *ʿayn* is the one caused by an envious person who does not say "*māshallah,*" since he passes by something that arouses his admiration. Discovering analogies, according to him, cannot be considered evil eye.

Some *saḥḥār*s, while sharing Wad al-Tōm's view, nevertheless pretend to comply with the subject's wishes. For example, Muḥammad al-Khayr ʿUmar said he would anticipate an interactant, whom he knew to fear his *saḥrah*s, by saying "*māshallah.*" (Incidentally, the way Muḥammad pronounced "*māshallah*" in this context approximated the pitch usually uttered by a frightened would-be victim of *saḥir.*) However, Muḥammad said he would still say to himself the *saḥrah* that came to his mind. I asked him, "Would you later tell him [the subject] of your *saḥrah*?"

"Of course, no."

"Why?"

"Because he wanted my *saḥrah* to be on the black market" (i.e., not available over the counter, through the usual, direct channels).

On the other hand, some *saḥḥār*s comply with *māshallah* demands and prohibitions much more stringently. Al-Duqāq, the poet, said he would ignore the *saḥrah* when it crossed his mind and busy himself in fortifying his faith by saying "*māshallah.*" Similarly, Nūr al-Dīn, a Rubāṭābī clerk who worked for Sudan Railways at its headquarters in Atbara, was forced to sign a "treaty" with his female office workers in which he promised to stop bewitching them. I interviewed Nūr al-Dīn while this "treaty" was still being observed. In narrating one of his old *saḥrah*s, he said, "One day they [the female office workers] were sitting *māshallah* . . ." Nūr al-Dīn was careful not to break the "treaty" even while he was reporting an old *saḥrah.*

A victim may also say "*a'ūdhu billah*" (I seek refuge in Allah), either by itself or in combination with other protective formulae such as "*Allahu 'akbar 'alayk*" (Allah is great on you), or may recite part or all of one of *al-mu'awwidhatān*.[3] Muṣṭafah 'Ayyūb said that some people would say "*a'ūdhu billah*" whenever he approached them, even when he had no intention of shooting a *saḥrah* at them. He added, "I for one will shoot whichever *saḥrah* comes to me if I see anyone's lips moving with the *ta'wīdhah* [utterance of '*a'ūdhu billah*']." The audience laughed in sympathy with his defiant spirit.

The meta*saḥrah*s relating to this formula abound. Ṣiddīq al-Ḥibayl said that he found Wad al-Tōm surrounded by people laughing at his *saḥir* and constantly saying "*a'ūdhu billah*" after each *saḥrah*. Al-Ḥibayl then likened Wad al-Tōm to a sack of red pepper, the smell of which makes people sneeze. In other words, he compared the *ta'wīdhah* expression that people utter excessively in the presence of a *saḥḥār* to the outburst of sneezing people suffer when they are around a sack of red pepper.

Other prophylactic formulae and rituals are also performed. The subject may approach the *saḥḥār* and surprise him to prevent him from concentrating his evil mental powers on the subject. The same result is said to be achieved by the subject showing his buttocks to the *saḥḥār*. The following extended, dramatic *saḥrah* narrated by Wad al-Tōm demonstrates not only the enactment of these particular prophylactic rituals but also how the *saḥḥār*s can be relentlessly vindictive:

> [They were attending] a *būghah* [a communal work project for cleaning up land, ploughing it, constructing water conduits and plots for irrigation, sowing it, and watering it for the first time], and with them was a "Sudanese" slave man. The slave was pitch dark and was a great laugher. . . . When he laughs his tongue becomes in fact the only thing that was not black around him. My maternal uncle Sīd 'Aḥmad said to him: "Hey, slave man. Stoop down and do some work, you with a tongue that looks like a candy cock [available for sale only on the twelve-day-long festivities on the occasion of the Prophet's birthday]." The slave man was the kind that is scared of the

> evil eye. In order to prevent the bad effect of the *saḥrah,* he said: "There is no power and no strength save in Allah," and immediately took off his pants and faced Sīd 'Aḥmad. Sīd 'Aḥmad said: "Hey, slave man! Having this penis [with testicles] that looks like the knife [in a sheath worn on the arm] and amulets [round or cylindrical leather purses containing protective Koranic and/or other magical texts usually worn around the arm]" [laughs]. The slave man then turned around and showed Sīd 'Aḥmad his bottom. Sīd 'Aḥmad said, "Hey, slave man having this anus that looks like the hole left by a peg that was on a water conduit [usually on dark clay soil]." Close to Sīd 'Aḥmad was ʿAbd al-ʿAẓīm, a *saḥḥār,* who said, "Sīd 'Aḥmad, by Allah, you have stung the slave man enough to make him look like a person who found a scorpion in his pants" [laughs]. Truly, it stings him wherever he turns.

On another occasion, the protective ritual of showing the buttocks was similarly turned into the subject of a meta*saḥrah.* A little boy was asked by his father to show his [black] bottom to a *saḥḥār* who was about to enter their home. The boy did so and the *saḥḥār* said, "Rise, boy having an anus that looks like a cavity resulting from a knot on [a black] waterskin," in reference to the practice of mending punctures in waterskins by inserting a pebble in the puncture and tying it up, with the knot to the inside of the waterskin, creating a cavity on the outside.

Grading a Saḥrah

Audiences penalize incompetent *saḥḥār*s for flaws in their display of competence either by making it clear that they are laughing out of courtesy or by not laughing at all. Poor *saḥrah*s are ignored and, therefore, do not become popular. Someone who attempts a *saḥrah* that fails with the audience may be asked to take it to Wad al-Tōm—the master of the genre—who will "grade" it for him. Further, a poor performance may be dismissed as a form of imbecility. Such failed *saḥrah*s are not uncommon with the mentally retarded among the Rubāṭāb. There is a certain retarded dependent of a wealthy man in the village who attempts *saḥir,* but his analogues are drawn exclusively from the attributes of his patron and his patron's property. The audience may find such *saḥrah*s amusing only insofar as they indicate the imbecile *saḥḥār*'s ignorance of the risks that performance of *saḥrah* entails.

Besides laughter, a successful *saḥrah* may be rewarded with praise for its precision. The criterion of exact similitude in discovering analogies is paramount for the audience. For example, a *saḥḥār* was asked by some of his audience to show them exactly how their unfinished village youth club, according to a *saḥrah* of his, looked like a kind of a waistcoat. To prove the validity of his comparison, the *saḥḥār* took them to the unfinished building and started showed them similarities between the two.

The idiom in which the audience expresses its appreciation of *saḥir* is homicidal. Their delight in the exactitude of the *saḥrah* is expressed in terms of shooting the target dead. Audiences normally punctuate their laughter with expressions such as "he killed him," "have mercy on him," or "you are really bad!" We have already seen how the evil bite of *saḥrah*s has been compared to the sting of a scorpion. I was a subject of a *saḥrah* one day, and one of the audience shouted to me: "Qaraḍōk![4] [they killed you]." Even when the *saḥrah* is later narrated to an audience, the narrator will preface the narration by saying, "Did you hear the one in which [a *saḥḥār*] killed [a victim]?"

An audience may also praise the power of a *saḥrah* by uttering the *ta'wīdhah. Saḥḥār*s themselves sometimes take such utterances as indicators of the audience's appreciation of their satanic-inspired power. Once Wad al-Tōm and another *saḥḥār* shot *saḥrah*s at a scrambled segment of a TV show they were watching at the home of a relative in the town of Omdurman. A power outage occurred immediately after the two *saḥrah*s were spoken. I asked Wad al-Tōm which *saḥrah* of the two had hit it right on the head. He said jokingly that his was probably the most effective because the audience had uttered a lot of *ta'wīdhah*s after it was said. Those around us laughed.

Speaking Blunts the Edge of Evil

The Rubāṭāb concept of *saḥir* (a term they use synonymously with *'ayn ḥarah* [evil eye]) emerges as a continuum ranging from the evil gaze to the metaphorically articulated *saḥrah*. However, the most evil *saḥir* is held to be the staring kind, that is, the one that has not been articulated. It is likened to a shot from a pistol with a silencer. (We will be dealing with more specimens of this ballistic idiom, which reinforces the homicidal idiom we mentioned earlier.) As ʿAlī al-Ṣāfī said, "The shot that you can hear does no harm; the one that is silenced is really bad."

When people in the villages speak of the silent, evil gaze they usually point to Nasr, a farmer in his late fifties. I had a long conversation with some villagers about Nasr. His reputation for having *ʿayn* goes back to the days when he worked on the railroad as a young man. The story I heard related that the young Nasr measured with his hand the bare, broad shoulders of one man and said that the man's shoulders would be a certain width in a certain number of years. Three days later, the broad-shouldered man died. When I asked the narrator whether what Nasr said was an expression of praise or envy, I was referred to Karār, who had witnessed the event. Karār denied that Nasr had said anything when he was measuring the man's shoulders.

Another drastic *ʿayn* attributed to Naṣr was not silent. He is said to have complained that a villager's water pump was too noisy for him to sleep. As a result, the piston of the water pump broke. Increasingly, the atmosphere of the session in which the stories were recorded became charged with hatred for Nasr, and stories were told about his childlessness and his rugged face. Muṣṭafah ʾAyyūb, a speaker of metaphoric *saḥir,* was present but did not participate in the discussion. On another occasion, however, he told me that Nasr, who "gazes and suppresses [the utterance of] his *saḥir,*" makes the kind of evil that is really harmful. According to Muṣṭafah, articulation blunts the edge of *saḥir.*

In addition, Muṣṭafah asserted that the people of the villages are not averse to his own *saḥir.* On another occasion, however, he described one villager, Wad Sūwār, as the kind that is really scared of *saḥir.* Wad Sūwār jokingly accused Muṣṭafah of being a "really bad" *saḥḥār,* and that his *ʿayn* (evil eye) "rubs dry the green [plant]." On another occasion, however, someone said in the presence of Muṣṭafah that his *saḥir* was harmless.

In addition, the stare is not necessarily silent. Muṣṭafah 'Ayyūb told of his uncle who was forced to withhold his *saḥrah*s. He added, "He comes along, stares at you and slips away. In so staring, he would simultaneously say to himself what crossed his mind, and vanish." We have already seen how Muḥammad al-Khayr 'Umar was pressured to suppress his *saḥrah*s. However, he said that he, too, would speak them all the same, adding, "The one that I suppress is harmful. They are better off if they allow me to speak it." It seems that statements like this express merely the *saḥḥārs*' feelings of defiance rather than their actual practice.

We have mentioned earlier how the *saḥḥār*s object to being accused of possessing the *'ayn,* and how they argue that *saḥrah*s stem from an irresistible imaginative urge and not from *fakar* (envy). Wad al-Tōm, for instance, argues that the *'ayn* stems from envy, whereas *saḥir* is merely guessing out analogies. According to *saḥḥār*s, *saḥir* is a *wanasah,* a joke; it is "just kidding," meant to make people laugh.

However, they admit that their *saḥrah*s can sometimes do harm. Thus Ḥasan Jaqalaybah of 'Atmūr village said that even though *saḥḥār*s speak *saḥir* for *wanasah,* harm may still afflict the subject as a result. Some *saḥḥār*s tell of *saḥrah*s shot by themselves or others in which the subject was harmed. Wad al-Tōm told how a *saḥrah* that he shot resulted in the death of a sheep; however, the audience pressured him to admit that it killed more than the one sheep.

*Saḥḥār*s often argue that their own *saḥrah*s are mild and attribute more dangerous powers to their rivals' *saḥḥār*s. A *saḥḥār* jokingly described the *saḥir* of one of his colleagues as *ka'ab* (really evil), while his own was only like a sting from a water crab.

Another man similarly described his *saḥir* as buckshot, compared to the bullets of other *saḥḥār*s. The self-image of a *saḥḥār* may be quite different from the view others have of him. Nūr al-Dīn, the urban Rubāṭābī *saḥḥār,* narrated some *saḥrah*s attributed to Wad al-Tōm, whom he does not know, in which Wad al-Tōm was depicted as a very evil *saḥḥār* whose metaphors harm drastically and instantaneously. However, Nūr al-Dīn would not accept this image as applied either to himself or to his late father-in-law, although his non-Rubāṭābī neighbors in Atbara had a similar or even worse image of him.

The Lonely Ṭalḥah *Tree*

An attractive hypothesis, espoused mainly by the *saḥḥār*s themselves, is that *saḥir* affliction falls only on those who are really scared of *saḥir. Fakī* Ibrahīm al-Qalubāwī of ʿAtmūr, for example, said that his teacher told him he was susceptible to being hurt by the *ʿayn* because he was afraid of it. Further, Wad al-Tōm characterized this kind of person as having an *ʿaqīdah* (belief) in the adverse effects of *saḥir,* "and what you are scared of harms you." He related a story about the slave man who was shot by four *saḥrah*s in a row and who had a temperature the morning after because of his belief that *saḥir* is fatal. To substantiate his hypothesis, Wad al-Tōm related how he cut a branch from a *ṭalḥah* (acacia) tree to use as an oar to row his raft down Atbara river. An *ʿArabī* (Arab, i.e., nomad) saw the branch and asked him whether he had cut it from *at-ṭalḥah al-farīdah* (the *ṭalḥah* that grows apart from similar trees) at a place he specified. Wad al-Tōm answered in the affirmative. The nomad was upset and warned Wad al-Tōm that he was headed for a misfortune by violating the taboo against cutting wood from such *ṭalḥah.* This warning alarmed Wad al-Tōm considerably, but, failing to find a substitute oar, he trusted Allah and used the oar he had originally cut. Happily, his raft arrived safely at its destination, and he even got a good price for the oar itself. "Had it been the nomad, his belief in the taboo about the *ṭalḥah* could have caused him harm," he said.

The same belief was shared by Khalīfah, who had been the subject of two *saḥrah.* He said, "*Saḥir* afflicts those who are scared of it. People used to *tashfaq* [fear] the effects of *saḥir,* but not anymore in this day and age." Similarly, ʾAḥmad ʾAyyūb, an attorney from ʾAwlād ʾAyyūb, argues in psychological terms that *saḥrah*s make subjects pathologically concerned about their well-being so that they readily see a connection between a misfortune and a *saḥrah*.

Wad al-Tōm argues the validity of his hypothesis forcefully and consistently. I interviewed him once in the presence of Mughdād, a shopkeeper, butcher, and farmer. Mughdād related the *saḥrah* about Abū Līkaylik, who met Muṣṭafah al-Tōm, a *saḥḥār*, while riding a jackass other than his own. Muṣṭafah pretended not to recognize the man and said, "Who is that? Is it Abū Līkaylik? What are you riding? A steam engine, or what!" This *saḥrah* alluded to the use of both steam and diesel engines at Abu Hamad junction. In other words, Muṣṭafah al-Tōm likened Abū Līkaylik to a train engineer who can take whatever engine is available. It is said that Abū Līkaylik immediately fell from the jackass onto the ground. Wad al-Tōm interpreted the cause of the fall as coming from Abū Līkaylik's belief rather than from anything intrinsic in the *saḥrah*. However, Mughdād, who is rational in his own way and a close enough friend of Wad al-Tōm to have a repertoire of his *saḥrah*s, argued jokingly that the *saḥrah* was responsible for the harm done to Abū Līkaylik. On another occasion, however, Mughdād adopted Wad al-Tōm's hypothesis and added that an affliction from a *saḥrah* is either a coincidence or a *sabab* (cause or agency), referring to the belief that every occurrence is predestined by Allah and that natural causation and people's actions are mere agents for the predestined to take place. He himself did not subscribe to this belief in predestination, or was at least ambivalent about causation.

This ambivalence is evident in the case of Muṣṭafah ʾAyyūb, the *saḥḥār*. He related a *saḥrah* in which he compared two men who carried their fishing nets on their shoulders every afternoon on their way to the river with railroad employees on their evening trips to light the lamps of the train's signaling devices. The reference here is to the routinization of the activity itself and to the fact that the fishermen used empty kerosene cans as buoys for their nets, whereas the railroad workers used the cans to carry kerosene. Muṣṭafah admitted that the fishermen suffered a misfortune as a result of his *saḥrah*. He said, "They were convinced that my *saḥir* afflicted their net. Anyway, whether that affliction was from 'The God of all people' or from me is of little import, but they never catch as much as they used to."

Generally speaking, I found the coincidence hypothesis more popular than the *sabab* explanation among the Rubāṭāb. Thus Muḥammad al-Khayr 'Umar said, "A *saḥrah* might hit the target or might miss it, just like a bullet." Further, Ḥasan Jaqalaybah said *saḥir* is like cowrie divination, which is neither true nor false all the time. Al-Duqāq, the poet, related the *saḥrah* that made him decide to consciously refrain from *saḥir*. An elderly *saḥḥār*, he said, saw a colorfully dressed five-year-old girl and asked al-Duqāq, "Who is this girl who looks like the little fish of Port Sudan [a Red Sea port]?" in reference to the dazzling colors of this fish compared to the drab Nile fish. Al-Duqāq continued, "It so happened that the girl was stung by a scorpion at that very same time. It is a coincidence, I know."

Saḥḥārs may point to a rational cause for an inadequacy or a misfortune held to result from *saḥir*. A few days before I arrived, Wad al-Tōm fell from a tree from which he was cutting a branch. People usually say that practicing *saḥir* for a long time immunizes the practitioner from its affliction, but on this occasion they suggested that Wad al-Tōm was bewitched by Ṣiddīq al-Ḥibayl. Ṣiddīq had been speaking *saḥir* at a gathering that Wad al-Tōm also attended. When people asked Ṣiddīq whether he was too afraid of Wad al-Tōm to bewitch in his presence, Ṣiddīq said, "Why should I be afraid as long as Wad al-Tōm is the reservoir from which we [*saḥḥārs*] pump gas?" in recognition of Wad al-Tōm as the authority in *saḥir*. Wad al-Tōm denied that this *saḥrah* had any effect on him, suggesting instead that old age made him fall.

Similarly, Muṣṭafah 'Ayyūb denied the accusation that his *saḥrah* of the youth club led to the complete halt of construction. He argued that the village people—and especially the youth—knew exactly what went wrong with the building; not only had the project run out of money, but the youth were too lazy to call for the community to help out. Muṣṭafah said that, although the youth concerned do not discuss the incompletion of the building in terms of *saḥir,* people who fear *saḥir* sometimes mention Muṣṭafah's *saḥrah* to passersby who ask why the building was not finished. In this way the *saḥrah* circulates and is embellished, and the idea of a causal connection between the speech act and the event is reinforced.

Who Shot the Old Airplane? The Culprit Identified

Accusations of *saḥir* are rife amongst the Rubāṭāb. I was annoyed at first to find that *saḥir* accusations are often humorously framed. I thought an accusation of harm was a terrible thing to toy with, and I doubted the seriousness of the accusers, who cannot sustain an accusation without bracketing it or laughing it off. However, I gradually became convinced that accusations may be humorously framed without detracting from their reality or currency.

A woman from the ʿAbaydab village recalled with exasperation a *saḥrah* shot at her father ten years previously when they went together to harvest a palm tree they owned in ʿAtmūr village. The *saḥḥār,* Wad al-Hadaʿ, Sr., likened her father with his back bent from old age to an airplane landing on a runway. The woman was upset and immediately asked her father to gather the dates quickly and leave before Wad al-Hadaʿ *yaqrushnah* (crunched them). This phrase describes *saḥrah* with a metaphor of gnawing that is related to the homicidal and ballistic idioms in which *saḥir* is couched in Rubāṭāb dialect. According to her story, this *saḥrah* had an immediate effect. The sack in which they carried the dates fell apart and the dates scattered everywhere. The long-term effects of the *saḥrah* were their abandonment of harvesting that palm tree thereafter and the ultimate death of her father. One of the audience suggested laughingly to the woman that her father might have died of his *yūm* (the day appointed by Allah for his death):

WOMAN: No, no! The *saḥḥār* killed him. He was never back to the palm tree after that. (laughs)

AUDIENCE MEMBER: You swear on that by Allah's name?
WOMAN: By Allah.
AUDIENCE MEMBER: You say he didn't live until the next harvesting season?
WOMAN: He didn't. (laughs)
AUDIENCE MEMBER: Is that so?
WOMAN: Wad al-Hadaʿ is an evil *saḥḥār.*

Similarly, ʿAbbās ʿAlī Muṣṭafah concluded his interview with me on a laughing note, saying, "This is the thing that befell me as a result of the *saḥir* of Wad al-Tōm." The first time I met ʿAbbās, at a funerary wake, he was affirming to those around him the adverse consequences of *saḥir.* In my interview with him he related two *saḥrah*s shot at him by Wad al-Tōm. As a Mayāyyīs, ʿAbbās is known to be an industrious, inventive farmer. One day he turned on the water pump, filled up the main canal, and then turned the pump off and started channeling the water from the main canal to the branch canals and to the watering plots. Wad al-Tōm, who knew of ʿAbbās's procedure, commented: "His mother has given him a pacifier," comparing the silence of the water pump and the water ʿAbbās stored in the main canal to a baby silenced by a pacifier. After he finished watering his land, ʿAbbās told me, he rode on a trailer connected to a tractor. Suddenly the hitch broke and the trailer toppled over, causing ʿAbbās to break his leg. The breaking down of the hitch "is unheard of before," according to ʿAbbās. In saying this, he seemed to suggest that *saḥir* has an independent effect that can break down a device as strong and permanent as a hitch.

ʿAbbās related another *saḥrah* from Wad al-Tōm in which the latter likened ʿAbbās's animal enclosure, which contained all kinds of domestic animals, to a zoo. As a result, he said, all the animals ended up either seriously injured or dead. The jackass kicked the young camel and broke its leg, "though they were living peacefully together in the enclosure for a long time." The jackass itself suffered from a leg rupture, "though it had been kept there for three years." ʿAbbās's argument here approximates the

Azande explanation of misfortune, in which natural causation (or godly designs, for that matter) are considered the "first spear," or cause, whereas witchcraft, the "second spear," explains the occurrence of the misfortune in the context of place, time, and the particular people or things afflicted (Evans-Pritchard 1980, 22–26). ʿAbbās seemed to suggest by his comments that had it not been for *saḥir,* the "second spear," the misfortunes could not have happened because there was nothing in the nature of the two situations to indicate that a "first spear" was in operation.

Although ʿAbbās has apparently structured his accusations coherently, he nevertheless prefaced them with a general disclaimer in which he stated categorically his belief in predestination. He said, "Everything is predestined by Allah. Nothing whatsoever is in the hands of man. A man claims nothing to be his doing, but all the same we say they [the misfortunes] are from these *saḥrah*s."

Muḥammad ʿAlī Muṣṭafah, the patriarch of Um Ghiday, was presented to me as somebody who is extremely scared of *saḥir.* Nonetheless, the interview I had with him also assumed this jocular frame. He related how one day he was watering a field of sorghum with a helper. During the day Muḥammad would take breaks and rest in the shade of a building on the farm. However, while resting, his ear was attentive to the flow of water in the conduit lest it should crack. Each time the conduit cracked, he pointed out to the helper the exact spot by shouting "Hey, Ṣiddīq, the conduit cracked here, it cracked there, it cracked again here, there, over there . . ." Unable to cope with the directions of the demanding farmer, Ṣiddīq did not show up for work the next morning. When asked why he did not show up, he said, "No one will ever be able to help this man, who acts like Ṭāha Ḥamadtū [a famous soccer commentator] commenting on a game of soccer." Interestingly, Muḥammad said laughingly that the yield of his sorghum was unexpectedly high that year (1968), which was called "the year of the American sorghum" because the national sorghum yield was so low that American sorghum was imported to meet the local demand.

Muḥammad related another *saḥrah* in which a *saḥḥār* likened the back-and-forth movement of a sowing team of his helpers to a jazz band (which in local parlance means a military band). Nevertheless, he said, the yield of the farm was again good. I asked: "This also was not affected by the *saḥrah*?" "No. But it really affected my sons," said Muḥammad. "On the contrary, it increased its yield," interjected a member of the audience.

Muḥammad went on to describe how his two sons were affected by the *saḥrah*. One of them had been complaining of his health ever since, while the other fled the village on his truck and returned only after the sorghum had been harvested. Muḥammad stated that Allah is his only protection against the evil of *saḥir*.

The Baker's Second Thoughts

Muḥammad Bābikir's case presents us with another instance of the humorously framed, bracketed, and yet vigorous accusations of *saḥir* among the Rubāṭāb. After staying in Berber for twelve years, Bābikir returned to the village and started a bakery business. We have already mentioned the *saḥrah* in which Wad al-Tōm likened Bābikir to *Iblīs* for peddling bread very early one morning. Besides selling bread, Bābikir also served cooked horse beans in his bakery. One customer, who liked his beans soaked with oil, used to bring his own oil from home in a glass cup. Muṣṭafah al-Hadaʿ, the *saḥḥār*, saw this customer with his cup of oil on his way to Bābikir's place and said, "Are you going to test your urine?" This *saḥrah* came four months after Wad al-Tōm's. Bābikir went out of business six months after the last *saḥrah*. In a brief encounter he told me that his business had failed because of the *saḥrah*s and the constant problem he had with flour supplies. In an extended interview I asked him whether he had been at all scared when he heard the *saḥrah*s. He said no; he had taken them as *hiẓār* (kidding). He had laughed when he heard the first one shot at him, and laughed again when the second was reported to him by the customer. According to him, the intentions of the *saḥḥār*s were good, "though some people are extremely annoyed by *saḥir*." He continued, "I was not scared, and I paid little attention to them. In actual fact my business was slowing down of itself. But, indeed, there are some people also who would say to me, '*filān* [i.e., X of the people] has bewitched you.' "

Although Bābikir himself would say at times that he had been bewitched, he still took *saḥrah*s lightly. Further, when I asked him how serious those who told him that *saḥir* had caused his business to fail were, he answered that nobody seriously suggested that. Had he been a believer in the harm of *saḥir*, he added, he would not have accepted the *saḥrah*s lightly and would have been mad at the *saḥḥār*s.

Bābikir's inconsistency wore my patience thin. Failing to get a clear-cut, firm accusational attitude to fit in my theoretical grid, I interrogated him further:

"The other day you discussed the matter differently. I remember you said 'these people [the *saḥḥār*s] caused me this failure or that [failure].' "

"I said there were many factors involved. I will also add this factor [i.e., *saḥir*] as a stumbling block that stood in the way of my business. I will also add it and will not discount it. I told you that. I told you that I will take it into consideration among the factors [that affected my business]. Yet still I am not [seriously] taking it into consideration. . . ."

"Did you say you still don't seriously take it into consideration?"

"Yes, I am still not seriously taking it into consideration. Nevertheless, I will add it as a factor among others. *'Ayn* affects. One shouldn't ignore that."

I did not hide my bafflement from Bābikir. I told him that accusing and still not seriously accusing did not make sense. He said, "Had the business stopped when all the necessary materials for it were available, I would have taken *saḥir* seriously into consideration. That is why I am uncertain about the effects of *saḥir* on my business. *Saḥir* might also have been a contributing factor because they were spoken at time when the conditions of my business were bad. Had it not been for these other factors, I would have attributed the failure entirely to the *saḥrah*s."

I realized later that my frustration with Bābikir was misplaced. In the brief encounter I had with him he appeared to me to be clear about his misfortune and who the culprits were. In the extended interview, however, Bābikir was not merely stating his belief; instead, he was grappling with it. For reporting convenience, scholarly investigations are preconditioned to report either clear-cut belief or disbelief, and they are therefore ill-prepared to accommodate a drama of reasoning with conflicting beliefs such as the one Bābikir tried to share with me.

As a *sunnī* (a follower of one of the four *madhhab*s [schools of jurisprudence] that follow closely the example of the Prophet), a Rubāṭābī is required to believe in the *ʿayn*. Thus Bābikir's statement that *ʿayn* affects and that it would be unwise to ignore it is a paraphrase of the widespread Prophetic tradition that says the evil eye is a reality. However, the existence of other factors attending the failure of his business accounts for Bābikir's vacillation in identifying what went wrong. He would like to retain his belief in *ʿayn,* but the realities of his business performance are too real to be dismissed. He clearly wished that those market realities were not there so that he would be able to say that *saḥir* was solely responsible for his going out of business.

Too Close for Legal Comfort

Some Muslim jurists hold the possessor of the *ʿayn* accountable for the harm he causes people, although others do not hold him accountable for this involuntary ill-doing. When such a person is repeatedly accused of having caused harm, he may be confined to his house by the Muslim ruler and be maintained by the state (al-Qaṣṭallānī 1971, 8:391; al-ʾAzraq 1905/1906, 161). Westermarck reports that in Morocco a man accused of the evil eye is punished by the governor by having the bridle of a mule put in his mouth and then having someone pull him around (Westermarck 1926, 1:424).

Rubāṭāb, however, cannot carry an accusation of *saḥir* to its legal conclusion. In a context of kinship they cannot afford these fine legalities. Two examples will demonstrate how much more highly kinship considerations are valued than the pursuit of the legal options open to villagers. I was told of a village carpenter who was boycotted by villagers for filing a suit against a shopkeeper who sold him overpriced merchandise. Ultimately the carpenter had to leave the village. Because of this precedence of kinship over legal means of redress, Wad al-Tōm applauded the idea of having a village cooperative. The cooperative was basically established to take over the sale of sugar (rationed because of short supply) from the village shopkeepers, who were rightly accused of running a black market. Wad al-Tōm said, "The village cannot be run without good judgment. If the villagers shy from filing suits against each other for fear of the bonds of kith and kin, it is only natural that they should hold what they have in common and supervise distributing it among themselves as a group."

The same social hazards apparently apply to *saḥir* accusations, since accusers must continue to interact with the *saḥḥār*s after the accusation is made. Most of the *saḥḥār*s under consideration are landed, well-connected individuals, and some of them are among the most successful entrepreneurs in the villages. Wad al-Tōm, for example, is an expert in cupping, treating burns, and circumcising. He is involved in the girls' high school project, the cooperative and primary school parents' association, and is on nearly all the village boards. Accusations here are a function of equal status (Evans-Pritchard 1980, 41).

Villagers may, however, impose unannounced sanctions, such as "taking another road if they happen to meet with *saḥḥār*s," as it is usually expressed. The severity of such sanctions may account for the decision of many aging *saḥḥār*s to quit this particular vocation.

The humorous frame in which accusations are sometimes delivered and discussed by the Rubāṭāb may indicate the general need to keep the machine of social interaction in motion after the temporary seizure caused by an accusation. This frame may be a tactical way of expressing one's belief that the *saḥḥār* is the source of one's misfortune without so far as seeking legal redress for the complaint.

The vacillating manner in which accusations are cast may also stem from the way accusers and community weigh them against a plurality of causes. As mentioned earlier, Bābikir would have been confirmed in his belief in the *ʿayn* if he had been able to trace his misfortune to *saḥir* in a direct and uncontaminated fashion. Both ʿAbbās and Muḥammad finally fell back on the powerful predestination dogma to downplay the role of *saḥir* causation. Further, villagers may resort to the *sabab* argument to relate *saḥir* to the predestination scheme.

Nevertheless, open accusations do sometimes occur. Ṣiddīq al-Ḥibayl of Kurgus was accused of bewitching the lighting project that was under way in the village in 1983, thus causing it to break down. The chairman of the project, described by Ṣiddīq as one of those who are scared of *saḥir,* brought up the accusation to the project board meeting. A close relative of Ṣiddīq who was on the board conveyed to him the board's anxiety over his subversive *saḥrah.* Ṣiddīq responded defiantly by bewitching the chairman himself. Nevertheless, he eventually met with the committee, apologized for the *saḥrah,* and expressed his good intentions toward the project.

Ḥasan Jaqalaybah et al.: Children of a Lesser Theory

Folklore and ethnography are founded on the assumption that the "natives" are better at acting on than at analyzing their symbolic realities. In this vein, the Azande are said to know better what to do when attacked by witchcraft than how to explain it (Evans-Pritchard 1980, 31–32). Mary Douglas was struck by the contrast between the clever, skeptical Azande and their toleration of discrepancies in their beliefs and the limitations of the kind of questions they ask about the universe (Douglas 1970, 121). This state of "suspended curiosity" produces what Malcolm Crick termed "conceptual synapses," which he defines as "beliefs which are not brought together, ideas which are not pushed to a conclusion, questions that are not asked. They are not contradictions for they lie precisely in areas which are not structured because the Azande see no point in thinking them out" (Crick 1976, 121).

Crick's characterization, if not merely an improved variant of the scholarly unwillingness to concede to the natives the ability to form a theory of meaning of their realities, can apply to all kinds of theoretical enterprise. Crick himself was quick to observe that "To a degree . . . our own legal notions operate by not following up certain lines of investigation." According to him, this results from the disparity between social knowledge and social interests (1976, 121–22).

The subversive power that the *saḥḥār*s set loose is so engaging that the search for a theory of *saḥir* is a continuing process among the Rubāṭāb. Al-Shaykh al-Ṣāyīm, a widely traveled *saḥḥār*, enumerated several local theories: "There are some people who are mentally equipped to describe [i.e., speak *saḥir*]. We do not know why. Some say to us it comes from intuitive insight. Others said this talent is *bon mot.* Yet some others said it comes from envy."

In my interviews I came across two evolving theories of *saḥir.* The first one, offered by Ḥasan Jaqalaybah, was documented in chapter two. In his theory, Ḥasan makes the association between *saḥir* and cannibalism. Rubāṭāb are susceptible to *saḥir* because they eat crocodiles, some of which were actually men who transformed themselves into this being to prey on women in order to be able to pay their taxes from the gold they wear. By eating the meat of such crocodiles, a man becomes a *saḥḥār* and can do harm even by looking innocently at things. Jaqalaybah was told this theory by a man he had met on a train, and we have seen how he went about matching the man's theory with his observation of *saḥir* among his people and succeeded in proving its validity.

If Ḥasan Jaqalaybah arrived at his theory through deduction, the *saḥḥār* Muṣṭafah 'Ayyūb used induction to develop his theory. I asked Muṣṭafah why *saḥir* was prevalent in his family. He said that he observed that all those who speak *saḥir* in his family had a "kind of something" that stuck out of their eyebrows. A member of the audience asked him, "Do 'Aḥmad 'Ayyūb and Ṣiddīq 'Ayyūb have it?" "Yes, they do," said Muṣṭafah. "Then you are right because they both speak *saḥir.*"

Muṣṭafah continued, saying that he noticed this "kind of something" on the eyebrows of his young children and knew they would ultimately speak *saḥir.* He added that he looked for that "something" whenever he carried the sons of his cousins, and that just a few days ago he had noticed it on some of them.

I can say nothing regarding the extent to which Jaqalaybah's and Muṣṭafah's theories have been accepted. However, the fact that they have been offered at all suggests that we reconsider the way we explore, find (or do not find), and assess indigenous theories of meaning. Central to this quest is the recognition that natives theorize, and any pronouncements to the contrary "reflect more the methodological problems of folklore [and ethnography] studies than the native powers of perception, distinction, and observation" (Ben-Amos 1976a, 225).

Persons and Actions

Saḥir belongs to a category of Rubāṭāb speech acts of dry humor known collectively as *al-rad al-sariʿ* (quick repartee). Language in this category is used for social discipline by a man of words. Generally speaking, in *al-rad al-sariʿ* the man of words employs his oral quickness to undermine the logic or position of an interactant. In striking the interactant dumb, the man of words emerges in full control of the situation. ʿAraydab al-Ḥāj, a literate farmer and a man of words himself, describes the Rubāṭāb homeland as a place of extreme misery because its people are "cunning, articulate, and have quick repartee."

Besides *saḥir,* this *al-rad al-sariʿ* category of speech acts includes *masākhah* (lit., saltlessness; insipid talk) and *mukhātah* (from *khātah,* to charge, to take offense). The use of similes is common to all these speech acts, including *saḥir,* which is by definition *mitil, mitil* (like, like), as the Rubāṭāb occasionally refer to it. However, *masākhah* and *mukhātah* are performed primarily as means of social control, whereas *saḥir* consists of social equations that map Rubāṭāb life and culture and comment on social inadequacies. Half of my field collection of *saḥir* may be labeled "depraise."[5] Included in this category are reprimands, ridicule, getting even, and so on. The metaphor of *saḥir* functions here as quick repartee that disarms the addressee and leaves him gasping for prophylactic formulae. The meta*saḥrah,* which I have already called the vindictive *saḥrah,* is the ideal domain for the social discipline function of *saḥir.*

Although the Rubāṭāb seem to distinguish between these three types of speech acts and their respective performers, they occasionally confuse or equate *masākhah* and *saḥir.* (The category of *mukhātah* is free of this confusion because it is apparently a woman's genre.) After narrating a *saḥrah* from Salmān Abū Ḥijil of the Ḥijūlah chiefly lineage, al-Shaykh al-Ṣāyīm compared *saḥir* to repartee when he commented, "The Ḥijūlah are famous for their *saḥir,* for their brightness and *al-rad al-sariʿ.*" Many *masākhah* episodes are attributed to members of the Ḥijūlah family. Further, a member of the audience who attended my interview with Muḥammad al-Khayr ʿUmar, the *saḥḥār* of ʾAmakī, said that Muḥammad is "a *masīkh* [speaker of *masākhah*] too."

The confusion of *saḥir* and *masākhah* also arose in an interesting collection session I conducted in al-ʿAbaydab village. One of those present said that someone called al-Nujūmī is scared of *saḥir.* The following dialogue took place:

TIJĀNĪ KIRIZ (of Kurgus village): How come, when he speaks *saḥir* himself?

ʾAḤMAD ʾAYYŪB AND ḤISAYN BĀJŪRĪ: No, he doesn't.

TIJĀNĪ: I don't remember his *saḥrah* well, but it was about some palms he was planting.

ḤISAYN: But this is a *masākhah.* (Some of those attending the recording session repeat his comment.)

ʾAḤMAD: Yes, it is a *masākhah.* That was the time when al-Nujūmī was digging a rocky part of his farm to plant some palms. A friend of his told him he was just wasting his time because palms would not grow on his rocky land. Al-Nujūmī pointed to some flourishing palms a stone's throw from where he was digging to plant his new palms and said to his friend, "And these palms are apparently planted on your head." I remember passing the other day with al-Nujūmī's friend by the palms, which succeeded anyway. I pointed to them and asked the friend, "Are these the ones that grew on your head? We had a good laugh together." But this is a *masākhah.* Al-Nujūmī is very good at *masākhah.* (ʾAḥmad narrated another *masākhah* from al-Nujūmī.)

These examples clearly show that the connection between *saḥir* and *masākhah* is recognized by the Rubāṭāb themselves.

In *al-rad al-sariʿ* speech acts, language is apparently conceived of as a form of action, a tool employed for social control. The story of Bakrī al-Khayr (fifteen years old) of Al-Zūmah village and his father's guest graphically illustrates the Rubāṭāb's concept of the power of language. A friend of Bakrī's bedridden father came to their shop. The father asked Bakrī to offer the man a cigarette. Bakrī did so, asking the man whether he had a box of matches or if he should bring him one to light his cigarette. The guest said, "Why should you think I have a box of matches? Do I look to you like someone who bakes bread?" The guest was upset by Bakrī's question because only women, whose job it is to bake bread, are expected to have a box of matches around in case a need for baking arises. I asked Bakrī how he felt after the guest's *masākhah.* He said he felt embarrassed and blamed himself for not simply taking the man a box of matches in the first place.

More important is the manner in which Bakrī's father used this *masākhah* event to make a point. Bakrī, who was the elder son, left school to take charge of the family's business because of his father's sudden partial paralysis. In my two visits to their home I gradually realized that Bakrī and his father had an ongoing argument over the son's worries about continuing his education, and over his desire to have more control in running the business. When Bakrī complained later to his father about the *masākhah,* the father replied, "Perhaps that will teach you something. Experience from people a *salikh* [skinning, grilling] that is more exacting than mine."

Even more than a form of social control, the Rubāṭāb view language, including *saḥir,* as a potential form of aggression. This conception of language is clearly revealed by Rubāṭāb metalanguage. We have already made reference to the ballistic and homicidal idioms in which descriptions of the effects of *saḥir* are couched. Similar metaphors are used to describe other genres of verbal art as well. For example, a line from a *sōmār* praises someone for "his answers that sound like shots." Another poet likened the competition of poets in improvising poems on a selected topic to "soldiers training to shoot at a target." Further, *yitdanah al-ḥadīth* (talking at close quarters) indicates an imminent outbreak of a fight. Additionally, *qaṣr al-ḥadīth* (shortened talk) is an idiomatic term for decisive action. *Yanṭaḥ* (to butt), *yalkid* (to elbow), *yaṭʿan* (to prick), *yakhatī* (to take charge), and *yanjiḍ* (to grill) are commonly used to describe various acts of speaking. Interestingly enough, *saḥir,* in an innovative tone, is sometimes said to have a corrosive effect like sulphuric acid.

By and large, the traditional idiom of the scorpion sting is still commonly applied to *saḥir.* The mayor who provoked the poetess to reveal his foreign origin complained about the incident to another person. However, he was reminded that he was the one who had "put his hand in the scorpion's hole." The same image was used to describe the slave who was repeatedly shot with *saḥrah*s; he was likened to a man with a scorpion in his pants that bites him wherever he turns.

An idiom of protection goes hand in hand with this conception of language as a form of assault. We saw earlier how a *saḥḥār* or those around him are said to be *maḥajjab* (protected by amulets), *maḥajjar* (fossilized, impenetrable), and *maṭaʿam* (immunized). Incidentally, amulets are specifically prescribed for scorpion stings and snakebites. In speaking of language in terms of amulets, the Rubāṭāb foreground their conception of it as a tool of aggression.

Identifying Saḥḥār*s*

In being called a *saḥḥār,* the shooter of *saḥir,* as we noted earlier, is automatically categorized with an order of actors and actions that define his person and power. The matriculation and hierarchy aspects of *saḥir* seem to set *saḥḥār*s apart as a category of persons endowed with deadly power.

We have already mentioned how *saḥir* is perceived as *'ayn ḥarah* or *ḥasdah* (evil or envious eye), and how the *saḥḥār*s question the truth of this perception. Further, the term *saḥḥār* is also used to designate those who supposedly give the evil eye merely by gazing. The *saḥḥār*s of the *saḥir* metaphors are thus believed by those who disapprove of their verbal actions to be casters of the evil eye.

We have also already alluded to another concept of *saḥḥār* that refers to people who have the ability to transform themselves into crocodiles and ogres that attack and eat other people. This association between *saḥir* and cannibalism is one reason why urban Rubāṭāb would prefer to call *saḥir*—their ethnic cultural specialty—*balāghah* (rhetoric) in order to avoid these unsavory associations.

Although many a Rubāṭābī—especially young men—try their hand at *saḥir*, the Rubāṭāb do not perceive all similes as *saḥir*. A man who actively shot *saḥir* metaphors whenever I ran into him was never identified as a *saḥḥār*. The identification of a certain category of people as *saḥḥār*s is evidenced by the fact that the Rubāṭāb commonly ask certain individuals to *yasḥar* (bewitch) targets that they name for them. Furthermore, we have seen how potential subjects of *saḥir* sometimes implore the same individuals not to *yasḥar* them, showing a marked exhibition of helplessness vis-à-vis a recognized, harmful power. The Rubāṭāb, of course, take into consideration the record of misfortunes attributed to a *saḥḥār* in identifying him as such.

Sometimes the Rubāṭāb view *saḥir* practice as almost a profession. Both hereditary and acquired powers are required for somebody to be matriculated into this profession. Mention has already been made of Muṣṭafah 'Ayyūb's theory in which he argued that those from his family who engage in *saḥir* were born with something protruding from their eyebrows. Similarly, Wad al-Tōm, who is an illiterate born to an illiterate father, gave high marks to the *saḥir* of Muṣṭafah 'Ayyūb and explained his talent by referring to the literacy of his family. Further, a father is reported to have described his son as a graduate (of *saḥir* school) by way of admiring a *saḥrah* the son had shot. Finally, the practice of referring a *saḥrah* that fails with the audience to Wad al-Tōm to "grade" it again underlines the Rubāṭāb conception of *saḥḥārs* as a special category of powerful persons.

Saḥḥārs and non-*saḥḥārs* alike are aware of a hierarchy within the *saḥir* "profession." *Saḥḥārs* apparently always have a "dean" recognized by his peers and by the community. This is attested to by the *saḥir* event we mentioned earlier in which "Dean" Wad ʾAyyūb tested other *saḥḥārs* on bewitching targets he selected for them. The goal of the test was to protect his "professional" reputation from being tarnished due to *saḥrahs* attributed to him by "unlicensed" and incompetent *saḥḥārs*.

The notion of hierarchy within the *saḥir* establishment is best illustrated by an encounter that took place in the fifties between Wad ʾAyyūb and Wad al-Tōm, who had moved recently to ʿAtmūr village from a Rubāṭāb settlement on Atbara river. At a wake at Wad ʾAyyūb's house, Wad al-Tōm, unaware that Wad ʾAyyūb was the dean of the *saḥḥārs*, began to speak *saḥir*. His friend Mughdād al-Rufāʿī drew Wad al-Tōm's attention to the inappropriateness of his speech behavior:

MUGHDĀD AL-RUFĀʿĪ: Where do you think you are? Stop it. This is Wad ʾAyyūb's house, if you care to know.

WAD AL-TŌM: Aha! You advise me then not to smoke at Shell (the gas station) (comparing his *saḥir*, which is like a lighted cigarette, to Wad ʾAyyūb's *saḥir*, which is like flammable gasoline).

WAD ʾAYYŪB (overhearing this exchange between Mughdād and Wad al-Tōm): Mughdād! May I ask you what school of *saḥir* your friend graduated from?

Interestingly enough, Wad al-Tōm, the present dean of *saḥḥārs*, was described by a *saḥḥār*, Ṣiddīq al-Ḥibayl, as "the tank from which they pump gas [i.e., *saḥir*]" in answering someone who had alerted him to the fact that he was indulging in *saḥir* while Wad al-Tōm was around.

5

Which Way Mimicry?

Words and Rituals

The question of the efficacy of words in magic has exercised the minds of ethnographers ever since Tambiah's reinterpretation of Malinowski's (1965) material on Trobriand magic (Tambiah 1968, 175–208). In this reinterpretation, Tambiah faults Malinowski for holding two conflicting, incompatible views concerning the efficacy of magical language. He argues that although Malinowski holds to the pragmatic function of words, he insists in the same breath that they also act because of their mystical associations (1978, 195).[1] In contrast, Tambiah maintains that magical language is simply a "heightened use of ordinary language" (1968, 188). This position, which has been largely adopted by subsequent writers (e.g., Rosaldo 1982, 203–37), finds an apt formulation in Weiner's statement that how magic works can be understood only from a theory of language use, not from a theory of magic per se (1983, 692).

However, subsequent scholars have found Malinowski's phrase "the creative metaphor of magic" (1965, 2:238) suggestive and useful. By this phrase Malinowski refers to the belief that the repetition of certain words produces the reality stated (1965, 2:238). He goes on to say that the essence of verbal magic consists in a statement that is untrue and which stands in direct opposition to the context of reality. But the belief in magic inspires man with the conviction that his untrue statement must become true (1965, 2:239). Tambiah and Rosaldo agree with Malinowski that magic authors what Basso would call a "world of make believe" (Basso 1983, 41). However, they are inclined to draw the make-believe world and reality closer and closer together because of their awareness of the performative aspects of language. They both hold that the magical world is patterned on reality to some degree. Tambiah maintains that the magical ritual is an imaginative, prospective, and creative understanding of the very technological operations and social activities the Trobrianders are preparing to enact (1968, 200). Rosaldo is even more explicit in viewing the magical spell as modeled on the experienced world (1975, 178). What appears as an incidental likeness in the metaphor, she argues, becomes the basis of a new orientation toward the experienced world (1975, 181), and consequently the spell organizes itself as it organizes experience. She goes on to say that the magician, in creating this metaphorical order, subordinates the natural world's diversity to a simple and compelling conception of a world that he can control through magic (1975, 178). The organizing function of the metaphor of magic and the kind of control the magician assumes through authoring it will prove to be crucial to our understanding of the Rubāṭāb *saḥir* metaphors.

The question of whether the efficacy of words in rituals draws from the intention of the speaker or from the conventions of performance has significant parallels in the ongoing debate between philosophers of language and ethnographers of speaking (Keane 1984). Intention is conceived of in this context as the feeling or the expression of that feeling, and convention is thought of as the propriety of the expression of feeling (Tambiah 1979, 125). Ethnographers of speaking are disappointed to see that, contrary to John Austin's position,[2] in which an illocutionary act is constituted by convention rather than by intentions (1962, 129), subsequent philosophers of language (especially John Searle) have largely and increasingly located the operative force of language in the speaker's intentions rather than in the social context in which meanings are born (Tambiah 1979, 123; Rosaldo 1982, 210–11). Rosaldo objects to Searle's use of the act of "promising" as a paradigm for our ways of doing things with words. She argues, "To think of promising is . . . to focus on the sincerity and integrity of the one who speaks" (1982, 211).

However, Rosaldo is very careful not to make intention and convention theories mutually exclusive. Instead, she presents her case in terms of what comes first—intention or convention (1982, 210). She does slip into extreme formulations, though. She argues that the Ilongot "lack 'our' interest in considerations like sincerity and truth; their lives lead them to concentrate, instead, on social bonds and interactive meanings" (1982, 222).

The expansion of speech act theory into ethnography has gone hand in hand with an increased emphasis on the conventional (Keane 1984, 14). Rosaldo notes with satisfaction that the writers who reworked the theory move in the direction of adding sociological and interactional dimensions to it (1982, 235), but this emphasis on the social and the conventional has not always been the case. Lately, ethnographers have become more inclined to explain the efficacy of magic in terms of intentions. Ahern has suggested a taxonomy of strong and weak illocutionary acts based on the presence or absence of the intentions that performers have with respect to the effects of the ritual (1979, 1–7). In addition, both Weiner and Brown look to the internal perspective of the actors for the sources of efficacy. Weiner examines how figurative language can be used to project the will from the narrow confines of "personal space" to the wider world of social relations and objects (1983, 692, 698, 703). Brown goes even further by arguing that "an emphasis on the rhetorical [pragmatic] possibilities of ritual utterance" leads ultimately to sterile conclusions (1984, 555). The efficacy of words, in his view, stems from the fact that they are "indices of structural mental operations" (1984, 554). Behind all the Aguaruna magic that Brown studied lies an explicit theory of how the self influences the external world of people and things. Of equal concern to the Aguaruna, Brown argues, are such factors as the internal state of the actor (1984, 553). In this perspective, intentions not only count but may even be primary.

It is evident that the assertions of the latter ethnographers contradict the position of Tambiah and Rosaldo with respect to the location of speech acts. The latter locate them primarily in the social arena, whereas the former are open to considering the primacy of the psychological factor. However, this contradiction can be resolved if reference is made to the forms of magic each side has in mind. Brown, for example, studied the Aguaruna magical hunting songs, in which emphasis is laid on "the act of holding the song in one's mind rather than the act of giving commands to presumed auditors" (1984, 552). This private magical procedure contrasts sharply with Tambiah's focus on public, serious, and festive forms of magic (1979, 139). As conventionalized actions, these festive rituals are distanced from spontaneous and intentional expressions (1979, 124). This fact, argues Tambiah, "jeopardizes the usefulness of the intentionality theory of meaning for understanding rituals" (1979, 123). Apparently, what is at stake here is the context of performance of magical rituals rather than an inherent explanatory power in either intentionality or conventionality as a source of the efficacy of magical words.

In this chapter we will analyze the anguish *saḥir* generates in its victims. We will pick up the argument advanced in chapter three about the conflict between *saḥir* and *sharīʿah*-minded discourse and other Rubāṭāb discourses to examine what threat *saḥir* metaphors pose to a Muslim Rubāṭābī. The specific Rubāṭāb conceptions of language as an agent of social discipline and of *saḥḥārs* as professional evildoers will be used to investigate *saḥir,* in Crick's parlance, as "actions" of "persons" in an articulated "moral space" (1976, 113). We will be looking at precisely what moral space these metaphors violate.

The Metaphors of Magic

Saḥir is essentially a "perception of similitude between two entities" (Abu Deeb 1979, 114), in recognition of which the Rubāṭāb sometimes refer to it pejoratively as *mitil, mitil* (like, like). The similitude may lie in the outer physical attributes of the two objects; Arab rhetoricians call this a *tashbīh* (1979, 145). Forty-four percent of my collection of Rubāṭāb *saḥrahs* belong to this category. The *tashbīh* may involve more complex imaginative activity in cases where the similitude lies in the psychological effect the attributes have on the recipient (1979, 145); Arab rhetoricians call this type of simile *tamthīl.* Twenty-seven percent of my collection belong to this category. Both types commonly use a similizing particle, but they can do without it. *Mitil* (like), the indigenous particle, is used in 36 percent of the *saḥrah*s I collected. The urban *zay* (like) is used in 16 percent of the cases. *Bla* ([does not look like anything] except), *'illa* (except), *yashbah* (look like), *biqat* (become like), and *bas* (just [like]) are not uncommon. In other cases a *saḥrah* may be what Arab rhetoricians call an *isti'ārah,* which is a borrowing of a name or a meaning to designate a referent other than the original meaning (1979, 145). The intention to make a comparison here is latent in the consciousness of the speaker: it is overt with *tashbīh* and *tamthīl* (1979, 151). Nonetheless, *isti'ārah* has the status of a branch of *tashbīh* (1979, 66). Thirty percent of my field sample can be classified as *isti'ārah.*

I have avoided entering into the long-standing controversy over whether a simile is a metaphor (1979, 227–28) and have considered all *saḥir* utterances metaphors. This avoidance is justified by the emphasis of the study on the word pictures these tropes create in their magical seizure of reality.

Although *saḥir* is essentially a simile, it does not operate according to the Frazerian sympathetic principle (like produces like, effect resembles cause) which is believed to underlie the metaphor of magic (Malinowski 1965, 2:232). *Saḥir* does not use the imperative form to transfer—in Tambiah's words—effects from a donor to a recipient object or person on an analogical basis (1973, 199). Thus, the alleged effects of a *saḥrah* are not limited by what is specifically named in the metaphor. A hand carrying an onion may be analogized to a microphone, but the range of misfortunes expected to result from this analogy are limited only by what the victim may claim. He could complain of hand trouble thereafter, as did the victim in the particular case, but he could just as well have complained of a headache. People may even have said that a victim's death is the result of the analogy.

The threat of *saḥir,* as we will argue in the following pages, rests on its being—in Tambiah's words—a persuasive "cultural equation" (1973, 218) predicating the world in an infinite "expansion of meaning" (1979, 219). In the presence of the perfect creation and word of Allah, such *saḥir* predications—to paraphrase al-Jurjani's basic statement—are unnecessary for either a better faith or a better life (in Abu Deeb 1979, 260). To adapt Basso's concepts, Allah's "primary text" cancels out the "secondary texts" of popular discourses. A *saḥrah,* as a metaphor, violates the rule of factuality espoused by *sharīʿah*-minded discourse. As a humorous genre, it strains and occasionally breaks down social interactions in which playfulness is discouraged, if not prohibited, by *sharīʿah*-minded discourse.

Drawing on Bateson and Goffman, Basso has lucidly developed his concept of the primary and secondary text to analyze Apache humor (Basso 1983, 41).[3] Primary texts, according to Basso, are the slices of unjoking activity that the joker employs as a model insofar as the joke is not entirely a product of the joker's imagination. This primary text furnishes the raw material from which the joking performances are fashioned. Consequently, any actual performance may be said to consist in the construction and presentation of a secondary text that is intended to be understood as a facsimile or transcripted copy of the primary text on which it is patterned (1983, 41).

We demonstrated in chapter three how the distinction between reality and lies reigns supreme in Rubāṭāb genre classification, as well as in identifying speech events. The contrast between reality and lies warrants our making liberal use of Basso's terms to label the Allah-inspired reality as primary text and to label as secondary text the *Iblīs*-inspired discourses, which include *saḥir* as a creative metaphor of magic. These discourses are parasitical secondary texts that gnaw at the elegance and completeness of the Allah-inspired primary text. The Rubāṭābī who rebuked the *maddāḥ* (an itinerant singer of the praise of the Prophet) saying, "In what aspect is the Prophet deficient to make his praise known?" said it all. Secondary texts are simply idle words.

Howling from Morning to Evening

Insofar as *Iblīs* is the author of all secondary texts, a Rubāṭābī takes special care not to succumb to his delusions. Amnah Dafaʿ

al-Sīd asked a young woman to set right a turned-over shoe because through it *Iblīs* enters a *wanasah* (casual talk event) and sows discord between the people. The *shaykh* (village head) of the ʿAbaydab village was nicknamed *Iblīs.* The man who nominated him to be the *shaykh* said he did so because the man is adept in making people fall foul of each other, a valuable asset for any ruler who wants to entrench his authority.

Furthermore, youth is believed to be deceptive because youth is the time when *Iblīs*'s texts appear most enchanting and irresistible. Jādallah (80 years old), a blind poet who spent an outrageous youth, says:

> Youth deluded us and then left us abandoned
> We neither fasted nor said our prayers
> We just succumbed to our sexual desires
> We abandoned our religious duties and the door of religion was [thus] locked up by *Iblīs*
> Our insatiable instincts pleaded to him that they had not had enough yet
> We raced after them howling from morning to evening

In addition, in one interpretation, slips of the tongue occur because *Iblīs* trades utterances with the hasty speaker.

Iblīs-inspired texts surround a Muslim Rubāṭābī. Praising someone to his face is considered an insult, and praising oneself is a sin because no one would praise himself except *Iblīs.* Conceit is believed to be from *Iblīs.* Furthermore, the glittering of mica, which abounds in the Rubāṭāb country, is called *taṣāwīr Iblīs* (*Iblīs*'s pictures) in recognition of the fact that not all that glitters is gold. Wet dreams are known as *bit Iblīs* (*Iblīs*'s daughter) in recognition that they are only illusions. Even a *bahlūl* (another name for a performer, *wannās*) was defined by ʿAbbās al-Ḥasan as the one who laughs you into giving him what he wants. The *bahlūl* was similarly described by another as *shayṭān khalāṣ* (of extreme satanic capability). Recall from chapter one that the periodic or permanent migrations that take the Rubāṭāb to urban centers or other lucrative projects are called *ṭashīsh* (losing one's way) in recognition of being lured away from home by *shayṭān.*

The degree to which a Rubāṭābī guards himself against secondary texts is evidenced by the many religious and secular[4] prophylactic formulae uttered when encountering these face-threatening texts. Piamenta (1979, 1983) presents an exhaustive tabulation of the religious formulae that constitute a system of "reality" and "danger" (1979, 2). Warding off the evil eye takes the lion's share in these formulae. *Istiʿadhah* is especially invoked to ask Allah's support against temptation, seduction and infatuation (1979, 94). When one Rubāṭābī used the *istiʿadhah* in anticipation of a *saḥrah* from a woman *saḥḥār,* she yelled at him, "Why are you uttering *istiʿadhah?* Am I a *shayṭān* [or what]?"

Interestingly enough, the Rubāṭab of ʿAtmūr have special "secular" formulas to mark and dismiss secondary texts arising out of intentional lies, as in tall tales or imbecility.[5] Two formulae are used to indicate that someone is engaging in lies or tall tales. "*Al-dagar*" (the snake) may be uttered to cut the tall tale speaker short. He may again be silenced by saying "*zolak liqah ʿadlū fī al-qaʿdah*" (he has the audience eating from the palm of his hand). The late ʾAḥmad ʿabd al-Qādir, a celebrated *wannās,* was said to be extremely vexed one day when this formula was said to him while he was engaged in telling a tall tale. He not only stopped the narration but also left the session, saying, "Is sitting on dirt what you call having an audience eating from the palm of my hand?"

Two other formulas are used to cut short imbecile texts. One may say "Bābikir, Bābikir," after a man who asked his imbecile relative, Bābikir, not to continue giving the speech he started because he was sure to mess it up eventually. Another formula villagers employ to censor an imbecile text is "*akolah yā,*" the hunters' cry after rabbits. The story goes that villagers were burying a dead man when a rabbit jumped into their midst. The brother of the dead man—of all people present—cried "*Akolah*" (there goes a rabbit!). In other words, the man was being foolishly inattentive to the real business at hand.

One example of how this formula is used occurred during my visit. A teacher from the Jaʿalīyyīn community was telling us about the burial customs of his ethnic group. He said at one point that his people do not bury their dead during the night, but prefer to wait until the morning. A villager commented, "Why so? Or are they afraid of wolves?" "*Akolah yā*" was uttered by the audience to distinguish the text of reality from this imbecile, secondary text.

Thus the negative, belligerent response to *saḥir* as a secondary text evidently falls within a semiotic of an uneven competition between Allah's primary text, the world of reality, and *Iblīs*-inspired secondary text, the imitation.

Jailing the Tongue

Envy, according to Islamic jurists, stems from *fuḍūl* (something in excess, inquisitiveness) in speaking and in the way one looks at people and things. *ʿAyn* is considered by these jurists to be a category of *ḥasad* (envy) (Ibn al-Qayyīm, 2:273). The Rubāṭāb, as mentioned earlier, identify *saḥir,* a form of excessive talk, as *fakar* (envy), and, therefore, view it as *ʿayn. Siḥr* (the standard Arabic word for magic, sorcery, and witchcraft) is basically a confusion of categories (al-Ṭabarī, 2:436). Its definition revolves around the axis of reality and falsity. Generally speaking, it is held to be the turning of a thing from its *ḥaqīqah* (true nature or form) into something else which is *khayāl* (illusion, imagination) with intent to deceive or delude (*Shorter Encyclopedia of Islam,* s.v. *siḥr;* al-Qaṣṭallānī 1971, 8:408). As a simile, the Rubāṭāb *saḥir* autocratically sets up relations in the world that turn the world into an uncertain meaning (Hamori 1974, 82). Therefore, it can be easily categorized as *siḥr.* Furthermore, we have seen how jurists indicate clearly that *ʿayn* is a category of that form of *siḥr* which they call the magic of the owners of compelling fancies, illusions, and strong psychic power. Such powers are described as being capable of affecting in concrete life what crosses the mind of their owners (Ibn al-Qayyīm, 2:233–34). The suggestion that the possessor of *ʿayn* is a *sāḥir* (another term for *saḥḥār*) is further reinforced by the popular Islamic medical manuals in which the same charms are prescribed for those inflicted by *ʿayn* as for victims of *siḥr* (al-ʾAzraq 1906, 161). Moreover, the associations of the two might have been further reinforced by the inclusion of *ʿayn* and *siḥr* in the same chapter in most of the scholarly books on Islamic sciences (e.g., al-Muttaqī 1971, 6:742).

Thus, *saḥir* can be seen as a violation of speech tact. It is not only an inquisitive, *Iblīs*-inspired discourse but also an expression of envy, that is, a revolt against the will and destiny of Allah (al-Rāzī 1872, 1:672). This is why jurists reminded Muslims of what their worthy forefathers said: "Nothing benefits more from a long term of imprisonment than the tongue" (Ibn al-Qayyīm, 2:273). Aside from the emphasis on observing tact in social interaction, the imprisonment of the tongue here is yet another instance of the need to apply the bridle of *sharīʿah.*

Limits of Playfulness

Saḥir is also perceived as ridicule. It arouses laughter. As mentioned earlier, *saḥḥār*s forcefully argue that their *saḥir* are jokes and should be taken as such. The subjects of their *saḥir,* however, are extremely reluctant to be the butt of the joke. They do not play along, and they complain of the physical harm the *saḥir* inflicts on them. In his strong aversion to being the butt of a joke, the subject has the support of *sharīʿah*-minded Islam, which holds that he should be immune from ridicule. Sura 49:10–12 of the Koran describes mockery, derision, and scoffing as ruinous to brotherhood among Muslims: "A believer who fears Allah will not scoff at any individual nor make the people the object of his jokes, scorn, sarcasm or mockery because this is nothing but pride, arrogance, and contempt for others, as well as ignorance of the scale by which Allah measures goodness" (al-Qaraḍāwī, 312).

Koranic attitudes toward humor put severe limits on playfulness, defined as the license to transform a primary text into a secondary text (Goffman 1981, 48). In fact, we may go so far as to say that Islam grants no license for joking at all. Secondary texts are unacceptable as long as the primary text is Allah's text and, as such, perfect and meaningful in every detail.[6] Joking makes its object look like a thing (Bergson 1911, 58) or a temporary plaything (Basso 1983, 42; Bakhtin 1981, 23). Making a toy of any of God's creatures—let alone man, who has been elevated by Allah—is blasphemous.

Where primary texts prove to be untransformable into secondary texts, the joking frame breaks down and the consequences can be explosive (Basso 1983, 43). The laughter of the audience makes the target of the *saḥrah* feel abandoned by the social body. We have seen how the audience shows their appreciation for the exactitude of the simile in *saḥir* by calling its subject "dead." In this experience the victim of *saḥir* confronts a situation more or less analogous to the one faced by an object of sorcery, as described by Lévi-Strauss:

> The victim yields to the combined effect of intense terror, the sudden total withdrawal of the multiple reference systems provided by the support of the group, and, finally, to the group's decisive reversal in proclaiming him—once a living man, with rights and obligations—dead and an object of fear, ritual, and taboo. *Physical integrity cannot withstand the dissolution of the social personality.* (1963, 166–67; emphasis added)

Stung and isolated by the disruptive *saḥir,* its target falls back on the *sharīʿah* discourse in order to return to the social setting from which he has been expelled. The prophylactic formulae he invokes serve this purpose in two ways. First, they provide him with the moral strength to cope with the embarrassing situation. When he utters "*al-taʿawdh*"[7] he asks for Allah's support against the seduction of the secondary text, the *saḥrah.* In uttering the *ḥawqallah* (Piamenta 1979, 23), he makes it known that his peace of mind has been disturbed by the whims of the *saḥḥār* and that he is finding it difficult to cope. The victim of *saḥir* may say to the *saḥḥār,* "*Allahu ʾakbar,*" which is the war cry of Islam. When invoked in the context of *saḥir,* this identifies the *saḥḥār* as an unbeliever and declares war on him.

Second, the prophylactic utterances persuade the audience to rally around the target of the *saḥrah.* The victim employs the formulae in order to present himself as a Muslim embattled in a holy war against infidels and the forces of evil. The audience sometimes utters the same prophylactic formulae, while at the same time enjoying the humor. The audience may also supplement this superficial support by asking the *saḥḥār* to have mercy on the victim. Sometimes, however, the strategies of the victims meet a more responsive audience that seriously reprimands the *saḥḥār* and asks him to make up to the victim by uttering "*māshallah.*"

Laughter, as conceived by Bakhtin, is the demolisher of fear and piety (1981, 23). In laughing one shows approval of the transformation of a primary text into a secondary text. Better still, laughter rewards this feat of transformation. The *sharīʿah*-minded person, then, abhors laughter because secondary texts are not permissible. A Rubāṭābī will ask God's forgiveness when engaged in laughter. In one of its extreme positions, *sharīʿah*-minded Islam equates laughter with blood. Some of the Prophet's companions are said to have laughed at a bedouin who was repeatedly tossed to the ground by his fractious camel. The camel kicked the bedouin so hard that it killed him. When the companions told the Prophet about the death of the bedouin, he admonished them, saying, "Yes, and your mouths are full of his blood" (al-Ghazzali 1965, 3:128).

As an *Iblīs*-inspired text, *saḥir* is an irreverence. As an expression of envy, it is even more irreverent; it is a revolt against Allah's will. As a joke, *saḥir* has no place in the *sharīʿah*-minded scheme of speaking because playfulness has no place in that scheme. We have seen how the *saḥir* metaphor threatens the moral space of the Muslim Rubāṭābī. The prophylactic response of the victim of *saḥir* is meant to disrupt the *saḥir* performance and nip in the bud the secondary text of the *saḥḥār*. In this text, to paraphrase Rosaldo (1975, 200–202), the *saḥḥār* subordinates Allah's creation to a compelling conception of a world which the *saḥḥār*, through his *saḥir*, can control. In the following section we will highlight the dialogue the Rubāṭāb conduct on whether *saḥir* projects the ill intentions of the *saḥḥār* or whether the victims are conventionally conditioned for such allegations of misfortune.

Intention: Your Riding Camel through Life

Saḥir provides us with a useful angle from which to look at the role of intention in the efficacy of words. We noted earlier how ethnographers have analytically relegated intention to a secondary position. Understandably, they prefer to view the efficacy of words primarily as a function of social facts. However, intention in *saḥir* is not just an analytical concept to be discerned and judged by scholars. The question of whether evil intentions lie behind the efficacy of *saḥir* is raised and discussed by the actors in *saḥir* events themselves. Some actors hold to the viewpoint that *saḥir* is motivated by bad intentions. Analysts cannot accept such a position, which locates speech in intentions, without putting their conclusions in jeopardy.

It is not difficult to see why the Rubāṭāb, as Muslims, should be concerned with intentions and actions. Islam requires that acts of *ʿibādāt* (ceremonial law), such as prayers, be preceded by *niyyah* (intention), a declaration by the performer that he intends to perform the acts (*Shorter Encyclopedia of Islam,* s.v. *niya*). Consequently, *niyyah* is defined as the "action of the heart" (al-Kirmānī 1933, 21). In this perspective *niyyah* is said to be more indicative of one's piety than action is. A Muslim can thus be rewarded for making his *niyyah* known even if the action did not follow (1933, 21). Strict jurists confine the function of *niyyah* to ceremonial acts. Nevertheless, they are not unaware that *ʾawām al-fuqhā* (ignorant jurists) tend to be less discriminating and stretch the function of *niyyah* to apply to all actions (1933, 20).

The Rubāṭāb also take *niyyah* into consideration to size up actions in domains other than ceremonial acts. A Rubāṭāb proverb states that *al-niyyah zamlat sīdah* (one's intention is his riding camel). In other words, one's enterprise in life stands and falls on one's intentions. Further, *niyyah* is described as either *sawdah* (black, evil) or *bayḍah* (white, good). In this perspective, mishaps are commonly attributed to the ill intentions of those who run into them, while having good intentions is ultimately rewarded. In this vein a Rubāṭābī adage recommends that for leading a happy life one needs to "whiten" (make good) one's intentions and lie (awaiting reward) across from *niyyah.* The paradigm of the heart, *niyyah* is thus crucial to understanding how the Rubāṭāb conceive of action.

Intentions loom large in Rubāṭāb discourse about *saḥir.* We noted earlier how victims of *saḥir* and others accuse *saḥḥārs* of *fakar,* which is basically an evil intention.[8] *Fakar* is specifically defined as admiring something and *istiktār* (thinking or feeling that it is too much) for its owner. We have seen how Bābikir, the village baker, apologetically described intentions of the *saḥḥārs* as good even though he believed that *ʿayn* is harmful and that it is unwise to ignore it. We have seen also Ḥasan Jaqalaybah, in the same apologetic vein, saying that although the *saḥḥārs* have good intentions, misfortunes may occasionally occur as a result of their *saḥir.* Finally, we indicated earlier how Ṣiddīq al-Ḥibayl was obliged to express his good intentions toward the village lighting project after a *saḥrah* of his was accused of causing the generator to break down. We are now familiar with the *saḥḥārs'* side of the story. They never cease denying that they harbor ill intentions behind their metaphors. We have seen them emphasizing that *saḥir* is not *ʿayn.* Further, they defend speaking *saḥir.* If *saḥir* is suppressed, they argue, it will turn sour and become really harmful. Utterances, in their view, should be taken as sharing their humorous thoughts with those around them; this is a token that their intentions are good and thus communicable. Comparing their *saḥir* to a shot from a regular pistol in contrast to one from a pistol with a silencer is intended by the *saḥḥārs* to show the good that comes from frankness.

It is clear that both the expression of feeling (intention) and the propriety of expressing it (convention) are built into the Rubāṭāb dialogue on the efficacy of *saḥir.* Victims of *saḥir* suspect the *saḥḥārs* of expressing their ill intentions in their metaphors. Conventionality, on the other hand, characterizes the response of the audience and the basic argument of the *saḥḥārs.* The audience announces that the victim of *saḥir* metaphor has been "killed" or "fatally injured" immediately after the shooting of the metaphor. Their judgment takes into consideration the propriety of performance: the right person (*saḥḥār*) performing the right action (the metaphor) in the appropriate frame. In cases where victims claim a misfortune either immediately or later on, these claims only confirm to the audience the competence of the performance. Furthermore, *saḥḥār*s attribute victims' claims of misfortune to a belief they have regarding the efficacy of *saḥir*. The *saḥḥār*s insist it is this belief that makes those who adhere to it susceptible to misfortunes from *saḥir*. In other words, speaking *saḥir* can be faulted—if at all—only for not observing the rules of speech propriety that this belief in the maleficent power of *saḥir* requires.

Similarly, *saḥḥār*s present another aspect of conventionality in *saḥir* performance. They are aware that people may not be so apprehensive of their metaphors when they have uttered "*māshallah*" first as a signal of deference to the *sharīʿah*-minded moral space. We have seen how some *saḥḥār*s are adamantly opposed to compromising their performance by adopting this formula, since accepting it would jeopardize their privilege to disrupt the existing relations in the world and recreate them according to their metaphors.

Rosaldo has rightly suggested that conventionality and intentionality are not mutually exclusive. But again, neither of them can be said to take precedence—as Rosaldo believes that conventionality does—in explaining the efficacy of words. Conventionality, as a social fact, can only be favored analytically as the "prime" factor at the expense of imposing the viewpoint of certain actors upon the rest of the actors in the social interaction. In our case this course of action would be like taking the views of the *saḥḥār*s and the audience while ignoring the views of the victims. For a better representation of the efficacy of *saḥir*, there is no alternative to considering the explanatory power of both convention and intention as they arise in the dialogue of the *saḥḥār*s, their victims, and their audience.

The remainder of this chapter will address the following question: Why is *saḥir* humorous, too? In our answer we will pay special attention to (1) how this metaphor of *saḥir* is related to other Rubāṭāb humorous genres; and (2) the manner in which the make-believe world of the metaphor is patterned on reality, and how it organizes itself and the community's experience through humor.

CHAPTER FIVE

Saḥir *and Humor: The Cutting Edge of Language*

We have noted that *saḥir* is a genre of Rubāṭāb dry humor that is essentially tongue-lashing. This humor preys on its would-be butt's exhibition of an inadequacy in speaking, coordination, positioning, or in observance of social codes of behavior. We have already seen how the *aṭ-ṭirī* poetic genre thrives on such inadequacies reported by audiences to poets. The punitive use of language abounds in these "cunning and articulate" people as we have seen them described. A Rubāṭābī of ʿAtmūr described the period of business partnership he had with a man known for his dry humor as "walking on the ledge of a wall." Furthermore, the idioms of infliction we have seen used in connection with *saḥir* graphically and literally illustrate the cutting edge of language. Even the names given to these genres are indicative of the bellicosity of language.

The *masākhah* (lit., saltlessness; insipid talk) genre of Rubāṭāb humor is largely a trickster situation, described by Denise Pauline as the complementarity of a trickster and a dupe (1977, 83). At one end is the *masīkh* (speaker of the genre), with his presence of mind and skill with words. At the other end is the dupe, who talks or acts unaware of the pitfalls he creates that make him vulnerable to *masākhah.* It is related that a man kept inviting his old, toothless uncle to eat from the dates the man had in front of him. The uncle repeatedly refused, saying that dates were too tough for his toothless mouth. After a while the man, unthinkingly, again said, "Take just one date, uncle." The uncle replied, "What am I going to do with it? Fumigate[9] with it, or what?"

Masākhah sometimes arise from an intentional literal interpretation of a statement. It is related that Malīk, the *saḥḥār* of Atbara, became weary of explaining to neighbor after neighbor how his *rakubah* (a patiolike construction made from wood, flattened wooden or cardboard boxes, etc.) fell flat to the ground. When a neighbor, whom Malīk did not like, came and asked how the *rakubah* fell Malīk answered, "It fell *daz* [crash]."

Masākhah is also used against members of other ethnic groups.

Thus the Rubāṭāb, collectively called *saḥḥār*s by other ethnic groups, are also referred to as *musākh* (pl. of *masīkh*). The Shāīqīyyah people are often the target of Rubāṭāb dry humor. Besides their inclination to use flowery, expressive language, the Shāīqīyyah compete with the Rubāṭāb for places in the passenger train that originates in Karīmah, the Shāīqīyyah terminal. This situation puts the Rubāṭāb at a disadvantage, and many stories are told of how *masākhah* humor, which the Shāīqīyyah often confuse with *saḥir,* is used by Rubāṭāb to negotiate for seats from the entrenched Shāīqīyyah.

The second genre of Rubāṭāb dry humor is *mukhātah* (from *khātah,* to charge, to take offense), which is conceived of as looking for argument and trouble. More women than men are known to speak this genre in ʿAtmūr. However, it is not uncommon for the genre to overlap with or shade into *masākhah,* for which more men speakers are known than women. Asyah, a speaker of the genre, took offense with the men digging a grave for a dead woman, with whom she had not been on good terms, because they were digging it very close to her mother's grave. She said to the men, "Hey men! What kind of crowding [of my mother's grave] do you think you are making?" When the story was narrated to me Madīnah al-Ḥāj scoffed at Asyah, for the space she wanted for her mother creates the impression that her mother was there to dance. However, Asyah justified her *mukhātah* by saying the space she wanted around the mother's grave should be reserved to bury her next of kin.

Mukhātah can prey on an inadvertent statement as well as on action. It is related that Asyah wanted to hire Bārkīn, a nomad Beja, to hand pollinate one of her tall palm trees. Bārkīn said he would do the job for a Sudanese pound. But Asyah offered him only half a pound. Finally, Bārkīn said that he would climb up the tree for half a pound and would climb down for another half pound. Asyah replied that it was all right with her for Bārkīn to climb up but that she would care very little if he ever climbed down.

What makes *saḥir* a humorous genre is apparently its preying on inadequacies, which is also basic to other genres of Rubāṭāb humor. Exposing one's failure to live up to the strict rules that govern verbal and motor behavior is evidently a humorous process among the Rubāṭāb. I indicated earlier that half of my field collection is "depraise," which includes reprimands, ridicule, getting even, and the like. Even natural failures such as being toothless or wearing dentures or glasses are picked on in *saḥir.* The extent to which inadequacies fuel the *saḥir* process is demonstrated by a meta*saḥrah.* It is related that a Rubāṭābī returned to the village for the first time with his crippled brother. The man was, however, advised to take his brother and leave because the village was "all bare power wires," that is, it is all *saḥir* that would "electrocute" the brother and compound his disability. The attraction of the brother's disability, according to the meta*saḥrah,* would be too strong for the *saḥḥārs* to resist.

Inchoate Pronouns

Inchoateness is often a kind of oddity, an object or a behavior that does not seem in tune with the context it occupies. An example of the oddities that people ask the *saḥḥār* to predicate upon is the case of the young "fundamentalist" Muslim who would dutifully carry the water all the way from the river but stop at the outer door and refuse to take it into the house in order to avoid seeing unrelated women.

I label 44 percent of my field collection "guess" when I was convinced that the analogy was drawn for the sake of analogy. However, such analogizing clearly predicates a sign-image upon an inchoate subject (Fernandez 1974, 120). In the case of the evil eye metaphors, these inchoate subjects are commonly picked up by the *saḥḥārs* for predication. However, in 7 percent of my collection the audience alerted the *saḥḥārs* to such subjects. Four percent of my collection are cases where *saḥḥārs* compete in predicating upon subjects of their choice. In 12 percent of the cases the subject of the inchoateness would himself draw the attention of the *saḥḥār* by imploring him not to bewitch him, as we have indicated earlier. In this connection, Wad al-Tōm states:

> An audience may draw your attention to *ḥājah shādhah* [an odd thing]. The audience may notice an odd thing at the same time you notice it. The audience would say, "Honestly, what did you say [by way of *saḥir*]?" and they wouldn't believe you if you deny saying something. For example, I passed one day by the water filter. . . . A man saw me and said: "Truly, what did you say [about it]?" I said, "Nothing." The man said, "I won't believe you. You must have said something, please." I said, "I said it is like . . ."

In preying on inchoateness, *saḥir*—even as mere analogy—partakes of the same stuff that is the target of other genres of humor among the Rubāṭāb.

The Chopping Block: A Delightful Shock of Recognition

Humor is experienced when elements originally perceived as unrelated suddenly fall into place (Keith-Spiegel 1972, 11). Metaphors, on the other hand, state an equivalence between two terms taken from separate semantic domains (Sapir 1977, 4). The pattern underlying humor has been commonly analogized to metaphor. Both humor and metaphor are seen to short-circuit two different domains of our understanding, making the hearers experience a delightful "shock of recognition" (Lévi-Strauss 1981, 657; Abu Deeb 1979, 198; Fernandez 1986, 79). The success or failure of a *saḥrah* rests on the intricacy and power of such a shock of recognition. From the narrated *saḥrah*s I collected this recognition seems to focus on the punch line of the *saḥrah*s. An informant related how a *saḥḥār* visited a butcher whose children were around helping him and occasionally snatching pieces of meat to roast and eat. The *saḥḥār* lifted the first child to kiss him and found that he smelled of meat. He did the same with the second child, who smelled the same. The *saḥḥār* then said, "What is the matter with you two smelling of meat like a chopping block?" The audience laughed solidly for several seconds, punctuating their laughter by repeating, "a chopping block." The laughter then broke down into subset laughter in which one of the audience would repeat the punch line to someone close to him and both would again laugh heartily. Then the narrator, still laughing, again said, "a chopping block." A boy among the audience repeated it. The narrator again said, "That on which you chop meat." Another man said distinctly, "You smell like a chopping block." The narrator again said, "He said you two smell of meat like a chopping block." An unsuccessful *saḥrah,* on the other hand, is punished by the audience, which leaves to the one who narrates it the burden of repeating the punch line later.

Saḥir: *The Poetics of Colonial Mimicry*

So far we have analyzed the humor *saḥir* generates in general terms, suggesting that it may be explained with reference to the general theory of metaphor. Furthermore, we situated it in the spectrum of Rubāṭāb dry humor, which preys on human inadequacies. Finally, we investigated how *saḥir* predicates inchoateness as a potential for humor. In the remainder of this chapter we will pursue our analysis of *saḥir* humor by focusing on the comparisons it makes between Rubāṭāb spaces and modern, European spaces, comparisons that are pervasive in *saḥir* metaphors. We will address the question of why Rubāṭāb find these comparisons funny. The concept of "colonial mimicry," emerging within the scholarship of postcolonial criticism, will be employed to account for the humor of *saḥir.*

We will illustrate these comparisons by the following example, which juxtaposes communal prayers and trains to underline the pervasiveness of these comparisons, as well as their complexity. Communal prayer, performed in straight lines of prayers and led by an *imām,* is usually compared to trains. A *saḥrah* tells that a group of people stood in line preparing to perform prayers but that no one stepped out to lead them in prayer. A *saḥḥār* commented, "Isn't there an engine to pull [these coaches]?" On another occasion the headmaster of the new girls' high school was courteously asked by the village *imām* to lead the Friday prayer in the mosque. A *saḥḥār* said about this change in leadership, "We have a diesel engine today," refering to the replacement of steam engines with diesel engines in the Sudan railway system taking place at the time. On a third occasion passengers were waiting for the train to come. When it appeared in the distance, a *saḥḥār* shouted to the passengers, "Straighten your lines, the *imām* is already here." "Straighten your lines" is idiomatic in preparedness for communal prayers, and Islam requires that Muslims should have their lines even before beginning their prayers.

Saḥir, a site of intricate distinctions between colonial and colonized spaces, can thus be described as a hybrid or mimic text in the senses used in postcolonial criticism. This criticism derived its nomenclature from Naryan Naipaul's *Mimic Men* and has since been painstakingly developed by Homi Bhabha (1984a, 1984b, 1985). Naipaul views mimicry as a permanent disability implicit in the colonial condition and texts. Colonialism, in his view, imposed disorder and inauthenticity on the margins of Europe. Subsequently, the life of the once colonized people is held hostage to distinctions they continuously make between the authentic experience of the "real" world and the inauthentic experience of the invalidated periphery they occupy (Ashcroft, Griffiths, and Tiffin 1989, 88). Colonial mimicry is thus the mimicry of the "original," "the true," which exists at the source of power (1989, 89).

The concept of mimicry has been refined by Bhabha. He maintains that the discourse is constructed around an ambivalence. To maintain authority over the colonized/other, imperial discourse delineates him as radically different from the colonizer/self. But to give value to this authority over the colonized other, the self must maintain sufficient identity with the other (Ashcroft, Griffiths, and Tiffin 1989, 103). The colonized is thus the subject of a difference that is almost the same but not quite (Bhabha 1984a, 126). The colonized is confronted, according to Frantz Fanon, by having to be white or having to disappear (1967, 138). However, Bhabha suggests that mimicry, that is, being white but not quite, is an ambivalent third choice before the colonized (Bhabha 1985, 103).

The comparisons *saḥir* make are, of course, not elegant, neutral juxtapositions of categories of Rubāṭāb and colonial spaces. Note here that Rubāṭāb space can include the steam train which was antiquated by the diesel train as we have seen it in the above-mentioned example of *saḥir.* The "poetics of contrast" (Comaroff and Comaroff 1987, 205) is embedded in a "disabling cultural framework" (Ashcroft, Griffiths, and Tiffin 1989, 93) in which metropolitan imperial artifacts and values are still the source of legitimation. In its proclivity, as a hybrid text, to contrast illegitimate Rubāṭāb space to the legitimizing metropolitan space, *saḥir* fixes the Rubāṭāb as a "partial presence, incomplete and virtual" (Bhabha 1984b: 127).

Rubāṭāb discourses are replete with this sense of the incompleteness of their space and usually summon a modern equivalent whenever mention is made to a Rubāṭāb artifact or practice. A narrator described the scene in a folktale where girls carried water from the river in their jars and then said, "That was before the introduction of the water taps." It is worth noting here that the project to supply village homes with running water is still incomplete, and we have seen how its neglect was a topic of a critical *saḥrah.* Further, when a storyteller comes to a gourd, a special kind of drum, or a term for "breakfast," he marks them as archaic. Mention of *marīsah* (indigenous drink) and *khalwah* (guest house or Koranic school) will immediately be followed by mentioning their modern substitutes: imported liquor, *daywān* (guest house), and school. Apparently, the raconteurs are engaged in describing a "quality space"—to use Fernandez's term—in which the metropolitan space is *the* space (1974, 124).

In Rubāṭāb discourses, their space strives for completeness by appropriating the colonial, real space. In lyric poetry, the lover emerges as the metaphorical embodiment of the Rubāṭāb quality space. A lover may be praised for having the color of German fabrics carried by Indian traders. Her cosmetic facial marks are lauded for being performed by a British surgeon. The sparkle of her healthy teeth are analogized to fire from Italian guns. Those who stand guard around her to keep away intruders and stalkers are "English men alerted every sunset." When she rarely speaks to the one who adores her he gets intoxicated by her words, which have the effect of a "cognac of beer" (a cup of beer). The lover is then rightly described as the "European sample that is [deservedly] overpriced." This situation of appropriating the colonial space is dramatically reproduced in this lullaby of a mother to her son, Jalal:

Jalal will never grow up to be a porter
Jalal will never grow up to climb up the mast
He will be a District Commissioner with an elevated scale
And make rounds of *al-ahālī* [the natives]

Rubāṭāb are embarrassed by the inauthenticity of their space. I experienced this embarrassment in a situation in which I was taken to represent the original space that exists at the source of power. A man was telling us about how the abrupt announcement of the Feast of Breaking the Ramadan Fast caught them completely unprepared. A merchant who was among the audience was upset by the content and idioms of the man's narrative. He told me, "Had he known your mission, he wouldn't have said what he said." The merchant was displeased with the man for using the archaic *hudūm* (clothes), *jar* (earthenware vessels for cooling water), and *kōz* (cup) instead of the modern *malābis, zīr,* and *kubayah,* respectively. He was especially annoyed to hear the man saying that he was so unprepared for the feast that he had no clean clothes to wear for the occasion. The merchant did not like the man to reveal how few clothes a Rubāṭāb farmer usually has.

This mimicry, or this textually dramatized permanent disability of a culture, evokes laughter even in non*saḥir* texts. Madīnah al-Ḥāj, the *sōmār* singer, laughed after reciting this line from a relatively old song: "He raised the six-year-old ox that is accustomed to drinking water from the river at noon." Madīnah said, "Past people considered having an ox as the epitome of wealth. Praise be to Allah. They did not live long enough to see these water pumps." All she needed was the laugh to make sense of the embarrassing juxtaposition. Having the metaphor work behind it, *saḥir* puts in sharp relief the mimicry inherent in the colonial situation.

6

A Corridor of Voices: The Genres of *Saḥrah*

In the previous chapter we saw the reality of *saḥir* vigorously debated by the Rubāṭāb. The *saḥḥārs* categorically deny that their metaphors cause evil to their objects. They argue forcefully, and sometimes in obviously hurt tones, that their intention in speaking *saḥir* is to make people laugh. *Saḥir,* they maintain, is a *nuktah* (joke), as the audience's laughing response confirms. Furthermore, the *saḥḥārs* describe those who accuse them of the *ʿayn* as victimized by some *ʿaqīdah* (belief). The metaphor victims, on the other hand, point to the harm they themselves have suffered as a result of *saḥir.* They dismiss as false the *saḥḥārs*' pet argument which distinguishes between the evil eye, which is real and harmful, and an "evil mouth," which is innocently humorous. In an attempt to silence the *saḥḥārs*, the victims fall back on the dominant *shariʿah*-minded model of speaking, which condemns *saḥir.* Victims' accounts of the afflictions they suffered from *saḥir* are cast in a personal experience story. The audiences are ambivalent toward *saḥir*—they enjoy the humor of *saḥir* but simultaneously object to its anticipated harm. In their uncertainty, the audiences tell about the *saḥir* events they know of as legends or jokes.

Previous research in *saḥrah* has been plagued by the problem of how to classify this protean form. Is it a form of humor, or is it a type of evil eye belief? Scholars have taken both positions. I first encountered the genre in 1966 when I conducted a survey collection of Rubāṭāb folklore. My collection of *saḥrahs*, recorded in a humorous session, was later published along with some *masākhah* episodes in a chapter entitled "*Al-Saḥir wa al-Nawādir*" (*Saḥir* and "Anecdotes") (Ibrahim and Nasr 1968, 57–64). The genre has thus been identified as humorous, which is how *saḥḥārs* and some narrators view it. However, from my personal experience as a native of the culture, I knew even then that *saḥrah*s could be identified differently. Muḥammad al-Diwayk called them *ḥikāyāt al-naẓal* (evil eye narratives) (1984, 1:76) in his study of folk narratives in Qatar. Most reporters have been interested in abstracting the belief in the evil eye from the *saḥrah*s they recorded (al-Diwayk 1984, 1:179; H. Ibrahim 1979, 149; Mohamed 1979, 38–39; Emra 1979, 7–8). In neglecting the polyphonic character of *saḥrah,* the genre was misrepresented because each reporter heard one voice and remained oblivious to the others.

Oral narrative accounts of *saḥrah* similarly fall into different genres of verbal art. Some people, especially *saḥḥār*s themselves, relate cases of *saḥir* shots in a form that may be identified as a joke. Others, particularly those opposed to *saḥrah* as evil eye, would relate the same cases as dire legends, while victims usually narrate their experiences in personal experience form. *Saḥrah*s also take the forms of riddles or proverbs, or may be displayed as comical episodes.

In this chapter we will compare and contrast the different genres in which accounts of *saḥir* are cast and show how they express the conflicting views of *saḥir* held by the different narrators. This enterprise will draw upon Bakhtin's concept of a dialogue of genres. We will look at how one utterance of *saḥir,* in Bakhtin's words, "builds on other utterances, polemicizes with them" (1986, 69). The issue here is not how these utterances are derived from a single event of *saḥir,* but rather how they derive from *saḥir* while reacting to one another (1986, 91), and how, as such, they are distinctively constituted in the dialogue of other utterances in their expressive field *saḥir.* In a word, how they become what they are in becoming "dialogic" in the Bakhtinian sense:

> Each utterance is filled with echoes and reverberations of other utterances to which it is related by the commonality of the sphere of speech communication. Every utterance must be regarded primarily as a *response* to preceding utterances of the given sphere (we understand the word "response" here in the broadest sense). Each utterance refutes, affirms, supplements and relies on the others, presupposes

> them to be known, and somehow takes them into account. After all, as regards a given question, in a given matter, and so forth, the utterance occupies a particular *definite* position in a given sphere of communication. It is impossible to determine its position without correlating it with other positions. (1986, 91; emphasis in the original)[1]

Genre research in verbal art is opening up to Bakhtin's dialogic principle. Dorst's application of Bakhtin's genre theory to neck riddles is a welcome and sensible start in this direction. Dorst has not only pointed out what inadequacy the theory can specifically address in genre research, but has also anchored the theory in the ethnographic strengths of verbal art. He argues that whereas previous research focused primarily on delimitations and consistencies of genres, the promise of the dialogic theory lies in dealing with the intrageneric and intergeneric instability (1983, 413–14). A theoretically grounded dialectics of genre, according to Dorst, is an unopened book in folklore studies. He goes on to say that "to open it would involve less a radical departure than a logical (and necessary) extension of the ethnographic enterprise already so firmly in place" (1983, 425).

The dialogic principle, unlike previous concepts such as theme, function, structure, and performance, is not to be used as a classificatory criterion for distinguishing one genre from another. Those concepts were used as axes along which—or polarities between which—to place respective genres, in order to describe and discover the distinctive features of each genre (Ben-Amos 1976b, xxxviii). In contrast, the dialogic principle is *relational;* it emphasizes the mutual awareness that different genres have of each other and their mutual reflection of one another (Bakhtin 1986, 91–92).

Folklore scholarship has largely overlooked the concept of the dialogue of genres because of undue emphasis on the distinctive unity of genres. Although an awareness of this dialogue is not lacking, the forms that pertain to it have been dismissed as transitional and mixed forms arising from misunderstanding. In its focus on generic stabilities, genre research is unequipped to accommodate the emergence, transformation, and obsolescence that arise from dialogue; instead, these are treated as forms of defect or as a breakdown in generic order (Dorst 1983, 413).

The case of the negative legend clearly demonstrates this inadequacy. Although folklorists are acquainted with negative legends, they have dismissed them as mixed forms, corruptions, or travesties of positive legends. They viewed negative legends as symptoms of the dissolution of the folk society and the crumbling of its old values (Degh and Vazsonyi 1976, 413). In other words, they related the negative legend genealogically rather than dialogically to the positive legend. They missed here the aspect of dialogue in legend-telling situations. According to Degh and Vazsonyi, the negative legend is as old as the positive legend. The born skeptics—who exist in all societies, including the most backward ones—have always told negative legends (1976, 413).

Degh and Vazsonyi's seminal research on the legend already approximates the dialogic model. Based on their extensive fieldwork, they pointed out the difficulty of delimiting the "capricious genre" of legend from other forms of folk prose (1976, 93). They pointed to the "frontier traffic between the genres" (1973, 46), which is reminiscent of Bakhtin's description of inner dialogism as "the choppers of borders between utterances" (1986, 119).[2] Degh and Vazsonyi's use of the term "rebuttal" (1976, 109)[3] to name the debate between the genres and the term "polyphonic" (1976, 117) to describe the voice of the legend are reminders of the terms "rejoinder" (Bakhtin 1986, 75–76) and "polyphonic" (Todorov 1984, 64) in their Bakhtinian senses. In Degh and Vazsonyi's perspective, truth and belief, long held to be the basic criteria for defining legend, are topics on which the legend "makes its case, takes a stand and calls for the expression of an opinion" (1976, 119). Debate, they argue, is an important criterion of the legend (1973, 8).

Borrowing this concept of a dialogue of genres, one can deal with *saḥrah* as a "corridor of voices" (Bakhtin 1986, 121), that is, as a set of competing attitudes, each of which gives rise to a different generic form. To identify the generic form in which *saḥir* utterances are constructed, we will focus primarily on what Bakhtin calls "the speaker's speech plan or speech will" (1986, 77).[4] This concept is not, of course, a novel idea, and Abraham's "rhetorical intent" (1968, 147) and El-Shamy's "narrator's intent" (1980, xliv)[5] are equally valid designations for the same concept. However, we will use this important concept in its Bakhtinian sense to identify the different generic forms subsumed under *saḥrah.* The concept is defined by Bakhtin as the subjective aspect of an utterance (1986, 77) in which the speaker expresses his worldview, evaluations, and emotions (1986, 90). Dialogically speaking, the speaker is, by such expression, responding to others' utterances and not just expressing his attitude toward the object of his utterance (1986, 92).

Set against each other dialogically, the points of view of the *saḥḥār,* the victim of *saḥir,* and the audiences who narrate their first- or secondhand knowledge of *saḥrah*s take the forms of the joke, personal experience, and legend *saḥrah*s, respectively. Other generic forms are generated within *saḥrah* as well.

Joke Saḥrah

The *saḥḥār*s' defense of their metaphors as jocular, involuntary statements is their major argument against those who accuse them of the *'ayn.* Thus, various speakers refer to *saḥir* as either jokes or funny stories. Before recording his repertoire of *saḥrah*s, 'Umar al-Ḥisayn of Mugrat Island asked, "Do you want me to narrate a *nuktah* [joke] from what I heard before?" Khiḍir Maḥmūd, a Rubāṭābī teacher and an avid collector and narrator of *saḥrah*s and *masākhah* genres, referred to the *saḥrah*s of Malīk al-Bashīr as *nawādir* (unprecedented and hence funny occurrences). This term is reserved by some for anecdotes that are a little longer than what they usually understand by *nuktah;* nonetheless, the humorous referent of both *nuktah* and *nawādir* does not allow for finer distinctions, and hence they are used interchangeably. *Nuktah,* the term the *saḥḥār*s use to describe their *saḥrah*s, apparently refers to terse humorous forms that conclude with a punch line of what the Rubāṭāb call *al-rad al-sari'* (quick at answering, repartee). After narrating a *saḥrah* from Salmān Abū Ḥijil of the Ḥijūlah chiefly lineage, al-Shaykh al-Ṣāyīm connected *saḥir* with repartee when he commented, "The Ḥijūlah are famous for their *saḥir,* for their brightness and *al-rad al-sari ʿ*." Generally speaking, the Ḥijūlah are praised for their rhetorical powers.

The joke is defined as an extremely succinct form limiting itself to "a dramatic dialogue or even to a question and answer sequence" (Degh 1972, 231). Similarly, a joke *saḥrah* can be compressed to a statement and a metaphor, as in the one that follows. Note how the narrative voice is indicated by the sequencing formula *baʿadayn* (after that), a common usage of Sudanese storytellers in narrative genres. We will give due consideration to this narrative device later in our study.

1.1

Date: 6/30/84.

Place: Kurgus West.

Narrator: Al-Ṭayyib Muḥammad ʾAḥmad al-Zākī (37 years old), a teacher.

Audience: Abu al-Qāsim Kiriz (32 years old), a farmer; ʿAbd al-Raḥmān Kiriz (24 years old), a college student; Al-Tijānī Kiriz (52 years old), uncle of Abu al-Qāsim and ʿAbd al-Raḥmān and the owner of the village bakery; collector (42 years old).

Situation: An open session for recording *saḥrah*s.

Original language: Arabic.

One day we were riding Kiriz's *lunch* [Engl., launch, engineboat]. *Baʿdayn* [after that] the *lunch* was green and rectangular. *Baʿadayn* we were dressed in white *jalābiyyah*s [loose, shirtlike garments] and huddling at the far end of the *lunch.* Ṣiddīq wad ʾAyyūb, the *saḥḥār,* saw us and said, "They look like a toothbrush." [audience laughs]

Although limited, the resources of the joke *saḥrah* need a sophisticated teller for the punch line to succeed with the audience.

A successful joke *saḥrah,* as we have seen in the previous chapter, sends the audience spinning around the punch line, repeating it with laughter and enjoyment.

The next example concerns a joke that did not succeed because the narrator, Abu al-Qāsim Kiriz, was too hesitant and apologetic to display his competence confidently. In delivering one *saḥrah* about some ʿAbaydab people, he said he was afraid that it might be *māmazbūṭah* (inappropriate) because he was narrating and recording it before an ʿAbaydab audience. He was not even encouraged when the audience said they did not mind. Weary of his hesitation, the audience suggested that he rehearse it, gauge the response, and then go ahead and record it, a procedure he followed to the detriment of his performance.

Earlier in the same session, Abu al-Qāsim actually asked for permission to perform from a competent narrator who was the spice of that recording session. Part of the failure of the following *saḥrah* may be explained by the fact that it was told in the shadow of that narrator. Note how, in narrating his *saḥrah,* Abu al-Qāsim seems to trip the punch line and then circle hopelessly around it.

1.2

Date: 6/5/84.

Place: Al-ʿAbaydab.

Narrator: Abu al-Qāsim Kiriz (see 1.1).

Audience: Muḥammad ʾAyyūb (40 years old), an attorney in Khartoum (the capital city), a good narrator of joke *saḥrah*s who had thus far dominated the session; Muṣṭafah ʾAyyūb (32 years old), a *saḥḥār,* farmer, and janitor at the intermediate school; Al-Ṭayyib Bājūrī (34 years old), a teacher at the girls' high school; Ḥisayn Bājūrī (32 years old), a teacher at the elementary school; Al-Tijānī Kiriz (see 1.1); collector.

Situation: A casual, extended session after a Ramadan evening meal called for by the Bājūrīs to introduce me to their ʿAbaydab community and for an ad hoc collection of *saḥrah*s.

> *Original language:* Arabic.
>
> *Baʿadayn* I remember a *saḥḥār* called ʿAwaḍ ʿAlī who bewitched the light when it was still new to Kurgus Island. People there were proud of it and they abandoned their lamps. *Baʿadayn* suddenly one day their power plant was down and that left them unhappy. On that day a wake was observed on the island and the people started talking, "The power plant is down and what not." He [ʿAwaḍ] asked [rhetorically], "Your power light is down?" They said, "Yes." He said to them, "You have no other way than to sail using your old oars" [narrator laughs]. That means go back to your lamps because electricity was no longer supplied. You had been sailing by the wind, but the wind stopped and people needed to use oars to sail the boat.

Aside from the lack of the laughing response that is the goal of such a narrative, the failure of this narrative is clearly revealed by the fact that the narrator explained his own punch line. The exegesis of the punch line is commonly the function of the audience. As addressees they delight in seeing the point of the metaphor, and they offer their exegesis as an appendix to the author's text and not as an integral part of it.

The joke *saḥrah* exhausts itself at the punch line. The narrator, however, may repeat the line as a sign of his ownership and pride in it. The audience, on the other hand, repeats the punch line in appreciation of the successful delivery of the joke. Before the punch line, confusion reigns (Lixfeld 1986, 236) and the tension built up by the joke is released only by that line. The joke *saḥrah* is apparently complete at the punch line. At the conclusion of the narrative, the narrator and the situation remain open to appended exegesis and laughter rewards.

A joke *saḥrah* does not tolerate a diachronic narrative in which events are narrated in the time sequence in which they took place (Dorst 1983, 426). This *saḥrah,* like any other joke, requires very little articulation of the plot to call on its audience's ability to analogize (Hockett 1977, 285–86). Its structure, like that of all jokes, is consistently directed toward the disclosure of the final, revealing punch line (Lixfeld 1986, 23).

The following joke *saḥrah* is not typical of the genre. It was selected to show what a joke *saḥrah* is not. The text is one of three I collected that record the same event of *saḥir* as perceived by a *saḥḥār,* the victim, and a third party. The *saḥir* event at hand is one in which Wad al-Tōm, the narrator of the following text, allegedly killed one or more sheep by drawing an analogy between the sheep and something else. The versions of the victim and the third party will be dealt with later (examples 3.1 and 2.1, respectively) to underscore the direct, dialogical relationship in which the three texts stand.

1.3

Date: 6/7/84.

Place: ʿAtmūr, Khiḍir's guesthouse.

Narrator: Wad al-Tōm (55 years old), a farmer, *saḥḥār,* and expert in traditional healing.

Audience: Khiḍir ʿAlī Muṣṭafah (64 years old) and his sons Bakrī (32 years old) and ʿUthmān (28 years old), who resigned from teaching to help their father in his expanding agro-trading business; Khiḍir's nephews Mughdād (55 years old) and Ḥāmid al-Rufāʿī (47 years old), the farmer-butcher and farmer, respectively; Bābikir Muḥammad Bābikir (35 years old), the baker; the collector; and an unidentified audience.

Situation: It was my first interview with Wad al-Tōm. The *saḥrah* came to him after he told the one in which he bewitched the combine of Muḥammad ʿAlī Muṣṭafah, the patriarch of Um Ghiday.

Original language: Arabic.

COLLECTOR: Is Muḥammad scared of *saḥir*?

WAD AL-TŌM: Yes, *lāḥawlah* [there is no power and no strength save in Allah].

COLLECTOR: What did he say to you after hearing of the *saḥrah* of the combine?

WAD AL-TŌM: Nobody told him about it [audience laughs]. He once chased me with regard to a *saḥrah* I said about his flock of sheep [audience laughs]. *Fī al-ḥaqīqah* [In actual fact] he had at that time a large flock of sheep. But he was visited by many guests. An automobile with guests in it came daily to his place. And they [his boys or clients] picked up a young sheep and slaughtered it. *Baʿadayn* I think he ran out of sheep or I don't know what. He asked me one time when he was visited by some guests, "By Allah, don't you have *ḍarībah* [something to kill for the guests]?" I said to him, "Have you run out of your watermelons?" *Al-ḥaqīqīyyah* [actually] it is common practice with the one who grows watermelons to cut one and present it to his visitors. I said to him, "The watermelons ran short." He really didn't like the *saḥrah*. He kind of chased me. *Baʿadayn* one of his young he-goats drank kerosene and he said my *saḥrah* was responsible for that.

KHIḌIR: Is it one young he-goat or a group of them; three or four perhaps?

WAD AL-TŌM: Truly, this he-goat . . . [the parts of Muḥammad's] tractor were rinsed . . .

KHIḌIR: Those who rinsed it were near the flour mill.

WAD AL-TŌM: That was near the tree that was in front of Muḥammad's home. When they untied here the flock to go and graze, this young he-goat went along with them, found the kerosene in a washbowl, and drank from it. *Ghāytū* [to cut a long story short] it instantly ran fast until it reached the flour mill and dropped. And Muḥammad said that was the result of my *saḥrah.*

Being the *saḥḥār* himself, Wad al-Tōm dwells at some length on his personal experience to build up to his punch line. In the text we see that Wad al-Tōm introduces this buildup twice with his own generic mark *fī al-ḥaqīqah* and *al-ḥaqīqīyyah* (in actual fact).[6] In an attempt to show an intimacy with Muḥammad, the patriarch, Wad al-Tōm expands this part by relating a self-serving encounter with him that Muḥammad himself does not mention in his version of the event (see example 3.1). Details of this kind are usually compressed in the joke *saḥrah* to the minimum required for the successful launching of the metaphor. Though atypical, Wad al-Tōm's joke *saḥrah* illustrates what the narrator has to slash down from the *saḥir* event to recast it as a joke. Space and time have to be compromised first in the joke genre.

To prove that Muḥammad is scared of *saḥir,* Wad al-Tōm had to mention, though in vague terms, how some of his sheep were allegedly affected by the *saḥrah.* Neither his first account of the event nor his rejoinder to Khiḍir states clearly that a sheep had actually died, whether as a result of or coincidentally with his *saḥrah.* He admits that "one of his young he-goats drank kerosene" and that "it dropped"—he stopped short of saying it actually dropped dead.

In addition, in his rejoinder to Khiḍir, Wad al-Tōm reveals a knowledge of place and time that he could not relate to the joke genre he had selected. He knows, for example, that parts of a tractor were rinsed near the tree that is in front of Muḥammad's house and not near the flour mill mentioned by Khiḍir. He seems to suggest that if Khiḍir cannot be trusted with places, he should not be believed as to the number of sheep that were affected, either. The details about how the he-goat encountered the kerosene washbowl will be repeated in the personal experience *saḥrah* as intrinsic to the narrator's plan. Here Wad al-Tōm has to appendix them in a *ghāytū* (glossed form) to his already finalized joke narrative.

Legend Saḥrah

A joke *saḥrah* exhausts its theme at the punch line. The plan of its speaker has no place for the statement of affliction claimed by the victims of *saḥir.* Hence the structure of the joke *saḥrah* falls short of what I call the "pinch line," the concluding part of a legend *saḥrah* (examples 2.1 and 2.2), which records the misfortune experienced by a victim of *saḥir.* The next case is an account of the same event Wad al-Tōm related in joke form above (example 1.3). In this case the narrator did not have direct knowledge of the event, but had heard about it from others.

2.1

Date: 5/29/84.

Place: Offices of Sudan Railways Research Department, Atbara.

Narrator: Nūr al-Dīn ʿUthmān (34 years old), a Rubāṭābī, a *saḥḥār,* a research assistant with the railways, and son-in-law of Malīk al-Bashīr, the famous Rubāṭābī *saḥḥār* in Atbara.

Audience: Collector. Nūr's colleagues in the office were going about their normal business and intervened with comment and laughter when one of the *saḥrah*s was directed toward one of them.

Situation: Nūr al-Dīn ʿUthmān demonstrated by the *saḥrah* how some *saḥḥārs*, such as Wad al-Tōm, can really be evil, whereas others—including himself—are harmless.

Original language: Arabic.

Wad al-Tōm is said to be really evil. People even disappear from his sight when their roads cross to avoid his *saḥir.* Among the evil things he committed, it is told that he once saw some goats in a boat, not goats but rather sheep. *Al-ḥaqīqah* [in fact] there were sheep in it and in it also were camels. The camels were made to kneel down on the boat floor. And the boat was filled by *hināy* [demonstrative particle, here indicating people] crossing from the east bank to the west bank of the river. Wad al-Tōm apparently had said "The people in their white dresses look like ginger among coffee beans" [in reference to the coffee-brown color of sheep and camels].

> When the goats, actually sheep, got out of the boat, climbed their way up and away from the river, they ran into a washbowl full of gasoline in which some people rinse out [the parts of tractors, water pumps, etc.]. They drank from that gasoline and were done for.

The narrator continued by narrating other similar drastic *saḥrahs* from Wad al-Tōm, including the one that allegedly killed his son. They all ended with a pinch line in which a misfortune was recorded.

Legend *saḥrah* is the most common form in which a case is made for the belief in the directly or indirectly harmful effects of *saḥir.* Nūr al-Dīn, a *saḥḥār* in his own right, delivered the text to prove his point that although in general *saḥir* is harmless, some individual *saḥḥārs* can be evil. However, a *saḥḥār* may resort to this same form to downplay or explain away the harm an audience has accused him of inflicting on a victim, as Wad al-Tōm did in example 1.3. In such cases a *saḥḥār* will attribute the pinch line to the victim and in this way confirm the *saḥḥārs*' basic argument that *saḥir* only affects those who are scared of it because of an *ʿaqīdah* (belief).

The legend *saḥrah,* like all legends, is "an inference that strives to reach *conclusions* from premises" (Degh and Vazsonyi 1976, 116; emphasis in the original). In the text under consideration (example 2.1), the narrator builds up the *al-ḥaqīqah* (the reality situation) introductory part just enough to launch the punch line (the metaphor), as in a joke *saḥrah.* He had to retract and cross out "goats" and introduce "sheep" and "camels" to give the right mix of colors for the revelation of the punch line. A narrator of legend *saḥrah* is never careless or casual about the punch line. It is apparently a prerequisite for a credible pinch line. To hit the target, the verbal missile has to be faultless.

The evil nature of *saḥir* is thus inferred from the finalization component of the legend, which in turn follows from the premise of *al-ḥaqīqah* and the punch line. Finalization refers to the way in which the speaker has completely said what he wishes to say and has exhausted his theme at a particular moment or under particular circumstances. The semantic exhaustiveness of the theme and the typical compositional and generic forms of rounding it up are two important aspects of finalization (Bakhtin 1986, 76–77).

The punch line here raises an interesting intergeneric relationship. Even in the negative tone in which a *saḥrah* legend is delivered, the punch line arouses laughter. True, this laughter is not of the magnitude or finality of the explosive laughter that the same punch line might have aroused in a joke *saḥrah.* The laughter in the joke *saḥrah* indicates that the text has satisfied the audience's expectations of a humorous text (Hoppal 1980, 12). However, laughter cannot always be viewed as general approval of the message of the joke (Lixfeld 1986, 238).

The punch line can be viewed as an "inserted genre" in the legend *saḥrah.* An inserted genre, according to Bakhtin, is an utterance that is introduced into another utterance wholly or in part, while retaining or reaccentuating its alien expression (1986, 91). Although the punch line continues to elicit laughter in the legend *saḥrah,* the pinch line is the real point of the narrative, what the audience expects. The irresistible, alien expression of laughter is reaccentuated by the pinch line in a way reminiscent of Hockett's statement: "We laugh despite ourselves, at least for a moment, before revulsion gets the upper hand" (1977, 283). Indeed, the function of the pinch line is precisely to arouse that revulsion.

The following portion of my interview with ʿAbd al-Mawlah ʿAṭah (32 years old) clearly shows how revulsion gains the upper hand over laughter when *saḥir* is performed:

COLLECTOR: What kind of response do you have when Malīk bewitches someone in your presence?

ABD AL-MAWLAH: We say, *ḥarām* [sinful], have mercy. This is *ḥarām ʿalayk* [sinful of you]. Perhaps the victim has children who need him. "Allah is great" on you. Ask Allah's forgiveness. Allah would give you a way out of your evil disposition. And so we start arguing with him.

COLLECTOR: You don't laugh, do you?
ʿABD AL-MAWLAH: No, we don't.
COLLECTOR: Really!
ʿABD AL-MAWLAH: In fact, we argue with him after laughing. We argue with him but not before having a laugh. We start then arguing with him and we accuse him of killing the victim and that he [the victim] will never be the same after his *saḥir.*

Apparently ʿAbd al-Mawlah is reluctant to admit the power of the punch line. But the fact remains that the truth of laughter "embraces and carries away everyone; nobody can resist it" (Bakhtin 1968, 99).

In non-Rubāṭāb communities, the legend *saḥrah*s usually take a cyclical pattern in which the formula "the Rubāṭābī said" is the mark of the genre. However, I encountered the conventional legend-validating formula, "I saw it with my own eyes," only three times. One informant swore "By Allah!" (truly) to validate his legend *saḥrah.* The following example illustrates the validation formula and shows how compressed a legend *saḥrah* can be.

2.2
Date: 7/7/1984.
Place: ʿAtmūr Senior High for Girls.
Narrator: Naʿīmah Ibrahīm (17 years old).
Audience: Senior class of ʿAtmūr High School.
Situation: I wrote it down from Naʿīmah when I discussed with the class whether *saḥir* has adverse effects.
Original language: Arabic.

There was a goat that had white twin kids. A woman said, "Like a pair of white socks." The two kids died. I saw that with my own eyes.

Certain tellers of *saḥrah*s can use either joke or legend *saḥrah*s to suit their particular experiences and convictions. Thus Mughdād, whom we have seen arguing for predestination and claiming that an affliction from *saḥir* is either a coincidence or an agency, delivers both forms. Of three *saḥrah*s of Wad al-Tōm to which Mughdād was an eyewitness, two have the legend *saḥrah* pinch line. The third ends at the punch line. However, the legend *saḥrah* is the favorite form for those who strongly and consistently believe that *saḥir* is evil. The narrator's ethnicity is one factor that helps to determine whether joke or legend *saḥrah*s are preferred. The conflicting speech plans that lie behind both joke and legend *saḥrah*s are best illustrated by the narratives of ʿAbd al-Mawlah ʿAṭah and Khiḍir Maḥmūd (33 years old), concerning *saḥrah*s attributed to the same Rubāṭābī *saḥḥār,* the late Malīk al-Bashīr. ʿAbd al-Mawlah is a Shāyqī who came in close contact with Malīk when they worked together as laborers for the track maintenance department of the Sudan Railways.

Ethnic groups like the Shāīqīyyah, who interact regularly with the Rubāṭāb, believe that each and every Rubāṭābī is an obnoxious *saḥḥār.* "They utter the *taʿwīdhah* after each word from a Rubāṭābī," said a Rubāṭābī, describing the attitude of these ethnic groups vis-à-vis the Rubāṭāb. Being from a different ethnic group than Malīk, ʿAbd al-Mawlah draws the following "satanic" image of him:

> He is a sort of a man who blows things out of proportion. He is quick at repartee, as people say. He is a *waṣṣāf* [describer, analogizer] of the first degree. He *yasḥār* [bewitches], causes people to laugh, full of jokes. He is all that in one. People would utter " 'Allah is Great' on you" to his face when they see him coming up towards them. He is evil and *maskhūt* [odious, cursed]. He is a *saḥḥār* and people were scared of him. He draws analogy too. [ʿAbd al-Mawlah then recited the *taʿwīdhah* he used to utter whenever he met Malīk.] Other workers also used to utter this *taʿwīdhah* either silently or openly. Even the overseer to whom Malīk reported was scared of him and uttered " 'Allah is Great' . . ." at him silently or openly. It is rare to find people socializing with him. It is really rare except for someone who did not know him for what he was. He would socialize with Malīk till the time he knew him better. When he got to know that Malīk was a *saḥḥār* he would avoid him like a plague.

According to ʿAbd al-Mawlah, people viewed the misfortunes suffered by Malīk just before his death in 1980 (three surgical operations in a row and running into a truck, the complications of all of which eventually killed him) as signs of God's wrath on Malīk for his evil. His eye surgery is especially emphasized in this respect because *saḥir* resides primarily in the eye. Interestingly, on surviving these misfortunes Malīk had analogized himself to a dress made from titron cloth: the stitches wear out in time, while the cloth remains intact.

The intragroup image of Malīk is totally different from ʿAbd al-Mawlah's intergroup view. Malīk's son-in-law Nūr al-Dīn describes him as a jovial, courteous man who opened his humble house (which lies precisely between the railway station and the hospital) to those Rubāṭāb who came to Atbara for treatment, to change trains, or to do business. According to Nūr al-Dīn, his *saḥir* was regarded as joking by his guests and by his many visitors from the Rubāṭāb community in Atbara. And as we saw earlier, Khiḍir Maḥmūd describes his friend Malīk's *saḥrah*s as *nawādir* (anecdote).

These contrasting intragroup and intergroup images of Malīk largely determined the genres that Khiḍir Maḥmūd and ʿAbd al-Mawlah selected to tell about their encounters with him. Khiḍir referred to Malīk's *saḥrah*s as *nawādir;* he narrated his eight *saḥrah*s from Malīk in the joke form, and his Rubāṭāb audience in ʿAtmūr village laughed heartily at them. ʿAbd al-Mawlah, on the other hand, recounted twenty-six *saḥrah*s from Malīk and selected the legend *saḥrah* form for nine of them. The statistical significance of this is obviously inconclusive; more significant, perhaps, is how ʿAbd al-Mawlah framed and conducted the entire interview I had with him. Judging by the tone of disgust directed toward Malīk that structured this interview, I would suggest that the fact that ʿAbd al-Mawlah did not mention the pinch line of the other seventeen *saḥrah*s can be explained with referencc to this tone. Whenever I asked him about what afflictions Malīk's *saḥrah*s had caused, he would readily come up with one misfortune or another. Three of the nine legend *saḥrah*s ʿAbd al-Mawlah delivered were shaped by such questions. I would argue, therefore, that the number of legend *saḥrah*s would have increased had I cared to ask about the afflictions more often.

In the interview, ʿAbd al-Mawlah would sometimes shift focus to make his point about the evil of Malīk. Five of these twenty-six *saḥrah*s were narrated to prove that Malīk was so cunning in his evil pursuit that he would miss hardly any opportunity to shoot a *saḥrah.* In reporting these *saḥrah*s, ʿAbd al-Mawlah was more concerned with the range of Malīk's destructive ability than with the individual misfortunes.

We have already pointed to elements of the dreadful picture ʿAbd al-Mawlah painted of Malīk. We have seen how he compared Malīk to a *saḥḥār* (here meaning a cannibal) because Malīk said he tasted blood when he finished conjuring up a *saḥrah.* In addition, he attributed to Malīk a "formulaic" *saḥrah* that I always encountered in situations where the evil of a *saḥḥār* was thought to be extreme. Malīk, ʿAbd al-Mawlah said, saw his two newly circumcised daughters lying in the same bed opposite each other, colorfully dressed in the ritual *qarmaṣīṣ,* and exclaimed, "They look like the queens of the playing cards." The daughters died the next day. This *saḥrah* is typically attributed to *saḥḥār*s whose *saḥir* is deadly as well as indiscriminate.

Moreover, Malīk's destructive powers were not only acknowledged but also sought after to effect desired damage. ʿAbd al-Mawlah told me how Malīk's workmates once asked Malīk to cause a bulldozer to break down in order for them to have a long break from work. Malīk emerges from ʿAbd al-Mawlah's account as a sinister *saḥḥār* whose evil doings were intentional and professional. In analyzing the structure of sentiment of ʿAbd al-Mawlah's interview, I sought to account for his failure to insert the punch line in most of the *saḥrah*s he narrated from Malīk. This failure, I would argue, resulted from ʿAbd al-Mawlah's conviction that nothing could have come from Malīk except harm. To him this fact was self-evident and needed no explicit statement in his narratives.

Personal Experience Saḥrah

The following example is a personal experience form of the bewitching of the he-goat event. We have previously heard it from the point of view of the *saḥḥār* (example 1.3) and a third party (example 2.1), in joke and legend form, respectively.

3.1

Date: 8/20/1984.

Place: Um Ghiday.

Narrator: Muḥammad ʿAlī Muṣṭafah (70 years old), the patriarch of Um Ghiday.

Audience: ʿAbbās ʿAlī Muṣṭafah (58 years old), Muḥammad's brother, owner of an agro-trade business; Wad ʿUmarah (85 years old), farmer; al-Shaykh al-Tijānī (55 years old), former commissioner of elementary education and presently owner of a bookstore in ʿAtmūr; Wad Ḥāj ʿAlī (60 years old), a tenant with the patriarch; the collector; and an unidentified audience of relatives and tenants of Muḥammad's agricultural scheme.

Situation: An interview to hear from Muḥammad the *saḥrah*s Wad al-Tōm shot at him or his property during the time he worked for him on the scheme. I came with a list of these from my interviews in ʿAtmūr, the older twin village of the enterprising, frontier-minded Um Ghiday.

Original language: Arabic.

MUḤAMMAD: Should I continue telling about Wad al-Tōm?

AUDIENCE MEMBER: Of course. Isn't he the hero of the play?

COLLECTOR: What is your story of Wad al-Tōm?

MUḤAMMAD: You want to hear then my story with Wad al-Tōm. It occurred at the time of the peanuts [when peanuts were first grown in Um Ghiday]. In fact, that was the first and most successful harvest of peanuts in this place. Subsequently people started coming to Um Ghiday to solicit money for different community projects and other missions. Some people came from Abu Hamad and said they wanted to build an institution for religious knowledge in the town. Ḥasan ʿUthmān [a leading, non-Rubāṭābī merchant in Abu Hamad] and other merchants were among them. *Baʿadayn* we asked them into the house and attended to their comfort. Then we sent for the boys [either sons or herd boys] and asked them to return from pasturing the flock of sheep and bringing back a male sheep that went out to graze with the flock [pause]. *Baʿadayn* they brought back the male sheep and butchered it. We had a feast in honor of the people of Abu Hamad, and they left. The next day some people from Nādī village came also and said they had a project to build a mosque and I know not what and so on and so forth. We sent for another male sheep and said to the boys, "Bring it back and come with it." They slaughtered the male sheep. The third day some people came from Marī island or from what or where I don't know. Years passed since then [c. 1966].

AUDIENCE MEMBER: Those were the people from the agriculture department at Berber [seat of the rural council under the jurisdiction of which the Rubāṭāb used to be].

MUḤAMMAD: What?

AUDIENCE MEMBER: Those were the people from the agriculture department at Berber.

MUḤAMMAD: True. They were the people from the agriculture department at Berber. They came to Um Ghiday. We sent for the boys to return with a third male sheep from the grazing flock. They brought another male sheep and slaughtered it. *Baʿadayn* there was Wad al-Tōm and others playing *sījah* [a game like checkers] under the *dom* trees that are opposite our home. *Baʿadayn* he kept seeing for three days in a row the male sheep that was sent for to return from grazing and was slaughtered. *Baʿadayn* he said to them [those around him], "Muḥammad's sheep are like watermelons; whichever one they tap [by way of testing its ripeness] they find it ripe and they cut it." [Narrator and audience laugh.] We had in the flock a castrated he-goat which we kept for ritualistic purposes. *Baʿadayn* that he-goat . . . The boys rinsed out the parts of the tractor and left the kerosene with which they rinsed out those parts in a washbowl that they left lying under the *sayyalah* [acacia raddianta] tree that stood in front of our house. The he-goat came and immediately bent over the washbowl and drank all the kerosene and filled up its stomach. The *taqah* [threshing floor] was very close to the mill. There was an Arab [nomad] guardsman at the threshing floor. *Baʿadayn* when the he-goat reached the guardsman it fell instantly to the ground. The Arab came fast to it and slaughtered it [i.e., according to the Islamic prescriptions because otherwise it will be a *faṭīsah,* the meat of which is religiously impure] and skinned it. And they took its intestines and viscera to the river. When they put them into the water the kerosene that came out of them drifted as far as this island that stands in the middle of the river. The question arose: Was its meat edible? They said it was. They took it inside the house for the womenfolk. None could put a single piece in his mouth. We decided to give it to the nomads, and our womenfolk succeeded in extracting the fat from the meat. It gave a lot of fat. Our womenfolk extracted it anyway and I would not know what they did with it [he laughs].

COLLECTOR: After how many days did the he-goat die?

MUḤAMMAD: It was a matter of . . .

COLLECTOR: After the *saḥrah*?

MUḤAMMAD: It died the second day after the *saḥrah.* It happened on the second day. Next day, for sure.

Unlike the joke or legend *saḥrah*s, in the personal experience *saḥrah* narrative diachrony is central. In this text Muḥammad pays special attention to locating his misfortune in time and place, whereas Wad al-Tōm refers to the time of the incident vaguely as the "the time when Muḥammad had a large flock of sheep." It is more specifically described by Muḥammad as the time of the first and most successful peanut harvest. The legend *saḥrah* (example 2.1) ignored time completely. Further, Muḥammad's narrative of the three prior episodes in which the guests were well received approximates the style of the folktale narration. Though repetitive and glossable, as proved by Wad al-Tōm's narration (example 1.3), the three episodes are nonetheless presented individually by Muḥammad. He apparently enjoys chronicling in full his generosity to his visitors. The trees take their proper name, place, and function in his personal experience *saḥrah,* although Wad al-Tōm mentioned them only after audience prompting. Further, Muḥammad gives a detailed description of the he-goat as castrated and kept for ritualistic purposes. Neither the plain, intruding he-goat of the joke *saḥrah* (example 1.3) nor the many but unidentifiable sheep of the legend *saḥrah* (example 2.1) are so special.

The narrative tide of the personal experience *saḥrah* sweeps resourcefully beyond the punch line and the pinch line at which the joke and legend *saḥrah*s, respectively, are exhausted. The victim of the *saḥir* is not left to lie there as a dying example of *saḥir,* as is the case in the legend *saḥrah.* The personal experience *saḥrah* continues to tell about some practically minded people who would not allow the death of the he-goat to be a total loss. First, it narrates how a guardsman killed it according to Islamic teachings to make its meat *ḥalāl* (religiously sanctioned). The stream of kerosene that dripped from the bowels of the he-goat to mid-river is a narrative delight. The story goes on to relate how the owners dispensed with its meat only when they realized it was inedible; however, its fat was salvaged by the womenfolk. The hierarchy of uses made of the he-goat is interesting in its own right. Being in a lower status, the nomads, on the one hand, had to rethink what they might get from the meat after its original owners found it distasteful. Women, on the other hand, process oil into lotions for massaging their husbands. Muḥammad's pretense—that he did not know what women could have done with the fat—has overtones of sexual innuendo. He laughed to mark this insinuation.

The joke and legend *saḥrahs* consume the narrative in the buildup of their punch line or pinch line. However, their audiences are compensated for the brevity of the narrative either by the humor or by the validation of belief in these finalizing lines. The personal experience *saḥrah,* however, does not expire at a punch line or a pinch line, and hence cannot afford compromising the narrative diachrony. It badly needs the story to make its point of personal misfortune and impress the audience. A narrator can live with a negative response for a joke or with a belief statement that did not convince the addressee, but failure to win the right response for a story of personal misfortune is difficult to bear.

The communicative hazards of the personal experience *saḥrah* are evident in the special way it turns to the addressee and the problems it runs into regarding finalization. The narrator of personal *saḥrah* needs the narrative diachrony to make his point about *saḥir* as *fakar* (envy). We have defined *fakar* as the act of simultaneously seeing and thinking in envious terms. *Fakar* is by definition attracted to efficient performances. It attacks people who are going diligently about their business and are completely oblivious of those who are watching them closely and enviously. Rubāṭāb define *fakar* as *khalah balū fihū* (lit., putting his mind in him, noticing him closely), like saying "This man works really hard" on seeing a hard-working man. The personal experience *saḥrah* uses the narrative device to present such efficient, oblivious performers before they were struck by the verbal missile. Thus Muḥammad works hard to relate the details of the activity of receiving guests that attracted the *fakar* of Wad al-Tōm, who was sitting idly under the *dom* tree.

The personal experience *saḥrahs* of ʿAbbās ʿAlī Muṣṭafah are a further demonstration of the attention to the details of the activities that preceded the launching of the *saḥir* metaphor.

3.2
Date: 8/20/1984.
Place: Um Ghiday.
Narrator: ʿAbbās ʿAlī Muṣṭafah (see 3.1).
Audience: Al-Shaykh al-Tijānī; Wad Ḥāj ʿAlī (3.1); the collector; and an unidentified audience.

Situation: A follow-up interview to personal experience *saḥrah*s the narrator had told at a wake a week before.

Original language: Arabic.

In '68 rain flooded *Wādī* [watercourse] ʿArab of Atbara River. *Baʿadayn* Muḥammad [his elder brother] was in Atbara but his tractors were here in Um Ghiday. He [Muḥammad] asked me to come driving the tractors to Atbara in order to go together to cultivate grain in *Wādī* ʿArab. I was tied here to my plots of peanuts because it was the planting season. I wanted to cultivate my peanut plots before going to the cultivation of grain. I was pressed to go to *Wādī* ʿArab, but I had still to plant my peanuts. I started working single-handedly because the tenants did not come up with me to plant peanuts. I worked single-handedly on my plots and sowed peanuts. The water pump was big, and during the Nile inundation no less than seven or eight men were needed to handle channelling the flow of water that it pumps out. I kept going down to the bank of the river, turning on the pump, filling up the main canal and the branch canal just enough to water my plots, and then turning it off. I kept blocking up water in the main canal, thus storing it, and then opening up for just enough water to go to the branch canal that I could handle in watering my plot. *Baʿadayn* Wad al-Tōm and company, who used to sit at noon under the *dom* tree Muḥammad mentioned earlier, were chatting as usual. That was a real hot midday in which I was watering my plot. They were talking here

> under the tree and were asking how ʿAbbās was managing pumping the water and irrigating the field at one and the same time. [We have already mentioned how his leg broke as a result of this *saḥir.*]

This scene of inventive, heroic absorption in work underlines the unexpectedness with which the deadly *fakar* takes ʿAbbās out of the active course of events. Speaking is again presented as parasitical on and detrimental to *shaghalah.* Useful and arduous activities unfold in myriad forms in different parts of the narratives. The playful Wad al-Tōm, however, is always spotted by the personal experience *saḥrah* under the shade of the *dom* tree, enviously watching working people. *Saḥir,* in the view of the personal experience *saḥrah,* is a source of hazardous disruptions in life. This view may account for the character of the personal experience *saḥrah,* which articulates the indeterminate world into meaning through the narrative (Dorst 1983, 424).

Addressivity takes on a special character in personal experience *saḥrah.* Addressivity is defined as the quality of being directed to someone, that is, taking into account the appreciative background of the addressee's perception of the speech (Bakhtin 1986, 95). In this example, the narrator addresses a female audience member directly using the feminine marker (*ti*) of the verb.

> 3.3
>
> *Date:* 8/9/1984.
>
> *Place:* ʿAtmūr.
>
> *Narrator:* Khalīfah Muḥammad ʾAḥmad (54 years old), farmer.
>
> *Audience:* Zaynab al-Fakī (65 years old), divorced, custodian of the saintly tombs of her grandfathers; Tāj al-Sir (53 years old), a farmer brought up in central Sudan who came to the village after the economic developments of the 1960s, now a farmer and janitor at the elementary school. Both Zaynab and Tāj are Khalīfah's cousins; ʿUmar (17 years old), Khalīfah's son, was also present.
>
> *Original language:* Arabic.

NARRATOR: Do you see this section of my field where I presently grow my clover? Did you [addressing Zaynab]? I planted this section that summer. The summer was really good. The plot could not contain the crop. That crop could have taken two plots. I cut the crop of the section in one go when I rose up early one morning and cut the crop down. Some women neighbors from——

ZAYNAB: What!

NARRATOR: I cut it down. I cut it down.

ZAYNAB: *Qash* [reeds].

NARRATOR: Yes. I cut down the grain. *Baʿadayn* the women came and started backbiting.

ZAYNAB: Were they women?

NARRATOR: Yes. Women from the neighborhood. They hit me with the evil eye. I gave the words they uttered due attention but soon completely forgot about their words. However, I gave them accusingly a very long stare and, finding themselves caught red-handed, they attributed their *saḥir* metaphor to Wad al-Ḥadaʿ [a famous *saḥḥār*]. By the belief in Allah and this is Tāj al-Sir here to bear witness to what I say. Tāj al-Sir was on his way at that time to harvest the *mushriqyyah* [a kind of date palm] of my uncle which was at the other end of the farm. I went to harvest my own *mushriqyyah*s and the women's words [*saḥir*] were resounding persistently in my heart. It was persistently resounding in my heart. The moment I got up from the palm tree I suddenly forgot [all about it].

ZAYNAB: You did.

Khalīfah went on to tell about how he finally fell from the palm tree into the water at the riverbank. Zaynab then intervened and said she was there and mentioned an attendant circumstance to prove it.

Narrators of this form apparently literally need someone to direct their utterance to. They invariably turn to address or to invite the participation of one individual among the audience. The narrative impetus of the personal experience *saḥrah* breaks the interview framework in which I entrapped the narrator. Faced with an alien collector, the narrators regularly bypassed me to address an audience with whom they could communicate in terms of time, terrain, and landscape. A personal experience *saḥrah* does not seem to succeed at all without this "dramatic" exchange, which introduces confirmation from a second source to help elicit a positive response from the audience.

This personal experience *saḥrah* also exhibits the generic attention to the details of the vigorous performance of the *saḥir*'s victim that made him vulnerable to the women's *fakar*. It is difficult to imagine how the narrative could have taken off without Zaynab. The audience to a personal experience *saḥir* is not there only to act as a credulous listener to the happenings of the narrative. Represented by a selected addressee, the audience is an inherent part of the structure of the personal experience *saḥir*. The narrator may implicitly invite an audience member to jump in by forgetting some details. Thus in example 3.1 the narrator, Muḥammad, omitted—either deliberately or forgetfully—the third group of guests. Similarly, ʿAbbās, the narrator of example 3.2, turned to the audience to aid his recollection in another narrative.

3.4
Situation: Same as 3.2.

ʿABBĀS: That was the time we used to grow peanuts. We grew peanuts here in Um Ghiday. *Baʿadayn.* There was in fact, in actual fact . . . Did we cultivate *Wādī* ʿArab in '68?

AUDIENCE MEMBER: Yes, '68.

In addition, audience members may voluntarily add details to the time or place of the narrative. Khalīfah, who narrated example 3.3, told another personal experience *saḥrah* at the same session. In that *saḥrah* his endurance in carrying sacks and jumping three times with the sacks on his back was likened to a typical jump of a jackass with its saddle on.

3.5
Situation: Same as 3.3.

KHALĪFAH: We were visiting Mahadī, son of Karrār . . .
TĀJ AL-SIR: Al-Mahadī, you said?
KHALĪFAH: Yes, al-Mahadī.
TĀJ AL-SIR: Was Wad Karrār [Mahadī's father] alive?
KHALĪFAH: Wad Karrār, Allah bless his soul, was alive then.

3.6
Situation: Same as 3.5.

KHALĪFAH: This son of mine ʿUmar . . . when they took me out of the water I wanted to swim but they prevented me and I came out of the water. On coming out of the water this son of mine ʿUmar [pointing to him] said, "*Bism Allahī* [in the name of Allah—surprised]. It is really my father. I thought it was a fish [laughter]."

These interactions between the teller and the audience help unfold the personal experience *saḥrah.* Its perception of time and space is too encompassing and seductive to allow an audience to wait lazily for the pinch line or punch line. Before the narrative is completed, many audience members can pitch in details of time or place by way of showing familiarity with the terrain, the dates, and the calamities.

The teller of the personal experience *saḥrah* usually contextualizes the punch line with the introductory part of his narrative. The teller and the audience may find the punch line funny but not final. Furthermore, the personal experience teller expands the pinch line by spelling out the details of the misfortune. An episode of salvaging the damage might be included, as in example 3.1. In his two personal accounts of his *saḥir* (examples 3.3 and

3.5), Khalīfah is very particular about the successful treatment he had for the harm *saḥir* had inflicted on him. Moreover, the teller might digress and include attending circumstances that are of doubtful effect to the impact of the story. Khalīfah includes in example 3.6 a "*saḥir* in the *saḥir*" episode in which his son shot a *saḥrah* at him.

The teller of a personal experience *saḥir* runs into difficulty when it is time to finish the story. Without a boundary line or a conventional formula to constrain him, the teller is left to his own devices to round off his narrative convincingly. It is evident from Muḥammad's narrative (example 3.1) that ending a personal experience *saḥrah* is neither easy nor predictable. As we saw earlier, Muḥammad concluded some of his personal experience *saḥrahs* with happy or ambivalent endings. In example 3.1 he is clearly tripping over the theme of what the womenfolk could have done with the fat they extracted from the he-goat. Of course, Muḥammad was only pretending that he did not know that fat goes into the preparation of ointment for sexual massages. My impression is that he needed his rhetorical question only to finalize his story.

The most common optional ending is "*ʿayn* is bad, the evil eye is bad," which is a brief reflection upon the moral of the story (Dolby-Stahl 1975, 182). Khalīfah concludes his two personal experience *saḥrahs* with this ending. However, this ending is optional, as is demonstrated by the two sessions in which ʿAbbās described his encounters with Wad al-Tōm. After a personal experience recorded at a wake, ʿAbbās used the formula "*al-saḥir kaʿab*" (*saḥir* is bad). In his interview situation, however, he ended one personal experience *saḥrah* by formally and laughingly stating, "There is the thing [the harm] that Wad al-Tōm caused me." He finished up the other saying, "The harm that resulted is from the *saḥir* of Wad al-Tōm. We recognized it as resulting from Wad at-Tōm. As a matter of fact, everything is predestined by Allah. Nothing whatsoever is in the hand of man. A man claims nothing to be his doing but all the same we said they [the misfortunes] are from these *saḥrahs*." This formal ending apparently echoes the question, "What *saḥir* encounter have you had with Wad al-Tōm?" with which I began my interview with him.

Riddle Saḥrah

Of my collection, 3.5 percent are riddle *saḥrah*s. Riddle *saḥrah*s fall into two categories. In the first category, an authority among the *saḥḥār*s may test the skills of other *saḥḥār*s in drawing analogies to objects he selects. The second most common category is that in which a *saḥḥār* would do the same to a junior member of his family. The riddling process is reversed in this genre of *saḥrah.* The riddler poses the answer in order for the riddlee to figure out the question, rather than the other way around, as in regular riddles.

4.1
Date: 6/2/1984.
Place: Kurgus West.
Narrator: Al-Tijānī Kiriz (see 1.1).
Audience: Al-Ṭayyib Muḥammad al-Zākī, Abu al-Qāsim Kiriz, ʿAbd al-Raḥmān Kiriz.
Situation: An open session for recording *saḥrah*s.
Original language: Arabic.

There was . . . al-Ṭāhir Wad ʾAyyūb, as a matter of fact, was a man who speaks *saḥir. Baʿadayn* he was among some people attending a wedding ceremony, and *saḥḥār*s were chatting with him. Some of those people and colleagues were also the type who express themselves [i.e., speak *saḥir*]. He [al-Ṭāhir] realized that some of these *saḥḥār*s indulge excessively in bewitching but attribute their *saḥrah*s to him, saying he said so and so. Al-Ṭāhir addressed them saying, "It is about time to test you in *saḥir,* and if you flunk the test you would be requested not to speak *saḥir* and say al-Ṭāhir said it. If you pass it then you are free to attribute your *saḥrah*s to me." They replied, "What is your test?" He said, "The test is that I want you to analogize the *ʿanqarayb* [a wooden bed, and

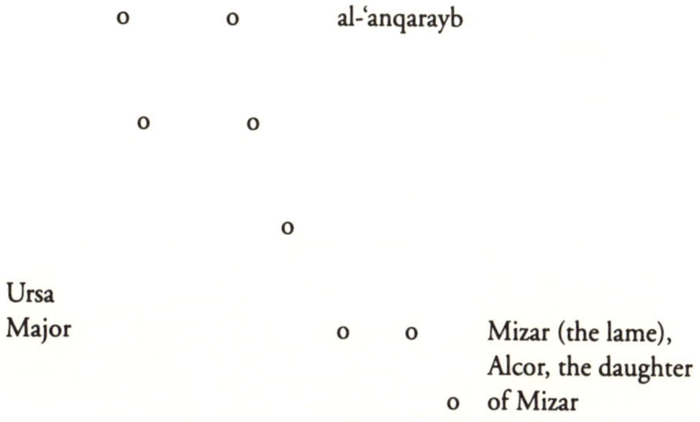

Figure 2 *Saḥir* work: The sky is the limit

also—as it is here—a name for part of *banāt naʿsh* (Ursa Major)] constellation, and to analogize also the clock of Atbara station. And, finally, analogize the turtle when skinned. What do they look like?" They couldn't come up with convincing analogies. Each attempted a description but failed to hit it on the head to the satisfaction of al-Ṭāhir. They gave up and asked him to solve the questions he posed. He said, "The *ʿanqarayb* is like a tractor, Mizar and others are like its disc, and the *ʿirayjah* [lame, diminutive; Alcor] is like the rudder of a tractor" [see fig. 2]. *Baʿadayn* the hands of the clock of Atbara station are like a jackass with his forelegs tied grazing on a grass plot, and who moves in jerks from a grazed section to a new one. *Baʿadayn* when somebody comes to skin a turtle he hangs it up, then lifts its upper shell . . . and its intestines will appear from above like an engine of a truck, the hood of which is lifted to check out the engine.

4.2
Date: 6/15/1984.
Place: Kurgus West.
Narrator: Ṣiddīq al-Ḥibayl (30 years old), a farmer, boatman, and trowel man.

Audience: ʿAbdīn al-Milāwī (28 years old), farmer; Abu al-Qāsim Kiriz; ʿAbd al-Raḥmān Kiriz; al-Tijānī Kiriz (see 1.1).

Situation: Interview to record his repertoire of *saḥrah*s.

Original language: Arabic.

A turtle was lying upright on the river bank. *Baʿadayn* our uncle said, "Bewitch that turtle." We said, "A *saḥrah* is a waste on it looking like a shovel that has no handle." *Baʿadayn* a little girl [his niece] said, "Like a pocket watch."

ABU AL-QĀSIM: Look, this is a *mubārah* [competition].

Although the time-sequencing *baʿadayn* surfaces in these accounts of riddle *saḥrah*s, they do not have such an elaborate plot development as the joke, legend, or personal experience *saḥrah*. As riddles, these riddle *saḥrah*s are also atemporal. The space between posing and solving a riddle, according to Dorst, is temporally void (Dorst 1983, 423). In mapping a culture's categories onto one another, riddle *saḥrah*s are deaf to time. Furthermore, if a riddle can take more than one answer, riddle *saḥrah*s can also take more than one answer, as is evident in example 4.2.

Proverb Saḥrah

A proverb is generically disloyal to the narrative from which it stems. It has to shed its story to make its gnomic potential usable. Rising from the debris of its narrative home, the proverb takes wing for eternity. The process by which proverb *saḥrah*s abandon their narrative in order to be applicable to other situations will be demonstrated by the following cases from my notes. Examples 5.1 and 5.2 are given to contextualize example 5.3.

5.1

Date: 7/14/1984.

Place: Khiḍir's *daywān.*

Source: Field notes.

Ibrahīm al-Kaddab (57 years old) is a villager who owns a lot of land and was the regional secretary of the government-sponsored Socialist Union. He told me that he objected to the idea of having a senior high school for girls in the village. He said that he told Khiḍir ʿAlī Muṣṭafah, the motivator of the idea, that he could see no reason for having the school at ʿAtmūr unless Khiḍir wanted to get its students' food contract. Most importantly, he objected because a girl might come to school pregnant from home but people would accuse the school and ʿAtmūr people of causing her condition.

5.2
Date: 7/23/1984.
Place: Funerary wake.
Source: Field notes.

At midday some ʿAtmūr men were teasing the headmaster of the girls' high school because his students, unlike those of the boys' high school, were absolutely useless regarding the school's self-help construction projects. They called him the "watchman of the watermelons," in reference to the fragility of his students.

Women are traditionally metaphorized as watermelons; thus in a folktale I collected, a mother was made to say that her seven daughters had become ripe watermelons. Someone from the audience interpreted this as reaching the marriageable age. However, the statement discloses the mother's worry that her daughters might pass that age without getting married. Such an old maid is called *baṭṭīkhah laqah* (soggy, overripe watermelon). Since the mid-1970s watermelons have become one of the main cash crops for the Rubāṭāb. They now grow them extensively to meet the demands of the town of Atbara. A Rubāṭābī described the hazards of depending on the watermelon economy by analogizing a watermelon to "bound water," that is, to water enclosed in cases. I once heard ʿAradayb al-Ḥāj, a literate, articulate farmer, persuading Khiḍir to expedite renting his truck so he could take his watermelons to the market, or else "my means of living, which is sheer water, would explode under the scorching sun."

The co-occurrence of the watermelon economy and the opening of the ʿAtmūr girls' senior high school has accentuated the women–watermelon metaphor. The headmaster was likened to a watermelon farmer who has to be constantly on the lookout to protect his watermelons from bursting from the heat. The villagers, of course, have seen the headmaster called time and again to the dormitories to see to the problems of the teenage girls.

5.3
Date: 7/23/1984.
Place: Khiḍir's *daywān.*
Source: Field notes.

Parents or guardians who accompany their daughters, nieces, or other relatives to ʿAtmūr girls' high school stay at Khiḍir's *daywān* until their return. A group of Manāṣīr people who had just checked their daughters in were settling in the *daywān* when I returned from the funerary wake (example 5.2). Embarrassed that he had taken this long trip for the sole purpose of checking in his daughter, a Manṣūrī said, "Surely, girls don't belong to children of Adam." Mughdād al-Rufāʿī said, "Girls are like a water conduit that cracks constantly. To make the water reach the plot that needs to be irrigated in the field, you have to carry dirt in a bucket to fill up the cracks." Mughdād drew here on a *saḥrah* of Muṣṭafah al-Tōm, which was identified as such by some of those around me.

Mughdād went on to tell about an embarrassing experience he had because of his zeal for girls' education. Before the opening of the girls' elementary schools in ʿAtmur and Kurgus, girls of school age were taken to Abū Hashīm school on the east bank of the Nile. Mughdād had volunteered to accompany fifty girls from ʿAtmūr and Kurgus for the first intake competition for Abū Hashīm school. He had agreed to accompany the girls because even their fathers were ashamed to appear in their company. "Not only that," he said, "but they poked

> fun at me for doing that." After that, people at the *daywān* continued talking about how parents would not want to be seen taking their daughters to schools. However, they said that things have changed dramatically. People not only are no longer ashamed of girls' education but they also follow them as far as Omdurman (one of the three towns that make up Sudan's capital city) in pursuit of that education. Mughdād stepped in saying, "And still carrying their buckets and filling up the cracks." The people there burst out laughing.

I was unable to record the narrative from which this punch line on girls and cracked conduits originated. Examples 5.1 and 5.2 clearly show that the self-help project of establishing a girls' high school in the village had created a conflict of ideals. Old metaphors on the fragility of women apparently resurfaced, efficiently utilizing the resources of the culture, such as the occasional discontent with the financial and voluntary labor obligations caused by an ambitious educational project, and the rise of the melon economy. New metaphors also emerge. The *saḥrah* of Muṣṭafah al-Tōm seems to have encapsulated the tensions and aspirations of the times such that it had a gnomic value independent of its narrative. It turned into a proverb, a generic signal of cutting the umbilical cord with its narrative womb.

The appropriateness of the punch line in joke, legend, and personal experience *saḥrah*s is judged by its function in the original narrative. In the proverb *saḥrah,* however, the punch line is answerable to the emerging situation it names. The performer of a joke *saḥrah* analogizes a *haqīqah* (real) situation to a metaphoric one, and the two situations fuse into a joke narrative. Even as an inserted genre, the punch line seems to hold together the perception of time and space in legend and personal experience *saḥrah*s. It is only in the proverb *saḥrah* that the punch line sheds its narrative to sponge on an evolving one. In examples 5.4 and 5.5 we see the text of a legend *saḥrah* and a joke *saḥrah,* respectively, and in example 5.6 we compare how their punch lines are used proverbially.

5.4
Date: 7/17/1984.
Place: ʿAtmūr girls' high school.
Narrator: Fatḥīyyah Wad al-Tōm (17 years old), student and daughter of Wad al-Tōm.
Situation: I wrote the *saḥrah* down in an open session for narrating *saḥrah* after a talk I gave to the students describing my mission.
Original language: Arabic.

Mention was made of a woman who has repeatedly married and divorced. Wad al-Tōm described it as today's slippers (clogs were in fashion then); you only need to change their uppers to keep them in circulation. The woman is said to have suffered from a rash as a result of the *saḥir.* Fatḥīyyah brought up the *saḥrah* to argue that *saḥir* and harm may be related coincidentally and not as a cause and effect.

5.5
Date: 7/14/1984.
Place: Kurgus Island.
Narrator: Ṣiddīq al-Ḥibayl (see 4.2).
Situation: I wrote the text down during a casual conversation.
Original language: Arabic.

It was low river season. A group of men wanted to wade across the river with their jackasses to Kurgus Island. Bābikir, the *shaykh* of ʿAtmūr, asked Ṣiddīq, the boatman, how deep the water was. Ṣiddīq said, "It won't reach the *khaṭṭāf*" [the plunger; here, the penis]. His answer referred to one mechanism of the water pump, which is held to be in working order if the tip of the *khaṭṭāf* only reaches the oil [see fig. 3]. By analogizing the penis to the *khaṭṭāf,* Ṣiddīq wanted to give Bābikir an idea of how deep the water was. It is said that Bābikir did not understand Ṣiddīq's point at first. After a few strides

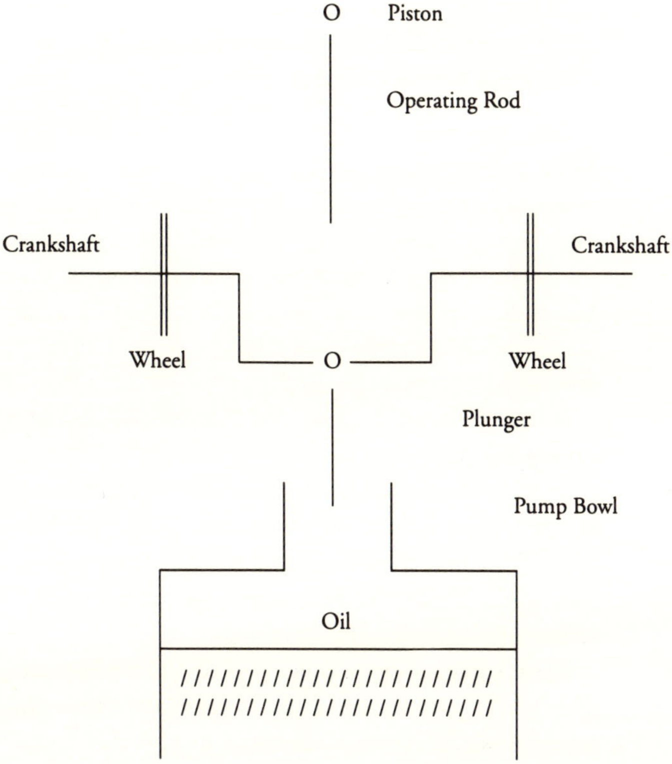

Figure 3 Machines as the measure of men

in the water, it dawned on him and he burst out laughing and had to seek the support of his jackass lest he fall in the water. Both of these *saḥrah*s were used proverbially on another occasion to tease a local man.

5.6

Date: 7/20/1984.

Place: ʿAtmūr.

Occasion: A wedding contract ceremony.

Audience: Among those present are Wad al-Tōm (see 1.3), Ḥasan Jaqalaybah (65 years old), ʿAradayb al-Ḥāj (63 years

old), and Khalīd (40 years old), all farmers; ʿUthmān al-Māḥī (42 years old), headmaster of the girls' high school.
Original language: Arabic.

The *wanasah* session took the *mulākadah* teasing form. It first focused on the newly married ʿUthmān al-Māḥī, whose procedures for moving his wife to his newly built house were closely observed by the villagers. ʿUthmān, however, asked his teasers to have mercy on him and to redirect their *mulākadah* to Khalīd. Khalīd's performance after his second marriage to a divorcée a few weeks ago was also under severe scrutiny from the villagers. Villagers noticed that Khalīd had abandoned calling for prayers as he used to. He also took unusual care of his appearance on the days of the week he went to his new wife, who lived on Jaʿdināt Island off Kurgus West. When mention was made of Khalīd's wife, Wad al-Tōm said, "That wife, the one he renewed her upper," in reference to the clog *saḥrah* of 5.4.

Next, someone mentioned how Khalīd held up the tip of his *jalābiyyah* (loose, shirtlike garment) in his hands when he waded through the water to his wife's home on Jaʿdināt Island. Another likened that scene to someone carrying a male sheep in his arms, in reference to the brown color of Khalīd's *jalābiyyah.* (Incidentally, carrying sheep in one's arms is formulaic in *saḥrah*s. The wading theme led to the *khaṭṭāf saḥrah* of 5.5.) Someone said that if the water level reached the *khaṭṭāf* when Khalīd wades his way back from his wife's home, Khalīd would not need to perform the ritual bathing required by Islam after sexual intercourse. Seeing that Khalīd had been excessively exposed to verbal stings, Wad al-Tōm described him as a person who found a scorpion in his pants, that is, it stings him wherever he turns.

In recalling these proverbial punch lines, the audience may not know or care about the original circumstances that gave rise to them. The ready-made punch lines were applied to a new, emerging situation to help it take off.

Displayed Saḥrah*s*

The proverbial use of a *saḥrah* depends mainly on recalling punch lines from previous *saḥrah*s. In the *saḥrah*s that are displayed, punch lines are usually improvised by *saḥḥār*s while physically enacting them to an audience. Wad al-Tōm and Muḥammad al-Khayr ʿUmar of ʿAmakī village are famous for performing together such acts of *saḥrah.* Muḥammad al-Khayr calls these acts *mujādaʿah,* which seems to cover all forms of artistic exchange. Seeing Wad al-Tōm, he said, inspires him with *saḥrah*s. He also pointed to al-Ḥasayn Wad ʾAḥmad, who spurs them on to start and continue the *saḥrah*s exchange. The role of such a hidden "scriptwriter" is the more interesting because it seems to be prevalent in the creation of verbal art among the Rubāṭāb. However, the role is especially conspicuous in the *aṭ-ṭirī* genre of Rubāṭāb verbal duels. The following examples illustrate this intricate use of *saḥrah*s.

6.1
Date: 8/6/1984.
Place: ʿAtmūr.
Narrator: Wad al-Tōm (see 1.3).
Situation: Interview.
Original language: Arabic.

Muḥammad al-Khayr came to offer his condolences at a funerary wake. The moment he raised the *fātihah* [the act of lifting the arms in a horizontal position with the hands open and reciting the first Sura of the Koran to the soul of the deceased], I hid behind a pillar. People asked me why I hid. I said, "I want to hide in this shelter to kill the crocodile, that is, Muḥammad al-Khayr." In hunting crocodiles the practice is that the hunter hides in a quiet place where a crocodile has been spotted. People then alerted Muḥammad al-Khayr to the fact that I was hid-ing in pursuit of him. *Baʿadayn* he got really scared, but the whole thing was a pretense of aggression.

6.2
Date: 8/22/1984.
Place: ʿAmakī.
Narrator: Muḥammad al-Khayr, a farmer.
Situation: Interview.
Original language: Arabic.

I was sitting at ʿAbd al-Raḥmān's home when Wad al-Tōm entered. He said to me, "You look jumpy today like a cat puffing up its tail on seeing a dog." He started staring at me. I looked and saw that his beard was not shaven and his hair had a greenlike grayness. I said to him, "You look like a *ḥamāmī* [green] jackass."

6.3
Date: 7/22/1984.
Place: ʿAtmūr, a funerary wake.

My entry for the day reads "People started telling stories about the encounters of Wad al-Tōm and Muḥammad al-Khayr. They narrated the one about the metaphor of cat and dog [6.2]. Muḥammad al-Khayr was said to have answered, 'I was told that you flew a wheel a few days ago,' in reference to the accident in which Wad al-Tōm fell from a tree while cutting one of its branches with an axe. The falling of the axe is likened to the wheel of the water pump, which sometimes flies from the pump because of poor maintenance."

The acting function that some *saḥḥārs* assume enhances their *wannās* role, which is viewed ambivalently by the community. By enacting their *saḥrahs*, the *saḥḥārs* are making a bid for an added measure of performative power. Bauman aptly characterizes this power:

Indeed, the physical acting out of the metaphors was intended as a means of enhancing their rhetorical power; the intersemiotic translation from the verbal to the physical codes enabled the act of communicating to seize the attention of on-lookers especially effectively, by making visible the semantic anomaly inherent in the metaphorical juxtaposition of subjects that belonged together only by a stretch of the imagination (Bauman 1983, 86).

Notes

Introduction

1. For early ethnographic and historical notes on the Rubāṭāb, see Crowfoot (1918) and Lorimer (1936).

2. The Jaʿalīyyīn is used in northern Sudanese genealogies in both a general and restricted sense. The former includes all the riverain dwellers between Dongola and the Six Cataracts such as the Bidayrīyyah, Shāīqīyyah, and Rubāṭāb. The latter is restricted to the Jaʿalīyyīn proper, who live between the confluence of the Atbara River and the Nile and the Six Cataracts (Hasan, 1967).

3. Shmuel Moreh, *Live Theater and Dramatic Literature in the Medieval Arab World* (Edinburgh: Edinburgh University Press, 1992).

Chapter One

1. Teaching, a major occupation for intermediate and high school Rubāṭāb graduates, was hit hard by this reversal of fortune in which farmers began to earn more than teachers. A farmer was poking fun of teachers in their presence, recalling those days when they were the cream of the villages. A teacher showed me a poem he composed as a rejoinder to a girls' song deprecating teachers and banishing them from the realm of dream suitors for Rubāṭāb girls.

Chapter Two

1. For a novel association between crocodile/*saḥḥārs* and the drama of spirit possession in northern Sudan, see Boddy (1989).

Chapter Three

1. In Rubāṭāb usage, *bidʿah* refers to something that has never been said or done before. The connotation of that, however, is negative. The Arabic root of *bidʿah* is *bdʿ*, from which the standard *bidʿah* and *ʾibdāʿ* (creation) are derived. Standard *bidʿah* refers in religious discourse to all innovated practices that have no sanction from the established religious or social norms. In literary discourse *ʾibdāʿ* covers all forms of artistic creativity.

2. The people of ʿAtmūr take pride in the fact that their village, unlike others, has no market day or marketplace where idle talk takes place.

3. *Aṭ-ṭirī,* or *aṭ-ṭaryān,* is my coinage based on the verb *ṭirah* (mention) which Rubāṭāb poets invariably use to denote their poetic project. A poet would say, for example, "*ṭirītū qultah*" (I mentioned him and said) to mark this kind of

poetry. There is no ethnic term for the genre. I ran into *ghunah* (singing), though the genre is rarely sung. The poem-duel is referred to as *mujāda'ah* (throwing at each other), but the term is used also to denote other forms of "singing" poetry where two or more persons are involved.

4. Neither 'Antarah nor Abu Zeid's *sirah* (romances) are narrated among the Rubāṭāb. Abu Zeid al-Hilali, Rubāṭāb of 'Atmūr village tell, came to the riverbank of their village. He could not reach the water because the bank was high. Thirsty and at "a dog's throw" from the Nile, Abu Zeid named the village "'Atmūr" (desert). You will hear little more than that about Abu Zeid. Romances about Abu Zeid are more likely to come from women. The episodes I collected in 1984 and the one I published in 1968 (Ibrahim and Nasr 1968, 42–64) were both narrated by women. The latter episode even took the *qālū*, the formulaic beginning of *ḥujah*.

5. The numinous refers to supernatural (or rather paranormal) beings, energies, and entities in the legend literature (Degh and Vazsonyi 1973, 18).

6. Negative legends denote narratives telling in their simple form a horrible experience that implies a supernatural encounter but releases the tension by finding sober explanations for the adventure (Degh and Vazsonyi 1976, 112).

7. "Ficts" is the technical term used by folklorists to cover these fictive notions, which, like popular beliefs, have the form of assertions. They include "taboo ficts," which describe the consequences of infringing a taboo (Von Sydow 1948, 87–88).

8. A byplay is a communicative medium that a subset of participants in an encounter create by withdrawing from the more inclusive encounter (Goffman 1981, 61).

Chapter Four

1. The notion of risk in performance is lucidly developed by Yankah (1985).

2. The length of the journey that makes it permissible for one to offer shortened prayers is one day and one night, or forty-eight miles. The period of stay during which one should offer shortened prayers is ten to nineteen days, according to different narrated traditions from the prophet (see *Ṣaḥīḥ al-Bukhārī,* 2:107–11).

3. The last two chapters of the Koran, *Al-Falaq* (The Daybreak) and *Al-Nas* (Mankind), both open with the words "*Qul a'udhū bi rabbī . . .* " (Say I seek refuge in the Lord of . . .) and are therefore known as *al-Mu'awwidhatān* (Piamenta 1979, 96).

4. *Qaraḍ* literally is "to gnaw." Later mention will be made of a "gnawing" idiom the Rubāṭāb use to describe the fatal effects of *saḥir.*

5. I assigned a *saḥrah* to be a "praise," "depraise," or "guess" from the textual, contextual, and textural indicators of the Rubāṭāb culture. I admit to a number of arbitrary identifications, which are unavoidable but which I hope underline the correctness of the general picture I attempted to draw regarding the topicality of *saḥir.* All the disclaimed *saḥrah*s were assigned to "depraise." I assigned a *saḥrah* to "praise," for example, when it was a positive, congratulatory statement such as the one in which a *saḥḥār* compared the successful planting of his

date palm shoots to a school that was famous for the success of its final class in entering to the higher stage. I considered "depraise" analogizing a school from which one pupil enters that higher stage to a kind of schoolboys' lottery. Judging by the texture of the Rubāṭāb male culture, I assigned two *saḥrahs* about the female gender as "depraise," though they may strike the reader as guessing. I assigned "guessing" to cases where no obvious ulterior sentiment is involved in the generation of the *saḥrah. Saḥrahs* of gnomic value are an example of this. Riddling with *saḥir* is another ideal situation of guessing.

Chapter Five

1. Malinowski describes the primary, associational function of words as acting in virtue of "their mysterious connection with some aspects of reality," not in "virtue of their ordinary colloquial meaning" (1965, 2:218).

2. Austin maintains that an illocutionary act is constituted not by intention or by fact, essentially, but by convention (1962, 129).

3. In his theory of play, Bateson's "territory" and "map" approximate Basso's "primary" and "secondary" texts, respectively (Bateson 1972, 182, 185). Goffman uses Bateson's distinction between territory and map to suggest his own "primary understandings" and "transformations" for analyzing play and fantasy. He defines "primary understandings" as an activity already having a meaning on its own terms, such as fighting. In play, he states, bitinglike behavior occurs but no one is seriously bitten. Because it is so keyed to differentiate it from fighting, play is said by Goffman to be a transformation or a transcription of "a strip of fighting behavior into a strip of play." "Key" is understood by Goffman to indicate the set of conventions by which a primary understanding (a "territory" in Bateson's terms) is transformed into something patterned on this activity but seen by the participants to be something quite different ("map" in Bateson's terms) (Goffman 1974, 40–44). Hoppal gives a useful background note on the related concept of "possible world" in modern text analysis (1980, 122–23).

4. These formulae are not exactly prophylactic in the religious sense. Rather, they are uttered to mark a text as a lie and to comment on its performance. They are not intended to protect the utterer except in a very general sense.

5. An imbecile text can also be considered as *Iblīs*-inspired. An imbecile is said to be *mabdūl* (changeling) in reference to the belief that because his family failed to attend to him as a child, the child attracted the jinn by his constant cries and the jinn substituted one of their own for him.

6. This is remindful of what Bakhtin says about the authoritativeness of authoritative discourse: "Therefore authoritative discourse permits no play with the context framing it, no play with its borders, no gradual creative stylizing variants on it. It enters our verbal consciousness as a compact and indivisible mass; one must either totally affirm it or totally reject it" (1981, 343).

7. For the varied contexts in which these formulae are used, see Piamenta (1979, 94, 155).

8. The Rubāṭāb have an image of themselves as being an envious people. They cite the tale type 1331 ("The Covetous and the Envious") in the Arne/Thompson folktale index in support of this negative image. The tale, as

summarized by Dundes, tells of two envious men. One is given the power of fulfilling any wish on condition that the other shall receive double. He wishes that he may lose one eye (1981, 278).

9. This what the Rubāṭāb do with a range of fruits, herbs, and charms that are prescribed for a cure.

Chapter Six

1. Bakhtin defines dialogical relationships as a special type of semantic relationship whose members can be whole utterances. Such a relationship can exist even between two utterances separate from each other in both time and space, knowing nothing about each other, if—in juxtaposition—they reveal some semantic convergence. These relations, according to Bakhtin, cannot be reduced to contradiction, struggle, or disagreement because agreement is one of the most important forms of dialogical relationships (1986, 124). Todorov uses the term "intertexuality," introduced by Kristeva in her presentation of Bakhtin, for the more inclusive meaning of "dialogical" (1984, 60).

2. The exact phrase is taken from an earlier translation of the same text published in *Soviet Studies in Literature* 3, no. 33 (Winter 1977–78): 23.

3. The article perceptively presents the folklore performance of a couple, a joke teller and a legend teller, who "seemed to be engaged in an everlasting never-to-be resolved debate, caused by the conflicting ideologies manifested by a rationalistic joke-teller and a mystic-transcendentalist legend teller" (Degh and Vazsonyi 1976, 109).

4. In connection with literature, Herandi calls this will the writer's "formative intention" (Kent 1986, 36).

5. El-Shamy argues that "the genre to which a tale belongs is reckoned according to the story's style and content, and, more importantly, according to the narrator's intent" (1980, xliv).

6. Other generic marks used by some narrators are *fiʿaln* (for a fact) and *ṭabʿan* (as a matter of fact).

Glossary

ʿālim (pl. *ulama*). custodian of Islamic traditions; canonist and theologian; preacher.

"ʿAllahu ʾakbarʾ ʿalayk!" "'Allah is great' on you!" "*Allahu ʾakbar*" is the war cry of Islam. When it is invoked in the context of *saḥir* it apparently identifies the *saḥḥār* as an unbeliever.

ʿaqīdah belief.

ʿArabī a nomad.

asḥar I bewitch.

aṭ-ṭaryān or aṭ-ṭirī a poetic genre of lampooning and ridicule.

"Aʿūdhu billah" "I seek refuge in Allah."

awlād son of.

ʿayn, al-ʿayn eye, evil eye.

ʿayn ḥarah "hot eye," evil eye.

ʿayn ḥasdah "envious eye."

baʿadayn after that.

bakḥarah a piece of paper on which Koranic verses and other healing formulae are inscribed; they are burned out and fumigated for healing.

baladīyyah town hall.

balāgh notification.

balīlah boiled beans or grains.

banāt naʿsh Ursa Major.

barashōt from "parachute"; the illegal border trade between Ethiopia and Sudan after World War II.

bidʿa (sing. *bidʿah*). something that has never been said or done before. The connotation is usually negative.

budaʿī speaker of things never heard before; an entertainer; a *wannās.*

būghah communal work.

daḥlūb a stone carved out for use as a receptable.

daywān guest house.

dom a type of tree.

faddān a square measure of 4200.833 m^2.

fakar seeing and thinking in envious terms; envy.

fakī or faqīr (pl. *fuqurah*). Koran schoolteacher; maker of charms and medical cures; a holy or religious man; or all three of these in one.

fanqas to kneel while sticking out one's butt; a form of witchcraft.

fāqah leisure.

al-fārghah empty words; refers disparagingly to folklore materials.

fatwah legal opinion.

fellahin Egyptian farmers.

fī al-ḥaqīqah in actual fact.

filān such and such of the people.

ghāytū	to cut a long story short.
al-ghinah	prosperity.
al-ghunah	singing; composing poetry; lyrical songs.
ḥaq	property or legacy.
al-ḥaqīqah	in fact.
al-ḥaqīqīyyah	actually.
ḥarām	sinful, not sanctioned by religion.
ḥarjal	African rye.
ḥarjamnah	not butchered according to Islamic regulations.
ḥasad	envy.
hiẓār	kidding.
ḥōsh	enclosure.
ḥujah	(sing. *ḥajwah*). *Märchen;* magic tales.
Iblīs	the principal *shayṭān* (devil).
istiʿadhah	utterance of "*aʿūdhu billah.*"
istiʿārah	metaphor.
istiʿmār	colonialism.
jalābiyyah	a loose, shirtlike garment.
kaʿab	really evil.
kadāyah	picnic; food eaten on such an occasion.
karāmāt	miraculous manifestations.
khadamnah	served.
khalwah	a studying and teaching center of Koran; guest house.

khaṭṭāf	a plunger of a water pump.
kirāyah	hired hand; working for money.
mabdūl	changeling.
maddāḥ	(pl. *muddāḥ*). an itinerant singer of the praise of the Prophet.
madhhab	(pl. *madhahib*). school of Islamic jurisprudence.
maḥajjab	protected by amulets.
maḥajjar	fossilized.
maqālāt	(sing. *maqālah*). narrative of real or presumably real occurrences; proverbs; folklore; an usual spectacle.
masākhah	(lit. saltlessness). insipid talk; a genre of Rubāṭāb humor.
māshallah	what Allah willed.
"Ma tasḥarnī"	"Don't bewitch me."
mathal	example or proverb.
mujadaʿaḥ	throwing at each other; two or more people taking turns performing items of the same genre of folklore.
mukhātah	from *khātah:* to charge, to take offense; verbal insult.
mulākadah	(lit. elbowing). a speech act of teasing.
nās al-balad	village people.
nawādir	(sing. *nādrah*). stories about rare or unprecedented occurrences and, as such, amusing.
niʿmah	blessing.
niyyah	intention.

nuktah	joke.
omdah	mayor.
qāl	said.
"Qāl Allah, qāl al-Rasūl"	"Allah said, [His] Messenger said."
qālū	they said.
qaraḍōk	they killed you.
qaṣr al-ḥadīth	shortened talk.
qaṭīʿah	backbiting.
qiṣṣah	story.
qiwālah	gossip.
"qūlnah wa qālū"	"we said, they said"; gossip.
quṣād	right to have prior claim to land that corresponds to one's *sāqyah* (farm).
ruṭānah	a gibberish.
sabab	cause.
saḥarak	he bewitched you.
saḥḥār	the shooter of the evil eye metaphor.
saḥir	the symbolic interaction in which the evil eye metaphor is shot.
sāḥir	the standard Arabic for magician, sorcerer, and witch.
saḥrah	the generic name for the oral reports of a *saḥir* event rendered by the *saḥḥār,* the victim of his metaphor, or the audience.
ṣaʿid	south.

salikh grilling.

sāqyah waterwheel, also metonymic for farm.

shaghalah work; "busy, busy" attitude; workaholism.

sharīʿah orthodoxy; the revealed, or canonical, law of Islam.

shaykh village head.

shayṭān devil.

shurād escape.

sīd owner.

siḥr the standard Arabic for magic, sorcery, witchcraft, and talisman.

sīyāsah politics.

sōmār a women's singing genre performed just before the circumcision of boys, in which the merits of the lineages to which the boys belong are summarized.

sunnah the saying and doing of Prophet Muhammad, later established as legally binding precedents.

ṭabʿan as a matter of fact.

tamthīl allegory.

tanaṣul disclaim.

ṭarīqah (pl. *ṭuruq*). a Sufi brotherhood.

tashbīh simile.

tashfag to fear.

ṭashīsh losing one's way.

taʿwīdhah or **al-taʿawdh** utterance of "*aʿūdhu billah.*"

tukum — a forked log of wood, the forked part of which is woven with ropes to provide a seat for those who drive the oxen.

wādī — watercourse.

walī — saint.

wanāsah — a speech event of casual talk; whiling away time.

wannās — adept in *wanāsah,* entertainer; *budaʿī.*

waṣif — analogy, description.

waṣṣāfīn — (sing. *waṣṣāf*). clever at drawing analogies, good at description.

yasḥar — to bewitch.

yisaʿlaw — a verb derived from *siʿlwah* (ogress), to transform into a *saḥḥār.*

yūm — the day appointed by Allah for one's death.

zikir — ritual swaying (dance) in Sufi gathering.

ziyārah — visit; a ritualistic visit to a *walī.*

Bibliography

Abdalsalaam, Sharfaldin A. 1983. *A study of contemporary Sudanese Muslim saints' legends.* Ph.D. diss., Indiana University.

Abraham, Roger. 1968. Introductory remarks to a rhetorical theory of folklore. *Journal of American Folklore* 81:143–58.

———. 1983. Interpreting folklore ethnographically and sociologically. In *Handbook of American folklore,* edited by Richard Dorson. Bloomington: Indiana University Press.

Abu Deeb, Kamal. 1979. *Jurjani's theory of poetic imagery.* Warminster, England: Aris & Phillips.

Abu-Lughod, Lila. 1986. *Veiled sentiments.* Berkeley: University of California Press.

———. 1990. Anthropology's orient: The boundaries of theory on the Arab world. In *Theory, politics and the Arab world,* edited by Hisham Sharabi. New York: Routledge.

Abu Zahra, Nadia. 1988. The rain ritual as rites of spiritual passage. *International Journal of Middle East Studies* 20:507–39.

Ahern, E. M. 1979. Problem of efficacy: Strong and weak illocutionary acts. *Man* (n.s.) 17:1–17.

Ahmed, Akbar S. 1987. Toward Islamic anthropology. *American Journal of Islamic Social Science* 3:181–230.

Arens, William. 1979. *The man eating myth.* New York: Oxford University Press.

Arkoun, Mohammed. 1988. Imaginaire social et leaders dans le monde musulman contemporain. *Arabia* 35:18–35.

Asad, Talal. 1986. *The idea of an anthropology of Islam.* Ocassional Papers Series. Washington: Georgetown University, Center for Contemporary Arab Studies.

Ashcroft, Bill, Gareth Griffiths, and Helen Tiffin. 1989. *The empire writes back.* London: Routledge.

Austin, J. L. 1962. *How to do things with words.* Cambridge: Harvard University Press.

al-ʾAzraq, Ibrāhīm. 1905/1906. *Kitāb Tashhīl al-Manāfiʿ fi al-Ṭib wa al-Ḥikmah.* Cairo: Maktabat al-Kutub.

Bakhtin, M. M. 1968. *Rabelais and his world.* Cambridge, Mass.: MIT Press.

———. 1977–78. The problem of the text. *Soviet Studies in Literature* 14 (Winter): 3–33.

———. 1981. *The dialogic imagination.* Austin: University of Texas Press.

———. 1986. *Speech genres and other late essays.* Austin: University of Texas Press.

Barber, Karin. 1991. *I could speak until tomorrow: Oriki women and the past in a Yoruba town.* Edinburgh: Edinburgh University Press.

BIBLIOGRAPHY

Barclay, Harold B. 1964. *Buurri Al-Lamaab.* Ithaca: Cornell University Press.

Basso, Keith B. 1983. *Portraits of "The Whiteman."* London: Cambridge University Press.

Bateson, Gregory. 1972. *Steps to an ecology of mind.* New York: Random House.

Bauman, Richard. 1975. Quaker folk linguistics and folklore. In *Communication,* edited by Dan Ben-Amos and Kenneth Goldstein. The Hague: Mouton.

———. 1977. *Verbal art as performance.* Rowley, Mass.: Newbury House.

———. 1983a. The field of study of folklore in context. In *Handbook of American folklore,* edited by Richard M. Dorson. Bloomington: Indiana University Press.

———. 1983b. *Let your words be few.* London: Cambridge University.

———. 1986. Performance and honor in 13th-century Iceland. *Journal of American Folklore* 99:131–48.

Ben-Amos, Dan. 1975. Toward a definition of folklore in context. In *Toward new perspectives in folklore,* edited by Americo Paredes and Richard Bauman. Austin: University of Texas Press.

———. 1976a. Analytical categories and ethnic genres. In *Folklore genres,* edited by Dan Ben-Amos. Austin: University of Texas Press.

———. 1976b. Introduction. In *Folklore genres,* edited by Dan Ben-Amos. Austin: University of Texas Press.

Bergson, Henri. 1911. *Laughter.* Translated by Cloudesly Breeton. London: Macmillan.

Bhabha, Homi K. 1984a. Of mimicry and man: The ambivalence of colonial discourse. *October* 28 (Spring): 125–33.

———. 1984b. Representation and the colonial text: A critical exploration of some forms of mimeticism. In *The theory of reading,* edited by Frank Gloversmith. Brighton, England: Harvester.

———. 1985. Signs taken for wonders: Questions of ambivalence and authority under a tree outside Delhi. In *Europe and its others,* edited by Francis Barker, Peter Hulme, Margaret Iverson, and Diana Loxley. Clochster, England: University of Essex.

Binder, Leonard. 1988. *Islamic liberalism.* Chicago: University of Chicago Press.

Boddy, Janice. 1989. *Wombs and alien spirits: Women, men, and the Zar cult in northern Sudan.* Madison: University of Wisconsin Press.

Bourdieu, Pierre. 1977. *Outline of a theory of practice.* Cambridge: Cambridge University Press.

Bousfield, John. 1985. Good, evil and spiritual power: Reflections on Sufi teachings. In *The anthropology of evil,* edited by David Parkin. New York: Basil Blackwell.

Brown, Michael F. 1984. The role of words in Aguaruna hunting magic. *American Ethnologist* 11:545–58.

Brown, Paula, and Donald Tuzin. 1983. *The ethnography of cannibalism.* Washington, D.C.: Society for Psychological Anthropology.

al-Bukhārī, Muḥammad Ibn Isma'il. See *Ṣaḥīḥ al-Bukhārī.*

Cantarino, Vicente. 1975. *Arabic poetics in the Golden Age.* Leiden: Brill.

Caton, Steven C. 1986. Salam Tahiyah: Greetings from the highlands of Yemen. *American Ethnologist* 13:290–308.

———. 1987. Power, persuasion and language: A critique of the segmentary model in the Middle East. *International Journal of Middle East Studies* 19:77–102.

———. 1990. *"Peaks of Yemen I summon": Poetry as cultural practice in a north Yemni tribe.* Berkeley: University of California Press.

Chereáchāin, Firinne Ni. 1992. If I were a woman, I'd never marry an African. *African Affairs* 92:241–47.

Ciardi, John. 1972. *Manner of speaking.* New Brunswick: Rutgers University Press.

Comaroff, John, and Jean Comaroff. 1987. The madman and the migrant: Work and labor in the historical consciousness of a South African people. *American Ethnologist* 14:191–209.

Coplan, David. 1992. History is eaten whole: Consuming tropes in Sesotho agriculture. Paper presented to the Seminar of the Institute for Advanced Research and Study of African Humanities, March 16, at Evanston, Illinois.

Crick, Malcolm. 1976. *Explorations in language and meaning.* New York: John Wiley & Sons.

Crowfoot, J. W. 1918. Customs of the Rubatab. *Sudan Notes and Records* 1, no. 2:117–45.

Degh, Linda. 1968. *Folktales and society.* Translated by Emily M. Schlossberger. Bloomington: Indiana University Press.

———. 1972. Folk narrative. In *Folklore and folklike,* edited by Richard Dorson. Chicago: Chicago University Press.

———. 1976. Symbiosis of joke and legend: A case of conversational folklore. In *Folklore today,* edited by Linda Degh, Henry Glassie, and Felix Oinas. Bloomington: Indiana University Press.

———. 1979. *Biology of storytelling.* Bloomington: Folklore Publications Group.

Degh, Linda, and Andrew Vazsonyi. 1973. *The dialectic of legend.* Bloomington: Folklore Publication Group.

———. 1974. The memorate and the proto-memorate. *Journal of American Folklore* 87:223–39.

———. 1976. Legend and belief. In *Folklore genres,* edited by Dan Ben-Amos. Austin: University of Texas Press.

Dionisopoulos-Mass, Regina. 1976. The evil eye and bewitchment in a peasant village. In *The evil eye,* edited by Clarence Maloney. New York: Columbia University Press.

al-Diwayk, Muḥammad T. S. 1984. *Al-Qaṣaṣ al-Shaʿbī fī Qatr.* 2 vols. Al-Doha: Markaz al-Turāth al-Shaʿbī Li Dūwal al-Khalīj al-ʿArabīyyah.

Dolby-Stahl, Sandra. 1975. The personal narrative as a folklore genre. Ph.D. diss., Indiana University.

———. 1985. A literary folkloristic methodology of the study of meaning in personal narratives. In Papers of the 8th Congress for the International Society for Folk Narrative Research, Bergen: 1984. A revised version was later published in *Journal of Folklore Research* 22:45–69.

Donaldson, Bess A. 1981. The evil eye in Iran. In *The evil eye: A folklore casebook,* edited by Alan Dundes. New York: Garland Publishing.

Dorson, Richard. 1972. *Folklore and folklike.* Chicago: Chicago University Press.

———. 1979. *African folklore.* Bloomington: Indiana University Press.

Dorst, John D. 1983. Neck-riddle as a dialogue of genres: Applying Bakhtin's genre theory. *Journal of American Folklore* 96:413–33.

Douglas, Mary. 1970. Introduction. In *Witchcraft: Confessions and accusation,* edited by Mary Douglas. London: Tavistock.

Dundes, Alan. 1966. Metafolklore and oral literary criticism. *The Monist* 50:505–16.

———. 1981. Wet and dry, the evil eye: An essay in Indo-European and Semitic worldview. In *The evil eye: A folklore casebook,* edited by Alan Dundes. New York: Garland Publishing.

Early, Evelyn A. 1993. *Baladi women of Cairo: Playing with an egg and a stone.* Boulder, Colo.: Lynne Rienner Publishers.

Eickelman, Dale. 1981. *The Middle East: An anthropological approach.* Engelwood Cliffs: Prentice-Hall.

———. 1985. *Knowledge and power.* Princeton: Princeton University Press.

Elworthy, Frederick. 1895. *The evil eye.* London: John Murray.

Emara, Yassine Anter. 1979. Looking for trouble. *Sudanow,* December, 7–8.

Encyclopaedia of Islam (New edition), s.v. *'Ayn.* Leiden: Brill.

Engels, F. 1972. *The origin of the family, private property, and the state.* New York: Passfinder Press.

Evans-Pritchard, E. 1980. *Witchcraft, oracles and magic among the Azande.* Oxford: Clarendon Press.

Fabian, Johannes. 1990. *Power and performance: Ethnographic explorations through proverbial wisdom and theater in Shaba, Zaire.* Madison: University of Wisconsin Press.

Fanon, Frantz. 1967. *Black skin, white masks.* New York: Grove.

Faruqi, Ismail, and Lois L. 1986. *The cultural atlas of Islam.* New York: Macmillan.

Favret-Saada, Jeanne. 1977. *Deadly words: Witchcraft in the Bocage.* Cambridge: Cambridge University Press.

Fernandez, James. 1974. The mission of metaphor in expressive culture. *Current Anthropology* 15:119–45.

———. 1986. *Persuasion and performance.* Bloomington: Indiana University Press.

Flores-Meiser, Enya. 1976. The hot mouth and evil eye. In *The evil eye,* edited by Clarence Maloney. New York: Columbia University Press.

Foucault, Michel. 1972. *The archaeology of knowledge.* Translated by A. M. Sheridan Smith. New York: Pantheon Books.

Furniss, Graham. 1992. Oral culture and the making of meaning. *African Affairs* 91, no. 363:271–76.

Galt, Anthony H. 1982. The evil eye as synthetic image and its meaning on the Island of Pantelleria. *American Ethnologist* 9:664–81.

Garrison, Vivian, and Conrad Arensberg. 1976. The evil eye: Envy or risk or seizure? Paranoia or paternal dependency. In *The evil eye,* edited by Clarence Maloney. New York: Columbia University Press.

Geertz, Clifford. 1988. *Works and lives: The anthropologist as author.* Stanford: Stanford University Press.

al-Ghazzali, Abū Ḥāmid M. 1965. *'Iḥyā' 'Ulūm al-Dīn.* 5 vols. Cairo: Al-Maktabah al-Tijarīyyah al-Kubrah.

Gilsenan, Michael. 1982. *Recognizing Islam.* New York: Pantheon Books.

Goffman, Erving. 1974. *Frame analysis.* New York: Harper & Row.

———. 1981. *Encounters.* Indianapolis: Bobbs-Merrill Educational Publishing.

Griffiths, V. L., and Abdel Rahman A. Taha. 1936. *Sudan courtesy customs.* Khartoum: Sudan Government.

Gwyndaf, Robin. 1984. Memorates, chronicates and anecdotes in action: Some remarks towards the definition of the personal narrative in context. Paper of the 8th Congress for the International Society of Folk Narrative Research, Bergen.

Hamori, Andras. 1974. *On the art of medieval Arabic literature.* Princeton: Princeton University Press.

Harfouche, Jamal K. 1981. The evil eye and infant health in Lebanon. In *The evil eye: A folklore casebook,* edited by Alan Dundes. New York: Garland Publishing.

Herzfeld, Michael. 1981. Meaning and morality: A semiotic approach to evil eye accusations in a Greek village. *American Ethnologist* 8:560–74.

———. 1982. *Ours once more: Folklore, ideology and the making of modern Greece.* Austin: University of Texas Press.

———. 1983. An indigenous theory of meaning and its elicitation in performative context. *Semiotica* 34:113–41.

———. 1985. Levi-Strauss in the nation state. *Journal of American Folklore* 98:191–208.

Hocart, A. M. 1938. The mechanism of the evil eye. *Folk-Lore* 49:156–57.

Hockett, C. F. 1977. *The view from language.* Athens: University of Georgia Press.

Hodgson, Marshall G. S. 1963. Islam and image. *History of Religions* 3:220–60.

———. 1974. *The venture of Islam.* 3 vols. Chicago: Chicago University Press.

Honko, Lauri. 1964. Memorates and the study of folk beliefs. *Journal of the Folklore Institute* 1:5–19.

Hoppal, Mihaly. 1980. Genre and context in narrative events: Approaches to verbal semiotics. In *Genre, structure and reproduction,* edited by Lauri Honko and Vilmos Voigt. Budapest: Akademiai Kiado.

Hymes, Dell. 1981. *Foundations in sociolinguistics.* Philadelphia: University of Pennsylvania Press.

Ibn al-Athīr Majd al-Dīn. 1893. *Al-Nihayah fī Gharīb al-Ḥadīth.* 4 vols. Cairo: Al-Maṭba'ah al-'Uthmāniyyah.

Ibn al-Qayyīm, Al-Jawzīyah. n.d. *Badāi' al-Fawāīd.* 4 vols. Cairo: Al-Ṭibā'ah al-Munīrīyyah.

Ibn Khaldūn. 1956–1961. *Tārīkh.* 7 vols. Beirut: Dār al-Kitāb al-Lubnānī.

Ibrahim, Abdullahi Alī. 1988. Breaking the pen of Harold MacMichael: The

Jaʿalīyyin identity revisited. *International Journal of African Historical Studies* 21, no. 2:217–31.
———. 1989. Popular Islam: The religion of the barbarous throng. *Northeast African Studies* 11, no. 2:21–40.
Ibrahim, Abdullahi A., and Ahmad A. Nasr. 1968. *Min ʿAdab al-Rubaṭāb al-Shaʿbī.* Khartoum: Sudan Research Unit.
Ibrahim, Hayder. 1979. *The Shaiqiya.* Wiesbaden: Franz Steiner Verlag GMBH.
———. 1991. *ʾAzmat al-Islām al-Siyāsī.* Cairo: Markaz Al-Buhuth Al-ʿArabīyyah.
Ibrāhīm, Muḥammad al-Makkī. 1963. Al-Mustaqbal al-Ḥaḍārī fī al-Sūdān. *Al-Rai al-Am,* Dec. 15.
Irvine, Judith T. 1974. Strategies of status manipulation in the Wolof greeting. In *Explorations in the ethnography of speaking,* edited by Richard Bauman and Joel Sherzer. London: Cambridge University Press.
Joseph, Roger. 1981. Vico and anthropological knowledge. In *Vico: Past and present,* edited by Giorgio Tagliacozzo. Atlantic Highlands: Humanities Press.
Keane, Edward Webb, Jr. 1984. The speech of spells: A consideration of Trobriand magic. M.A. diss., University of Chicago.
Keith-Spiegel, P. 1972. Early conceptions of humor: Varieties and issues. In *The psychology of humor,* edited by J. H. Goldstein and P. E. McGhee. New York: Academic Press.
Kent, Thomas. 1986. *Interpretation and genre.* London: Associated University Press.
Khalid, Mansour. 1990. *The government they deserve: The role of the elite in Sudan's political evolution.* London: Kegan Paul International.
al-Kirmānī, Muḥammad Ibn Yūsuf. 1933–1962. *Ṣaḥīḥ Abī ʿAbd Allahī al-Bukhārī Bisharḥī al-Kirmānī.* 25 vols. Cairo: al-Maṭbaʿah al-Bahīyyah.
Kishtani, Khalid. 1985. *Arab political humor.* London: Quartet Books.
Launay, Robert. 1992. *Beyond the stream: Islam and society in a West African town.* Berkeley: University of California Press.
Lévi-Strauss, Claude. 1963. *Structural anthropology.* New York: Basic Books.
———. 1981. *The naked man.* Translated by John and Doreen Weightman. New York: Harper and Row.
Lewis, I. M. 1989. The cannibal's cauldron. In *Magic, witchcraft, and religion: An anthropological study of the supernatural,* edited by Arthur C. Lehmann and James E. Myers. Mountain View, Cal.: Mayfield Publishing Company.
Lindenbaum, Shirley. 1983. Cannibalism: Symbolic production and consumption. In *Ethnography of cannibalism,* edited by Paula Brown and Donald Tuzin. Washington, D.C.: Society for Psychological Anthropology.
Lixfeld, Hannjost. 1986. Jokes and aggression. In *German volkskunde,* translated and edited by James R. Dow and Hannjost Lixfeld. Bloomington: Indiana University Press.
Lorimer, F. S. 1936. The Rubatab. *Sudan Notes and Records* 19, no. 1:162.
McCartney, Eugene S. 1981. Praise and dispraise in folklore. In *The evil eye: A folklore casebook,* edited by Alan Dundes. New York: Garland Publishing.

MacDonald, Donald A. 1972. Collecting oral literature. In *Folklore and folklike,* edited by Richard M. Dorson. Chicago: Chicago University Press.
Maclagan, R. C. 1902. *Evil eye in the western highlands.* London: David Nutt.
MacMichael, Harold M. 1922. *A history of the Arabs.* 2 vols. Cambridge: Cambridge University Press.
Malinowski, Bronislaw. 1965. *Coral gardens and their magic.* 2 vols. Bloomington: Indiana University.
Maloney, Clarence. 1976. Don't say "Pretty baby" lest you zap it with your eye—The evil eye. In *The evil eye,* edited by Clarence Maloney. New York: Columbia University Press.
Marx, Karl. 1964. *Pre-capitalist economic formations.* New York: International Publishers.
Mauss, Marcel. 1967. *The gift.* New York: The Norton Library.
Medvedev, P. N., and M. M. Bakhtin. 1978. *Formal method in literary scholarship.* Baltimore: John Hopkins University Press.
Meeker, Michael. 1979. *Literature and violence in Northern Arabia.* Cambridge: Cambridge University Press.
Messick, Brinkly. 1986. The mufti, the text and the world: Legal interpretation in Yemen. *Man* (n.s.) 21:102–19.
Mohamed, Osman S. 1979. An eye for an eye. *Sudanow,* October, 38–40.
Muhammad, Akbar. 1985. The image of Africans in Arabic literature. In *Slaves and slavery in Muslim Africa,* edited by John Ralph Willis. London: Frank Cass.
al-Muttaqī, ʿAlī ibn ʿAbd al-Mālik. 1969. *Musnad ibn Ḥanbal wa Bihāmishihi Muntakhab Kanz al-ʿUmmāl.* 6 vols. Beirut: Dār Ṣādir.
———. 1971. *Kanz al-ʿUmmāl wa al-ʾAfʿāl.* 16 vols. Aleppo: Maktabat al-Turāth al-Islāmī.
An-Naʿim, Abdullahi A. 1986. The Islamic law of apostasy and its modern applicability: A case from the Sudan. *Religion* 16:197–224.
Nelson, Kristina. 1985. *The art of reciting the Quran.* Austin: University of Texas Press.
Obeyesekere, Gananath. 1992. "British cannibals": Contemplation of an event in the death and resurgence of James Cook, explorer. *Critical Inquiry* 18, no. 4:630–54.
Oyler, D. S. 1981. The Shilluk's belief in the evil eye. In *The evil eye: A folklore casebook,* edited by Alan Dundes. New York: Garland Publishing.
Pauline, Denise. 1977. The impossible imitation in African trickster tales. In *Forms of folklore in Africa,* edited by Bernth Lindfors. Austin: University of Texas Press.
Piamenta, M. 1979. *Islam in everyday Arabic speech.* Leiden: Brill.
———. 1983. *The Muslim conception of God and human welfare as reflected in everyday Arabic speech.* Lieden: Brill.
Poole, Fitz John. 1983. Cannibals, tricksters and witches: Anthropophagic images among Bimin-Kuskusmin. In *The ethnography of cannibalism,* edited by Paula Brown and Donald Tuzin. Washington, D.C.: Society for Psychological Anthropology.
al-Qaraḍāwī, Yusuf. n.d. *The lawful and prohibited in Islam.* Indianapolis: American Trust Publications.

al-Qaṣṭallānī, ʾAḥmad Ibn Muḥammad. 1971. *ʾIrshād al-Sārī Fī Sharḥ Ṣaḥīḥ al-Bukhārī.* 10 vols. Baghdad: Maktabat al-Muthanah.

Ranke, Kurt. 1981. Problems of categories in folk prose. Translated by Carl Lindahl. *Folklore Forum* 14, no.1:1–17.

al-Rāzī, Fakhr al-Dīn. 1872. *Mafātīḥ al-Ghayb.* 8 vols. Cairo: Al-Maṭbaʿah al-Amīrīyyah.

Redfield, Robert. 1985. *The little community and peasant society and culture.* Chicago: Chicago University Press.

Rosaldo, M. Z. 1975. It's all uphill: The creative metaphors of Ilongot magical spells. In *Socio-cultural dimensions of language use,* edited by Mary Sanches and Ben Blount. New York: Academic Press.

———. 1982. The things we do with words: Ilongot speech acts and speech act theory in philosophy. *Language in Society* 11:203–37.

Rosenthal, Franz. 1956. *Humor in early Islam.* Philadelphia: University of Pennsylvania Press.

Ṣaḥīḥ al-Bukhārī. 1979. 9 vols. Chicago: Kazi Publications.

Sahlins, Marshall. 1981. *Historical metaphors and mythical realities.* Ann Arbor: University of Michigan Press.

Sanday, Peggy Reeves. 1986. *Divine hunger: Cannibalism as a cultural system.* London: Cambridge University Press.

Sapir, J. David. 1977. The anatomy of metaphor. In *The social use of metaphor,* edited by David Sapir and J. Christopher Crocker. Philadelphia: University of Pennsylvania Press.

Schoeck, Helmut. 1981. The evil eye: Forms and dynamics of a universal superstition. In *The evil eye: A folklore casebook,* edited by Alan Dundes. New York: Garland Publishing.

Seligmann S. 1910. *Der bose blick und verwandtes.* 2 vols. Berlin: Hermann Barsdorf Verlag.

al-Shaʿarānī, ʿAbd al-Wahāb. 1903/1904. *Kitāb al-Yawāqīt.* Cairo: Al-Maktbaah al-Azharīyyah.

al-Shahi, Ahmed. 1986. *Themes from Northern Sudan.* London: Ithaca Press.

al-Shahi, Ahmed, and F. C. T. Moore. 1978. *Wisdom from the Nile.* Oxford: Oxford University Press.

Shahid, Irfan. 1983. Another contribution to Koranic exegesis: The Sura of the Poets (xxvi). *Journal of Arabic Literature* 14:1–12.

El-Shamy, Hasan. 1967. Folkloric behavior: A theory for the study of the dynamics of traditional culture. Ph.D. diss., Indiana University.

———. 1980. *Folktales of Egypt.* Chicago: University of Chicago Press.

al-Shawkānī, Muḥammad. 1978. *Nayl al-Awṭār.* 10 vols. Cairo: Maktabat al-Qāhirah.

Shorter encyclopedia of Islam, s.v. *Niya.*

Siebers, Tobin. 1983. *The mirror of Medusa.* Berkeley: University of California Press.

Silaymān, Ḥasabū. Interviewed by Maḥjūb Abd al-Ḥafīẓ for al-Sahafa, 22 August 1983.

Smith, W. C. 1957. *Islam in modern history.* Princeton: Princeton University Press.

Spooner, Brian. 1976. Anthropology and the evil eye. In *The evil eye*, edited by Clarence Maloney. New York: Columbia University Press.

Stein, Howard F. 1976. Envy and the evil eye: An essay in the psychological ontogeny of belief and ritual. In *The evil eye*, edited by Clarence Maloney. New York: Columbia University Press.

Strathern, Andrew. 1982. Witchcraft, greed, cannibalism and death: Some related themes from the New Guinea highlands. In *Death and the regeneration of life*, edited by Maurice Bloch and Jonathan Parry. Cambridge: Cambridge University Press.

al-Ṣuyūṭī, Jalāl al-Dīn. 1969. *Tanwīr al-Ḥawālik.* 2 vols. Cairo: al-Maktabah al-Tijarīyyah al-Kubrah.

al-Ṭabarī, Abu Jaʿfar. 1955-1969. *Tafsīr.* 14 vols. Cairo: Dar al-Maʿārif.

Taha, Mahmoud Mohamed. 1987. *The second message of Islam.* Translated by Abdullahi A. An-Naʿim. Syracuse: Syracuse University Press.

Tambiah, S. J. 1955. Changing customs of the Riverain Sudan. *Sudan Notes and Records* 36:146–58.

———. 1964. Changing customs of the Riverain Sudan. *Sudan Notes and Records* 45:12–28.

———. 1968. The magical power of words. *Man* (n.s.) 3:175–208.

———. 1973. Form and meaning of magical acts: A point of view. In *Modes of thought*, edited by Robin Horton and Ruth Finnegan. London: Faber and Faber.

———. 1979. A performative approach to ritual. *Proceedings of the British Academy* 65:113–69.

Todorov, Tzvetan. 1984. *Mikhail Bakhtin: The dialogical principle.* Translated by Wald Godzich. Minneapolis: University of Minnesota Press.

Trimingham, J. S. 1949. *Islam in the Sudan.* Oxford University Press.

al-Turābī, Ḥasan. 1989. *Al-Ḥarakah al-Islāmīyyah fī al-Sūdān.* Khartoum: Maʿhad al-Buḥūth wa al-Dirāsāt al-Islāmīyyah.

Turner, Bryan. 1974. *Weber and Islam.* London: Routledge & Kegan Paul.

Turner, Victor. 1974. *Dramas, field, and metaphors.* Ithaca: Cornell University Press.

Von Sydow, C. W. 1948. *Selected papers on folklore.* Copenhagen: Rosenkilde & Baggar.

Weiner, A. B. 1983. From words to objects to magic. *Man* (n.s.) 18:690–709.

Westermarck, Edward. 1926. *Rituals and belief in Morocco.* 2 vols. London: MacMillan.

White, Luise. 1992. Vampire priests of Central Africa: African debate about labor and religion in colonial Northern Zambia. Paper presented to the Seminar of the Institute for Advanced Study and Research in the African Humanities, Feb. 26, Evanston, Illinois.

———. 1993. Cars out of place: Vampires, technology, and labor in East and Central Africa. *Representations* 43 (Summer): 27–50.

Yankah, Kwesi. 1985. Risks in verbal art performance. *Journal of Folklore Research* 22:133–53.

Yassin, M. Aziz. 1978. Personal names of address in Kuwaiti Arabic. *Anthropological Linguistic* 20, no. 2:35–63.

Youssouf, Ibrahim Ag, Allen Grimshaw, and Charles Bird. 1976. Greetings in the desert. *American Ethnologist* 3:797–82.
El-Zein, Abdul Hamid. 1977. Beyond ideology and theology: The search for the anthropology of Islam. *Annual Review of Anthropology* 6:227–54.